CHINESE RELIGIONS

Chinese Religions

Julia Ching

ORBIS BOOKS

Maryknoll, New York 10545

The Catholic Foreign Mission Society of America
(Maryknoll) recruits and trains people for overseas
missionary service. Through Orbis Books, Maryknoll aims
to foster the international dialogue that is essential to
mission. The books published, however, reflect the opinions
of their authors and are not meant to represent the official
position of the society.

First published in Great Britain 1993 by
THE MACMILLAN PRESS LTD

Published in the USA and Canada 1993 by
ORBIS BOOKS
Maryknoll, New York 10545

Third printing, September 1999
Fifth printing, August 2001
Sixth printing, March 2002
Seventh printing, November 2002
Eighth Printing, March 2004
Tenth Printing, March 2005

Library of Congress Cataloging-in-Publication Data
Chinese religions / Julia Ching
    p. cm
    Includes bibliographical references and index.
    ISBN 0–88344–875–0 (pbk.)
1. China–Religion–History. I. Title.
BL1802.C458 1993
291'.095–dc20   93–2896
                                              CIP

Printed in China

This book is dedicated to my sister Priscilla

Contents

Acknowledgments

It is my pleasure and privilege to thank the people who have been helpful with the writing and completion of this book. I think naturally of my sister Priscilla and her family, who offered me a home away from home during the final weeks of 1991 and the first week of 1992, when I checked the semi-final manuscript. I think also of colleagues in Hawaii and David Chappell, who helped to get me library privileges for the final checking, and Roger Ames, with whom I had useful discussions. I think especially of the generations of students who took the course of Chinese religions with me at the University of Toronto. There are also many others, former students, friends and colleagues, including Raymond Dragan, who gave useful information. And I wish also to thank Vanessa Graham, who represents the publisher, and Anthony Grahame, the editorial controller, and many others, including Glyn Richards and Kristofer Schipper, who have inspired or assisted me.

Last but not least, I think of my spouse and colleague, Willard G. Oxtoby. He has always stood by me, not only with a wealth of information about world religions in general, and also responded to my own ideas in gestation. He is especially there in difficult moments whenever my computer skills prove insufficient, and my diction or style is less than felicitous.

JULIA CHING

Note on Transliteration

The transliteration of Chinese names and terms is complicated by the fact that scholars use several systems; which system is chosen depends on each scholar's special interests in the field of Chinese studies. I decided to follow as a rule the modified Wade-Giles system of romanisation, as is still done by specialists working on traditional Chinese culture in the United Kingdom and in North America. But place names are usually rendered according to known, customary usage. There are a few exceptions – for example, proper names of people and places from contemporary mainland China – that are given according to the newer Pinyin system of romanisation now in use there, which is derived from the International Phonetic Alphabet. In the case of technical terms, the Pinyin form is usually given together with the Wade-Giles form the first time each term is introduced. However, with bibliographical citations, the Wade-Giles form is always followed in the case of titles of books or articles.

Chronological Table

Dates and entries before 840 B.C. are traditional.

LEGENDARY PERIOD

The Three Sovereigns
The Five Emperors   (Yellow Emperor, Yao, Shun, etc.)

ANCIENT CHINA

Early Royal Dynasties (3rd to 2nd millennium)

Hsia Dynasty	Mythical Founder Yü, the Flood-controller
Shang Dynasty (c. 1766–1123 B.C.)	Founder: King T'ang The religion of antiquity (oracle bones)
Chou Dynasty (1122–256 B.C.)	Rise of humanism Bronze inscriptions Spring-Autumn period (722–481) Confucius (c. 551–479) Lao-tzu? Warring States period (403–221) Mo-tzu (c. 468–376) Mencius (c. 321–289) Hsün-tzu (c. 298–238) Chuang-tzu (?) (Legalism, Yin-yang School, etc.)

IMPERIAL CHINA

Early Period (3rd to 5th cent. B.C.–5th cent. A.D.)

Ch'in Dynasty (221–207 B.C.)	A united empire Burning of books (213 B.C.)

Han Dynasty
(206 B.C.-A.D. 220)
	Confucianism as 'state religion'
	  (2nd century B.C.)
	
	Introduction of Buddhism
	  (1st century A.D.?)
	Taoism as religion

(Chang Tao-lin: 2nd cent. A.D.)
The Three Kingdoms (A.D. 220–280)

The Six Dynasties   China separated
(420–581)   Kumārajīva in northern China
                           (402–413)
                           Spread of Buddhism and of Taoism

Middle Period (6th to 9th centuries)

Sui Dynasty   Buddhism as state religion in Japan (594)
(581–617)

T'ang Dynasty   Climax of Buddhism (7th to 8th cent.)
(618–907)   Nestorians in China
                           (Hsüan-tsang, 596–644)
                           (Hui-neng, 638–713)
                           Persecution of Buddhism (845)

Later Period (10th to 20th cent.)

Five Dynasties
907–960

Sung Dynasty   (Jurchen rule in northern China,
                               1115–1234)
(960–1279)   (Jews in Kaifeng)
                           Climax of Neo-Confucianism
                           Chu Hsi (1130–1200)

Yüan Dynasty   Mongol rule
(1260–1367)   Kublai Khan (r. 1260–1294)
                           Tantric Buddhism dominant
                           (Franciscan missionaries in China)
                           (Marco Polo in China)

Ming Dynasty   Wang Yang-ming (1472–1529)
(1368–1644)   Jesuit missionaries in China)
                           (The Christian century in Japan)

Ch'ing Dynasty   Manchu rule
(1644–1911)   Opium War (1839–42)
                           (Return of Christian missionaries)
                           T'ai-p'ing rebellion (1850–64)
                           Boxer rebellion (1900)

REPUBLICAN CHINA

Republic 1912–49	May Fourth Movement (1919) Founding of Communist Party (1921) Sino-Japanese War (1937–45)
People's Republic 1949–	(Expulsion of Christian Missionaries) Cultural Revolution (1966–76) (Anti-Confucius campaign, 1973–74) Fall of the 'Gang of Four' (1977) (A policy of modernisation and of religious toleration)

Introduction

1 Europe and China Compared

For thousands of years, Europe and China each thought of itself as the centre of its known and inhabited world. The Greek term was *oikoumene*, and the Mediterranean area called itself this. China, on the other hand, was to its own people 'all under Heaven' (*T'ien-hsia/Tianxia*) or the 'Middle Kingdom' (*Chung-kuo/Zhongguo*), a civilised oasis surrounded by what was thought to be a cultural desert. And while today's Western Europe utilises the same Roman alphabet even with the various national scripts, the West of the past was united in the use of Latin as the language and writing system of its educated élite. In China's case, we see today the cementing force of the same writing system which has been in use for millennia, and that of a standard spoken language called Mandarin with its spreading influence over a multitude of dialects.

There are also the differences with Western European civilisation. We find in China a uniquely coherent and integrated civilisation, both ancient and enduring, which developed more or less independently of other civilisations. With this comes the consciousness of both uniqueness and even superiority, a consciousness strengthened by the fact that the Chinese civilisation spread its benefits to the whole of East Asia. As centre of its world, China had a low regard of all that is called foreign, also called barbarian. While this has its parallel with the custom in ancient Greece to call 'barbarian' what is not Greek, Chinese culture has enjoyed a more continuous and less interrupted history over a larger continental land mass, and spread over to Japan, Korea and what is now Vietnam, whereas Greek culture served more as an impetus than as the actual content of what we call today, Western civilisation.

2 The Meaning of Religion: Western Term, Chinese Context

The English word 'religion', coming as it does from the Latin *religio*, is usually taken to signify a bond between the human and the divine. Scholars have had difficulty applying this sense to the Chinese context, and some even go so far as to say that the

1

dimension of transcendence is itself lacking in the Chinese spiritual universe.

Actually, the word 'religion' (*tsung-chiao/zongjiao*) did not exist in the Chinese vocabulary until the late nineteenth century, when it entered through Japanese translations of European works and terminology – the Japanese and the Chinese having shared historically, and sharing even now, the 'ideograms' or characters that make up the Chinese script. This was true also for the word 'philosophy' (*che-hsüeh/zhexue*). Before that, the custom was to represent 'doctrines' (*chiao/jiao*) of various spiritual and intellectual lineages, which functioned very much like philosophical and religious teachings, as there had not been a clear distinction between the two traditionally. But this could also be said of the European tradition, at least until the eighteenth century.

What of the argument that the long *absence* of the word 'religion' in traditional Chinese language signifies the absence of religion itself historically, or of any understanding of the phenomenon as it has been known in the West? I agree that in some cases one could argue that the lack of a word or term signifies some lack of strength of a concept it represents, or even more likely, a different perception of a similar concept. But to argue that a phenomenon like religion was not part and parcel of culture without examining the evidence is a different matter. It would assume a position of linguistic determinism which, by association, implies that the Chinese also never developed any 'humanism', since the term *jen-wen chu-yi/renwen zhuyi* or *jen-tao chu-yi/rendao zhuyi* is also a modern coinage. And yet, those who object to describing the Chinese as religious and other-worldly usually represent them as humanistic and this-worldly. I prefer to argue that while China never produced a Western-type religion, one can find in the Chinese tradition what is functionally equivalent to religion or religions in the West, and that such *Chinese religions*, much less distinct from the rest of Chinese culture than Western religions and Western culture, have much to tell us about the uniqueness of the religious phenomenon itself.

We could also analyse the implications of the question posed earlier: *must* religious belief necessarily model itself after the belief in the Jewish-Christian God, and *is* this necessarily a 'personal' deity? Even in the latter case, one might refer to the cult of Heaven in China as a testimony to religious belief. Besides, the very disagreement between missionaries and scholars of the past and present is enough to cast suspicion on monolithic answers. Why and how can one characterise a people and a civilisation with a long historic past, and stretching across half a continent, as 'having always been', and 'by necessity' irreligious and atheist? Is it not possible that there are, and have been, *both* believers and non-believers in God in China? Is it also not possible, that a more personal notion of God was predominant at certain periods and within certain circles, while a more *transpersonal* notion became prevalent at other periods and within certain other circles?

We are not merely seeking similarities between Chinese religion and Western religion. We acknowledge many differences exist. Here we should note that the newly coined term for religion (*tsung-chiao*) is itself revealing. For the first word *tsung* refers to the veneration for lineages, an important element in East Asian philosophies and religions. Not only have the Chinese always respected antiquity and historicity, they have also esteemed the teacher–disciple relationship so central to every religious and doctrinal lineage. In our own context, we shall argue that the 'doctrinal lineages' have also been concerned with those ultimate questions that make them *religious*.

The Religions of Harmony

It has also been said that the religions of the world all emerged in the so-called East. Certainly, Christianity, Islam and Judaism all share Near Eastern origins and are sometimes called the Abrahamic religions after the Hebrew patriarch venerated by all three traditions. Hinduism and Buddhism are the best-known examples of other living religions that have their roots even further east, in South Asia and among the so-called 'East Indians'. When comparing and contrasting with Chinese traditions and their separate roots, we discern that the Near East and South Asia share a common Indo-European cultural and linguistic past. Chinese civilisation is once more different, being further removed from the West.

When compared in terms of contents and orientations, the Abrahamic religions, with their beliefs in a God of Revelation, have been called 'prophetic' and the Indian religions, with their emphasis on the interior and mystical life, 'mystical'. Such a distinction had originally a theological justification involving even the sense of superiority of the prophetic over the mystical. I am referring to the German scholar Friedrich Heiler's influential and pioneering study, in which he actually abstained from specifically calling the mystical traditions 'religions'. According to this view, the prophetic religions offer a clear sense of a belief in the one God, and a strong dimension of transcendence above this life and this world, whereas the mystical religions tend to absorb the individual in himself or herself, even with the discovery of the divine within.[1]

Friedrich Heiler made a real contribution to comparative religion in spite of certain time-bound considerations that he manifested. Today, we may use the terms prophetical and mystical religions without subscribing to any triumphalist presupposition or sense of superiority. We can discern a clear distinction between the two familial groups within the great Indo-European tradition. But Heiler could not place Chinese religions in either of these two categories.

The Swiss theologian Hans Küng describes the religions of the world as three river systems: the Abrahamic or Semitic-prophetic religions, the Indian and mystical religions, and the Chinese religions which arose especially in the Yellow River basin, and which set great value on a wisdom tradition. Although some people may find the use of the term 'river system' in English as applied to religions unusual and perhaps also uncomfortable, this represents an attempt to look at the Chinese tradition as representing a distinct and different kind of religion. We may call these the 'religions of harmony' because of the known Chinese effort in directing attention to harmony between the human and the cosmic as well as harmony within society and within the self.

Mention of the word 'harmony' brings to mind certain arguments against the Chinese tradition as having any religious character. It has to do with whether Chinese civilisation ever possessed a dimension of transcendence. If harmony is cosmic, that is, between the human and the natural, or social, or even introspective, where is the superhuman, the supernatural, the super-social dimension?

Transcendence and Immanence: Are they Compatible?
It is difficult to speak so early of transcendence and immanence in the Chinese tradition, since we have not yet laid out the evidence. For the sake of clarity, we wish nevertheless to touch upon this subject at once. We wish especially to assert that these two terms are not necessarily mutually exclusive.

Frequently, the term transcendence is applied to Western religions like Christianity and Islam because of the centrality of the belief in God as the Other, and the clearness of a separation between this life and this world and the life beyond. In contrast, the Chinese tradition and its humanism appears to offer a clear alternative of immanence or of harmonising oneself with nature or with others rather than worshipping the divine or wrestling with the question of the divine. But is reality that simple?

We may respond in two ways. The first is to show the presence of the transcendent dimension in an apparently immanent world view. We may show, as we shall, that mainstream Chinese humanism has a certain openness to the transcendent, even if humanists themselves might be theists or atheists or agnostics. The other is to offer evidence for the presence of a strong religiosity in China's antiquity, and then to argue that this religiosity never completely disappeared, even if it was transformed and subsumed by the early development of humanistic culture. We shall do this as well. And we shall also maintain that the idea of God, however different that is from the Hebrew Creator, was present from the very beginning of Chinese civilisation until our own times, even if this idea has undergone evolution and transformation. We shall also demonstrate that, even as this has moved intellectually from a more personal understanding to a more transpersonal one, a practical and devotional theism has persisted in popular religious consciousness.

In writing a book on Chinese religions, we are not presuming that religion is necessarily good. Our description of the religion of antiquity in China, with its similarities to the religion of antiquity in the Near East and elsewhere, will demonstrate the morally ambiguous character of religion itself. We have in mind especially such a practice as human sacrifice, found in antiquity in both Israel and China, which clearly indicates the transcendence of the divine over all life, and is so diametrically opposed to all humanism.

Our theme has to do with the interaction between transcendence and immanence. We seek to interweave the various religious traditions China has produced and witnessed, in a very 'religious' context. Going back now to the Latin term *religio* as the bond between the human and the divine, we intend to propose that the Chinese maxim, *T'ien-jen ho-yi/Tianren heyi* or 'Heaven and the human are One' (in Chinese the word *jen* (human) stands for both men and women), arose out of a primeval experience: that of the human being possessed by the spirit or spirits, in a moment of trance. We could call this a kind of shamanic experience, and we shall be speaking much more about the shamanic aspect of ancient religion, as well as about the surviving importance of ecstasy and of theistic beliefs in today's popular religion. This maxim was to become better known in the later traditions, such as in Confucian and Taoist philosophies, to represent less a union between the divine and the human, and more a continuum or a communication between the two orders, moving more and more away from the originally anthropomorphic, to an increasingly pantheistic sense.

In Taoist religion (and in today's popular religion), however, both in its supreme Three Pure Ones and in the pantheon of deities in the heavens as well as in the human body, the anthropomorphic character of the deity has been quite visible.

The harmony between the human and the heavenly orders, perceived simply as natural or cosmic or social harmony, made some observers dismiss the presence of any transcendence in Chinese civilisation. They have not bothered to probe this sense of harmony, to understand its original impulse and inspiration, and to plumb its very depths of experience during the millennia of time that have passed, and even today, when we still have living witnesses to the fact of Chinese religion and religiosity. After all, scholars on one or the other side of the transcendence / immanence debate are not so much in fundamental disagreement about Chinese religion as they are about the *definitions* of such terms as transcendence and immanence, and whether these should always be considered as mutually exclusive. Here we touch upon a topic that itself requires much more discussion and debate than can be allowed in this Introduction.

The history of Chinese religion has seen changes and shifts in beliefs and attitudes, to the introduction of foreign religions and their gradual acculturation. To use the maxim of *T'ien-jen ho-yi*, we may speak of moments when religion teaches or promotes a greater union between God and man, such as in antiquity, in the teachings of the fifth-century Mo-tzu, in religious Taoism and in Pure Land Buddhism, not to mention also missionary Christianity, Chinese Islam and popular religion. There are other moments when religion teaches or promotes a greater harmony between the divine and the human orders, such as in Taoist philosophy, in the humanism of Mencius, of Neo-Confucian philosophy, as well as Chinese Mahayana Buddhist philosophy, especially of Ch'an (or Zen). Except for certain cynics and sceptics, like the Legalists of the past and the Marxists of the present (and there are fewer and fewer today who are genuine Marxists), the ideal of 'Heaven and man are One' has always been respected.

Which version of 'Heaven and the human are One' has been more dominant on the whole? It is not easy to answer this question. On the basis of the texts, one would say that there appear to have been more intellectuals who are more pantheist than theist, preferring harmony as an ideal, than those who are more theist than pantheist, preferring union as the goal. But religious life is not only based on texts, and not always recorded in texts. (If we include the grass-roots population, we are no longer sure.) While, superficially, Taoism is not a religion that can count on numerical strength among its clergy today (I was told in 1986 that there were only about one thousand priests in all of mainland China), nevertheless its clergy is kept extremely busy by a population needing its services during the unfolding of the annual liturgical calendar as well as on special occasions of life. In addition to this, many visitors to Taiwan as well as residents there might presuppose that Taoism is its principal religion, given the great number of temples, large and small, as well as the bustling activities carried on there. With its focus on meditation and intuition, the agnostically or pantheistically inclined Ch'an (or Zen) Buddhism, has always been attractive to those intellectuals and artists for whom the rational is not enough, but could hardly be counted as a religion of the masses. On the other hand, devotional or Pure Land Buddhism, which has so many parallels with the Christian religion, has always had more adherents in both China and Japan.

Communication between the human and the divine signifies a religious life in which *spirituality*, much more than speculative philosophy, occupies a dominant place. I have italicised the English word, which has a foreign ring. The French *spiritualité* would be preferable. But this in itself shows how spirituality is not properly understood by the Anglo-Saxon mentality, which confuses the occult with the spiritual. In this book, our assertion is that a striving for moral and spiritual perfection, for authenticity, and for self-transcendence marks both philosophy and religion in the Chinese tradition. In this regard, comparison can be made with important developments in Christian thought. I have in mind a theological argument with consequences for spirituality: that over grace and freedom. In the fifth century, St. Augustine was decisive in establishing a sense of human wretchedness and the preponderant importance of grace in the human quest for holiness. He thus put to rest the claims of the British monk Pelagius, who emphasised the possibility of achieving sanctity by voluntary action, an allegedly Stoic position as well. But the controversy did not stop there. Among other things, Augustine's influence tended to be within Latin Christianity, whereas the Greek fathers, with their reliance on biblical allegories and mystical insights, maintained a more positive role for human beings as divine images. In the Chinese context, we see a parallel in the focus on the Confucian striving for sageliness and the Buddhist quest for enlightenment. (We may even add the Taoist quest for immortality and salvation.) In all cases, the belief in human perfectibility triumphed – with the mainstream Confucian position closer to the Byzantine one than the Latin, and with Pure Land Buddhism most approximating Augustine, and we may add, Luther and Calvin with their insistence on justification by faith alone.

Comparisons sometimes diminish the issues themselves, when they are forced upon them. In this case, however, they serve to heighten our understanding of the central issues in both East and West. Both are concerned with human striving for perfection (or for union with God). On each side, some emphasise what human striving itself can achieve ('self-power', Japanese: *jiriki*), others emphasise what divine help alone can achieve ('other power', Japanese: *tariki*). It is to be expected that a revealed religion like Christianity would tend to emphasise divine help, whereas a humanism open to religion like Confucianism would tend to emphasise human striving. Nevertheless, the interaction between transcendence and immanence is itself present in such striving.

Philosophy and Religion: Where are the Borderlines?
In discussing the continuum between the heavenly (or cosmic-natural) and the human orders, we are also discussing a theme common to both religion and philosophy, as we have already hinted. This happens because the lines of demarcation between religion and philosophy are not so clear in the Chinese tradition – the situation resembles that in Europe before the eighteenth century, that is, before a parting of ways between philosophy and its erstwhile mentor, theology. The Chinese term for *philosophy* (*che-hsüeh/zhexue*) also entered the Chinese language through translations from Western languages in the recent past. In this book, we are covering many schools of thought with philosophical content as well as religious thrust. In doing so, we follow mainly a history-of-religions approach which is akin to the history-of-ideas method. We shall not single out for discussion the school of logic in traditional Chinese philosophy – also called the School of Names (*ming-chia/mingjia*). This too is an age-old tradition going back to the fourth century B.C. or even earlier, with extant texts attributed to Kung-sun Lung as well as scattered in *Mo-tzu*, *Chuang-tzu* and *Hsün-tzu*. The discussions of logic, however, were largely outside the context of religion and have little religious significance. Readers who have an interest in this subject can pursue it elsewhere.[2]

This is not to say that our book only covers Chinese religious philosophies. Obviously, the book is organised around religious traditions and religious concerns. But the book also goes into some depth in the discussion of these traditions and concerns, as reflected in the attention given not only to topics like transcendence and immanence, but also to the philosophical interaction between the various schools of thought, whether indigenous, or between indigenous traditions and those of foreign origins.

Since we are aware of the diffuse character of indigenous Chinese religion(s), we prefer to call them *traditions* to avoid giving the impression that they are just like institutional religions in the West. That is why we speak of indigenous Chinese traditions and religions of alien origins. This brings us to the subject of the book's organisational structure.

3 Organisation of this Book

The problem of cultural assimilation is obviously the other sub-theme of this book. For this reason, and to highlight the main theme of harmony, we are organising this book around three parts: the indigenous traditions (including the religion of antiquity, Confucianism and Taoism); the religions of foreign origin (Buddhism, Islam, Christianity), with Neo-Confucianism considered as China's response to Buddhist influences; and the legacy of syncretism representing the fruits of union between the native and the non-native. This will enable us to focus clearly on the religious character of ancient Chinese society, explain the early development of Chinese humanism and highlight its religious dimension. The comparison and contrast of the native and the foreign elements in traditional China will help as well to indicate the similarities as well as differences between Chinese religions and Western religions, especially Christianity, but in some respects also the other Abrahamic religions. I refer to the Hebrew religion and even to Islam – which is after all much more 'occidental' than 'oriental'. The broadly chronological chapter sequence is also pedagogically useful. And we shall review briefly the religious situation under the Chinese Communist government. We are conscious of the fact that, in the name of Maoism, Chinese Marxism once attracted the attention of quite a few scholars of religion. But living now in a world which has so recently witnessed the unravelling of Communism in Eastern Europe and in the erstwhile Soviet Union, we shall deal with Communism in China more as a political and historical reality than for any religiosity it once attempted to project. We shall also refrain from dealing only with history or textual traditions; we shall give consideration to popular religion, both in terms of its Taoist or Buddhist aspects and in terms of what can better be called shamanic, the modern survival – if only in fragmented forms – of an ancient legacy. Indeed, in many ways, popular religion represents the vitality of syncretism in a tradition that is thriving in highly industrialised societies like those of Hong Kong and Taiwan, and has even spread to the West with the *émigré* Chinese population. We shall then conclude by seeking to answer the question concerning the future of religion in China, in the context of a surviving Marxist ideology. But we shall not dwell long on the contemporary scene, since our major concern is with a span of four thousand years.

The Comparative Perspective
The structure of ideas in this book is cast in a comparative mould. To facilitate understanding, certain themes are singled out, such as divination, ecstasy, sacrifice and kingship in ancient religion, and these are discussed in a context that includes ancient Hebrew religion as well as Japanese religion. Ritual and Morality characterise Confucianism, making it both religion and philosophy. The struggles between Confucianism and Mohism, on the one side, and Legalism on the other, are an echo of the Pauline talk of love and the law, except that the law on the Chinese side is very much a secular thing. Taoism is presented both as a philosophy with religious meaning, and as a religion of salvation with mystical overtones. The entry of Buddhism was facilitated by the translation of its scriptures, while exegesis and hermeneutics led first to the articulation of Chinese Buddhist philosophical schools, and then beyond to the development of mystical Ch'an and devotional Pure Land – with the two of them eventually mixing. Neo-Confucian philosophy is interpreted as a response to Buddhist philosophy, which brought with it a metaphysics of morality as well as a philosophical spirituality with a religious character. And then, turning attention to those religions of West Asian origins like Islam and Christianity, a contrast is made between Islam's success in surviving as an ethnic religion with minimal assimilation and Christianity's dilemma in choosing between cultural adaptation and non-adaptation. Popular religion is then examined in terms of its vitality as a tradition of syncretism which blends not only Confucianism, Taoism and Buddhism, but also Christianity and Islam.

While grounded in the structure of thought itself, the comparative dimension in this book serves more as a horizon than as a focus. Analogies have limited usefulness, and should be used with caution. Besides, this book treats a multiplicity of traditions which together make up Chinese *religions*. To focus on thematic comparisons alone would entail a disruption of this multiplicity. This might be more feasible were one writing on Confucianism or Buddhism or Taoism alone, rather than on all of them together. It is also the author's firm conviction that sufficient knowledge and information must precede any useful and intelligent comparative effort (or, if one wishes to use the more theological term, any 'dialogic' effort). What comes to mind here is the German theologian Paul Tillich's visit to Japan for 'dialogue' with Buddhists (1960). According to reports, he found it a frustrating experience, because his 'partners' could not even understand where his specific questions were coming from, since they had different assumptions and used different categories, and because they represented more than one *kind* of Buddhism.[3]

We shall nevertheless allow ourselves some comparative suggestions, offering them as partial clues to the understanding of the contents of this book, and we shall do this in the context of comparative religion rather than of theology. Following history as well as the structures of religious phenomena, we shall compare the ancient Chinese religion with the Hebrew religion. When presenting Islam, Christianity and other religions of West Asian origins in China, we shall focus more on historical encounter than on comparative analysis – again, as the structures dictate. Indeed, such themes as acculturation and indigenisation *imply* a comparative mould of thought which becomes somewhat simplistic when made explicit.[4]

We must be mindful that, when compared to Christianity, the Chinese religions all together represent a much older and complex whole, comprehending a vast corpus of scriptures and divergent traditions. On first examination, indeed, differences might appear much larger than similarities, and there are scholars who claim that the only 'religion' in China is its theistic equivalent in Pure Land Buddhism. However, in the broader perspective that this book represents, we have already referred to nuances in understanding the term *religion*. We may add that institutional Taoism (which has become much better known in recent years) and the popular religion still thriving today (which is related to Taoism) both present interesting parallels to institutional Christianity, with the cult of saints and immortals, and an implicit doctrine of creation, fall, and salvation.[5] In the case of Confucianism and other traditions, specific parallels are harder to find, but we may yet argue that the quest for sageliness is not only evidence of transcendence, but also in itself 'soteriological'. And indeed, within both Confucianism and Chinese Buddhism, the mainstream thrust has been that of universal access to sagehood or salvation.

We have referred here to some of the ideas that have already been presented in the book *Christianity and Chinese Religions*, which follows basically a dialogue format between myself as a China scholar and Hans Küng as a Christian theologian. This book is nevertheless different from the work that was the result of an earlier collaboration. This one represents an effort of description and also of interpretation, without making Christian apologetics. It incorporates new materials and insights, such as those about antiquity, brought to light by more recent archaeological discoveries, and about the various traditions, especially with subjects like Neo-Confucian philosophy and Taoist meditation and healing methods, which the page limitation of the earlier work forbade. Effort is also made in this book to highlight attitudes and actions regarding gender, in religious traditions that are clearly patriarchal. The central theme of *T'ien-jen ho-yi*, to which we made only occasional reference in the earlier work, is also more prominent in this work. But having this focus does not exclude having a context as well, which permits comparative references to other religions and traditions. We believe that it is a more comprehensive book, at a point in time when very few such works exist.

Part One
The Indigenous Traditions

1

The Ancestral Cult and Divination: The Dawn of Ancient Religion

1 Archaeology and Ancient Religion

People living in the Near East, in Greece and in Italy sometimes discover archaeological records and remains by digging in the ground or by throwing stones into caves. And our knowledge of the religions of antiquity in these areas has especially been enriched and revolutionised by the archaeological research done by scholars during recent centuries. For example, the Dead Sea Scrolls shed light on Hebrew religion and early Christianity, while the Nag Hammadi manuscripts in Egypt illuminated Christian Gnosticism. China is also an ancient country, and offers a very fruitful field for scholars interested in remote antiquity.

China's rich history makes the country an archaeologist's paradise. Archaeological findings have yielded us the records of an early civilisation going back at least four thousand years. I am speaking here of the oracle bone inscriptions which offer evidence of unmistakable early religiosity, including ancestral cult, divination, sacrifice, priesthood and shamanism. We shall recount a few of these findings and the new world of antiquity they have uncovered.

2 Dragons and Dragon Bones

Dragons have different meanings in East and West. This mythical beast represents mainly an evil force in the West, as depicted in the New Testament's book of the Apocalypse and in stories of St. George as the slayer of the dragon. In China, it represents chiefly a benign if fearsome power, associated with storms and

15

clouds, rains and fertility, rivers and marshes, and especially with imperial power. It is believed to be life-giving and rain-giving, and at the same time fear-provoking because it is capable of bringing destruction. At festivals like the lunar Chinese New Year (in late January or in February), dragon dances often attract attention, not only in the old country but also in overseas Chinese communities. While this dragon motif is actually shared by many other peoples in East (Japan and Korea) and Southeast Asia (Vietnam, Thailand, even Indonesia), it seems especially prominent in the Chinese consciousness.

Dragon Bones and Oracle Inscriptions

In traditional Chinese pharmacology, there is an item called 'dragon bones'. Some of these came from tortoise shells and animal bones. Interest in such dragon bones has led to important discoveries, including the dawn of Chinese civilisation itself.

In 1898 (or 1899), Wang Yi-jung, then Chancellor of the Imperial University in Manchu China, found that the surfaces of certain fragments of the 'dragon bones' displayed engraved characters. He concluded that the hieroglyphic writings, which he did not understand, went back to a period more ancient than that of the bronze inscriptions with which he was familiar. After his death in 1900, his friend Liu Ô, a noted writer, inherited his findings and continued the task of searching and collecting, and published in 1903 the results in a six-volume work based on an assemblage of 1,058 pieces. This led to the eventual unearthing in 1911 of the ruins of the ancient royal Shang capital at Anyang, making possible a scientific reconstruction of an ancient civilisation that had a profoundly religious orientation. In this case, the fragments in question are found to carry oracular inscriptions going back some four thousand years.[1]

As an archaeological find, oracle bone and shell fragments carrying inscriptions may be compared to the Dead Sea Scrolls of Qumran, discovered between the years 1947 and 1951, some of which are extant only on fragments which had to be deciphered and pieced together. Both have religious significance, the Dead Sea Scrolls disclosing especially the strong Jewish influence on early Christianity. But the Chinese fragments represent a more revolutionary discovery, bringing with it the unpacking of an entire ancient civilisation. Besides, the oracle inscriptions were written as well in a script that was till then unknown, whereas the Dead Sea Scrolls were legible to Hebrew and Aramaic scholars.

Chinese Antiquity as an Open Frontier

Archaeological discoveries have thrown light on the religious character of prehistoric China, putting it in the company of the ancient Near East. For the late fourth and early third millennium B.C., we have evidence of potters' marks resembling writing, of scapulimancy (etymologically, 'shoulder-bone divination') using a variety of animal bones, and of clay phallus objects apparently involved in ancestral worship.

Very recent archaeological discoveries are also revolutionising our knowledge of ancient China as a whole. One can no longer speak of its ancient civilisation as having arisen basically in the Yellow River Basin, since many very early finds have been unearthed far away from that area. In 1986, archaeologists made certain discoveries of altars and other remains in Chekiang (Zhejiang) dating back to five thousand years ago, that is, long before the Shang dynasty. They also unearthed remains in San-hsing-tui (Sanxingdui), Szechuan (Sichuan), dating back three thousand or more years, back to the early Chou dynasty, but at a time before this region was incorporated into Chou China. Among the unearthed figures, there is especially a beautiful large bronze figure from Szechuan, with protruding eyes and double pupils, as well as very large ears, that came out of burial pits arranged in the shape of five stars. The special eyes and ears connote special skills and powers, and the scholar Jao Tsung-i speculates that this find represents a 'sage' figure to whom sacrifices were offered, that is, a deity figure rather than a priestly or shamanic one.[2]

Archaeologists have begun to speak of Chinese civilisation as having had very possibly multiple origins. Perhaps it is more accurate to call this civilisation the composite of many regional cultures, each with its special features. If no writing system earlier than that of the oracle bones has been definitively discovered or deciphered, even that may yet come.

3   The Ancestral Cult and Ancient Religion

Ancestral veneration is part and parcel of many religions, including ancient Roman religion, African tribal religion, as well as the religions of East Asia. As practised in different forms, it is therefore not uniquely a Chinese phenomenon. In the later nineteenth century, scholars thought that it was possible to find historical evidence for the existence of one primitive religion for all humankind. Many agreed with the Englishman Herbert Spencer that the ancestor cult could be considered as the root of every religion.[3] However, the French sociologist and China scholar Marcel Granet insists that the ancestral cult came later, emerging from an earlier association with holy places, and appearing only when societies were more developed. He also argues for a later divinisation of the forces of nature. In our own case, the question is moot, as we are simply interpreting the ancestral cult and the cult of nature deities without probing into their pre-history.[4]

The ancestor cult might have arisen out of psychological needs or attitudes, including the fear of the deceased, as well as feelings of piety toward them. It was already widespread among the Indo-European people from the time of the Paleolithic and Neolithic periods. Behind the cult stands the belief in survival after death, in whatever form that might be. This cult was deeply rooted among the Greeks and Romans, with some striking parallels to the Chinese case. Indeed, filial piety was not only important in the patriarchal religion of China, but also in that of Israel, with its deeply rooted sense of filial duty toward father and mother, as mirrored in the Fourth Commandment.[5]

While the ancestor cult still underlies much religious practice in China, Korea and Japan, the term 'ancestor' does not today always refer to the lineal progenitor, and may rather represent a close, deceased relative. The practice has been little observed in mainland China since the Communists took power in 1949, but memories of it linger. Formerly, wooden tablets were used, bearing the names of the deceased ancestors, male and female, of the extended patriarchal family. In front of these, anniversary feasts were held, complete with prostrations and libations. Today, photographs or paper tablets sometimes replace these on family altars. But the consciousness of ancestors remains strong in a society where age still commands respect.

In comparing ancient China with ancient Israel and Christianity, it could be said that Judaism and Christianity were *religions of the Fathers*, that is, patriarchal religions, whereas Chinese religion was not only a patriarchal religion but also an *ancestral religion*. In contrast with China, Israel believed in the God of its Fathers, but not in divinised Fathers. On the other hand, among the ancient Chinese, the God of the Chou dynasty appeared to have been an ancestral spirit of the ruling house. The belief in *T'ien/Tian* (Heaven) as the great ancestral spirit differed from the Judaeo-Christian, and later Islamic belief in a Creator God. For this reason, there are those who claim that the Chinese and the Christians worship *different* Gods, or that the ancestral cult does not offer enough transcendence to the Chinese religion. We have foreseen some of these arguments and shall discuss them again. Here we wish merely to mention the consequences of the ancestral cult for the cult of the dead. In early Christianity, the Church Fathers pointed out that prayers and sacrifices to the dead were opposed to the First Commandment, which reserved all worship for the one God, who did not permit any quasi-gods, to whom prayers could also be made. But Judaism, Christianity and Islam never forbade praying *for* the dead; indeed, this practice was often recommended.

In comparing religions, there is also the question of the belief in immortality or the after-life. Here it appears that the ancients in China, both in the Shang and in the Chou, had a world view quite similar to that of the ancient Jews. For example, they believed in a heavenly abode for the good. Both the oracle inscriptions and the *Book of Poetry*, a classical text, make mention of the deceased kings as rising to Heaven and becoming physically close to the Lord-on-high.

The Ancestral Cult in Antiquity

If we go back four thousand years to the dawn of Chinese history, we find a society where ancestral religion is central, and the royal ancestral temple was the centre of political administration. There, the great feasts were held, the weapons of war were stored, and the vassals were enfeoffed. And for each of the great occasions, the gods and spirits were also invited to participate. True, there were other beliefs, besides that in the departed ancestors. Many other spirits were worshipped, including a supreme deity, astral spirits and other spirits of nature – of the mountains and rivers.

Together with the dragon, there were also other mythical animal figures popular in cult and as art motifs. These include the *t'ao-t'ieh/taotie*, a stylised ogre mask with wide open jaws and other feline characteristics. The suggestion has been made that it resembles a tiger which served as a guardian of graves against evil spirits, and even perhaps that it points to the earth as a divine force, from which we all come and to which we shall all return. A third popular animal figure, real rather than mythical, was the tortoise, which was so important in divination rituals. It is especially interesting that the tortoise was not native to northern China, and had to be imported from southern regions to serve this exalted end.

Practices like divination, which was consultation by the living of

spirits of the dead and other spirits, permeated daily life. Extant
'oracle bone inscriptions', be these made on tortoise shells or
the shoulder blades of cattle, continue to tell the tale of a
literate civilisation, that of the Shang dynasty, with its kings
and nobles, commoners and slaves. The leaders of Shang society
took important decisions only after having consulted the diviner-
mediums, who, in turn, sought counsel from ancestral spirits, or
from the supreme being, called Lord-on-high (*Ti/Di*), or *Shang-
ti/Shangdi*), from whom blessings and protection were expected.

Such testimony to the *religious* character of early society is corroborated by that of the somewhat later ritual bronze inscriptions,
which come from the early part of the Chou dynasty, when the court
diviners had diminished in influence but the ancestral religion was
still going strong. So too was the belief in a supreme being, by then
more often called *T'ien/Tian* or Heaven.

Textual references, such as in the Confucian classics, offer evidence of the performance of ancestral rituals. Often, the son had
to serve as the family priest, while a grandson or nephew was
appointed, after divination, to serve as *shih/shi* (literally, 'corpse')
or ancestral impersonator, that is, to act as a living reminder of
the ancestor to whom sacrifice was being offered. In fact, this
impersonator was much more than an actor in a drama. He was
regarded as the carrier of the ancestor's soul, the *shen-pao/shenbao*,
'possessed by the soul of the ancestor', just as shamans were called
ling-pao/lingbao, 'persons possessed by spirits'. It was believed that
the ancestor spirit received in this person the offerings made to
him, and also spoke in person through this mouthpiece, expressing
gratitude for the offerings and promising protection and happiness
to the family.

The following verse from the *Book of Poetry* gives a vivid description of a royal ritual offered to ancestors, at which more than
one impersonator was present:

> In due order, treading cautiously,
> We purify your oxen and sheep.
> We carry out the rice-offering, the harvest offering.
> Now baking, now boiling,
> Now setting out and arranging,
> Praying and sacrificing at the gate.
> . . . .
> The Spirits enjoyed their drink and food
> They assign to you a hundred blessings. . . . [6]

We get from this the impression of a happy family feast, where a group of people worked together on preparing the animals for their meat, which was consumed after the ritual sacrifice by the family group. The verse lends some substance to the possibility that, in a mood of intoxication, ancestral spirits appeared, at least sometimes – to descend into their impersonators – and commune ecstatically with their descendants.

The Origins of Filial Piety

Speaking of happy families and the ancestral cult, we naturally think also of the virtue of filial piety, usually perceived as central to Confucian teachings. But how did this virtue take up centre stage? Had that to do with the ancestral cult? Here again, the study of antiquity is helpful, and gives surprising finds.

The word for filial piety is *hsiao/xiao,* and comes to us not from oracle inscriptions, but from later bronze ones presumably of the Chou times, where it is depicted as a hand resting upon the head of another person. This image may represent an older person supported by a younger one, and may also evoke a feeling of affection. Interestingly as well, some of the older bronzes were cast by Chou rulers as acts of filial piety to ancestors, and other less old ones were presented to parents and grandparents, and even to other living members of the family. Thus it appears that the scope of filial piety has been widening beyond the circle of direct ancestors.

When the historian examines ancient attitudes toward ageing and the aged, as well as toward death and dying, he or she is in for surprises. On the one hand, death and burial rituals have always been more elaborate than those surrounding birth. On the other hand, while sorrow has always been associated with death, as shown in oracle inscriptions from the Shang, there is also evidence there of the custom of clubbing the aged to death, carbon-dated at a site to 5630 B.C. Similar customs have been found elsewhere in the world as well.[7] Scholars have linked this with possible cannibalism, and/or with a ritual to release the soul of the victim, which would make such an act euthanasia. Working with similar evidence and textual references, scholars have also concluded that unwanted children, especially female infants, were often disposed of at birth or even earlier.[8]

After the initial shock, we may conclude that even if filial piety as a sentiment goes back to early time the forms through which it was expressed went through transformations. And this includes not just the attitude toward one's parents, but also the attitude toward one's children. Unfortunately, female infants have been for a very long time the victims of a patriarchal society where the virtue of filial piety makes the male heir the foundation of the ancestral cult.

4 Mythology and Ancient Religion

Whereas Greek, Roman and Japanese mythologies have survived largely intact, Chinese myths of antiquity remain scattered and fragmentary, frequently interspersed in later texts bearing the mark of a demythologiser's editing. Archaeological discoveries have disclosed a past of war and violence, when warriors were buried with horses and chariots. Mythological records support an age of legendary gods and heroes, especially of those sage figures traditionally known as the Three Sovereigns (*San-huang*) and the Five Emperors (*Wu-ti*), also venerated as ancestral leaders of the Chinese people.

Sage Kings: Ancestral or God Figures?
There is a place for wisdom in every religious tradition. In the case of the Hebrew religion, a forerunner of Christianity, we know of the Wisdom books of the Old Testament, attributed often to one of the great kings, whether the mighty David or the wise Solomon. Even more than for the Jews, sages or wise men occupy a very important place in Chinese culture in general, and in antiquity in particular. The world knows of the sage Confucius (literally, Master K'ung) as a wise and humane teacher, and the anti-Confucius campaign that took place in Communist China (1974) shocked everyone, including those in the People's Republic itself. The world also knows of the sage Lao-tzu (literally, Old Master) as a wise man who couches his love of the natural and his disdain of the artificial in apparent riddles. While neither Confucius nor Lao-tzu was ever a ruler or a king, many dynastic founders and imperial families demonstrated their veneration of these men, sometimes even trying to invent genealogical links to one or the other.

Besides these sage teachers, the Chinese also venerate certain more remote figures as ancient sage rulers. The best known is the Yellow Emperor, the alleged ancestor of the Chinese people. But there are also others. And the association of Chinese civilisation with sage rulers has been such that European philosophers of the seventeenth and especially the eighteenth century loudly praised the Chinese people for their alleged legacy of philosopher kings. It has been said that what the Greek philosopher Plato preached was literally practised in ancient China.

In the classical texts, the term *sheng* or 'sage' refers to a wise and virtuous man, usually a ruler in remote antiquity. Etymologically, the oracle bone graph is made up of a big ear and a small mouth. It is closely associated with acute hearing, perhaps hearing the voice of the spirits, and perhaps also communicating something of what has been heard. The names of the so-called Three Sovereigns reveal their legendary character as well as their contributions to culture. They are sometimes called the Heavenly Sovereign (*T'ien-huang*), the Earthly Sovereign (*Ti-huang*), and the Human Sovereign (*Jen-huang*). They have also been identified with such figures as Fu-hsi ('Animal Tamer'), Sui-jen ('Fire-maker') and Shen-nung ('Divine Farmer'), who bear names that bespeak their merits. As a group, these figures might represent the personifications of certain stages in the development of early culture, and are hailed as culture heroes in later texts.

The Five Emperors refer to another group of figures, usually including the Yellow Emperor, Chuan-hsü, his obscure grandson, and the famous Yao, Shun and Yü. We shall introduce each of these briefly:

- The Yellow Emperor is often portrayed as the conqueror of evil forces and the bearer of civilising benefits, including the invention of the compass needle. His wife allegedly taught the people to rear silkworms, while his chief minister invented writing.
- Chuan-hsü is little known, and is sometimes said to be another name for Emperor Yao, the third of the group of five.
- Yao is remembered as a benevolent ruler who decided to pass the throne on to the most worthy man in the realm – Shun.
- Shun is the legendary filial son who had a blind father and an evil step-mother. In his turn, he made his heir Yü.
- Yü is the great Flood-controller. On account of constant overflowing of its banks, the Yellow River flooded large areas. In Yü we have the model hard worker who laboured for thirteen years and finally succeeded in channelling the waters of the Yellow River into the ocean. He was also the founder of the first dynasty, the Hsia, since he was allegedly urged by a grateful populace to depart from tradition and pass the throne to his own son.

About fifty years ago, a group of critical Chinese historians proposed the theory that these legendary sages were god-figures. Their hypothesis was founded upon their critical examination of the fragmentary materials in the early texts, be these classics, history or mythology. Their theories associated the Three Sovereigns – and sometimes the Five Emperors as well – with the primeval Great One (*T'ai-yi*), which in turn represents the supreme being called God. According to them, the Three Sovereigns and the Five Emperors belong to the realm of mythology, but became regarded as human beings after a process of reverse euhemerisation during the later Chou period.

Should we consider the ancient sages human or divine? The answer depends on whether we refer by the term 'divine' to a supreme being, or to an ancestral spirit or deity of a tribal group. Scholars who consider the ancient sages as deity symbols do not always agree as to what it means to be a deity. Scholars like Ku Chieh-kang and Yang Shang-k'uei think that the Three Sovereigns (and perhaps also the Five Emperors) all represented a supreme being, a personal God. But others prefer to regard the same sages as ancestral spirits or god-ancestors, occupying a position lower than that of the supreme being. This is closer to a totemic theory, in which an animal or plant species is associated with a particular tribal group's identity. When the term 'totemism' is applied to ancient China, it is thought that oracle and bronze inscriptions bearing a number of pictographs derived from animal symbols are to be associated with totemic clans. The sage Shun is associated with the phoenix, and has been regarded as the ancestor of the Bird Tribe, while the Flood-controller Yü (with Dragon connections) has been called the ancestor of the Reptile Tribe. But then, whether ancient China may be called a totemic society depends very much on how such symbols are interpreted.

In any case, the primordial sages were obviously ancestral figures in a country where the people considered themselves as children of a divine or semi-divine order. They point to an age when communications between the human order and the divine were central to all life, with sages either representing the divine order or serving as mediators – and also as ancestral spirits.

Queen Mothers and Female Deities
What was the role of women and the feminine in ancient religion? What does mythology say, and what does archaeology reveal?

There is little that we can say for certain about a very ancient matriarchal society. However, the study of Chinese surnames and clan names reveals two layers of history: earlier surnames usually have the word 'female' or 'woman' (*nü*) as radical and indicate at least a matrilineal origin. Such was the surname of the Chou house, Chi. Later surnames tend to come from place names, and presumably had more to do with the father's origin. At work was actually a social-historical process confusing clan names and family names.[9]

Archaeology has unearthed evidence in Europe, India and Africa that a female deity, often called the 'mother goddess', was worshipped in many parts of the world in Paleolithic, Neolithic and early historical times. Such a figure had its place in the ancient civilisations of Sumer, Babylon and Egypt. Recently, in 1986, an equivalent figure was found also in Liaoning province, north-east of Beijing, at excavation sites of the Hongshan culture dating back to about 4,500 to 2,500 B.C. The area is in today's Inner Mongolia. The finds were of small statues of a pregnant goddess figure often surrounded – significantly – with jade dragons, tortoises, birds and cicadas. Somewhere north-west of this main site, in Niu-he Liang, a life-sized head of a female figure dating from 3,000 B.C. was unearthed and is being considered the oldest deity figure discovered in China and possibly the first tangible evidence of an archaic female goddess cult.

The meaning of this find is still being studied. The site of the discoveries is somewhat removed from the Yellow River Basin, long believed to be the cradle of Chinese civilisation. Pre-dating these finds, there has been known textual evidence of female deity figures, such as the mention in oracle inscriptions of a 'Western Mother' and of an 'Eastern Mother'. And there are diverging descriptions of the 'Queen Mother of the West' in such texts as *Chuang Tzu* and *Huai-nan Tzu*, as well as in *Lieh Tzu*, and in *Shan-hai ching* (Classic of Mountains and Oceans) – a text that contains some parts going back to 400 B.C., and other parts to about 300 A.D.

The problem of linking records to remains is that the texts do not speak clearly of this goddess figure in fertility terms even though the findings do. Nevertheless, the textual figure has a clear connection to life and to motherhood, and would later represent the power and wisdom connected with longevity. Certainly, these findings have given reason for pause and reflection to those scholars who assert the absence of any mother goddess figure in ancient China.

Mythology also yields us another female deity figure: Nü-wa (etymologically, suggesting 'woman'), sometimes alleged to be the consort of Fu-hsi, the culture hero. Her name comes up first in the 'Questions to Heaven' (*T'ien-wen*) section of *Ch'u-tz'u* (Songs of the South), where the question was posed as to who made her physical body. A commentary notes that she was supposed to have a human head and a serpent's body. She figures in the later *Shan-hai ching* as a goddess who transforms herself seventy times daily. In a passage coming from a lost second-century-A.D. text, she is described as having made human beings with the yellow earth; when she got tired, she just strung many figures together with mud. Hence it is said that the nobles were the ones made with some care, while the commoners were strung up with mud. The second-century-B.C. text *Huai-nan-tzu* also describes an early cosmic catastrophe involving a male god who broke the pillar attaching earth to heaven. Nü-wa's task was to repair the universe, which she did, using multi-coloured pebbles to mend the blue skies, cutting turtle legs to establish the four compass points, killing the black dragon that was causing a flood.[10]

Humankind was created by a goddess – this makes a good feminist story, even if it enshrines social distinctions between nobility and lesser folk. Moreover, if it took a male figure to bring catastrophe to the universe, it took a female deity to restore order and completion. While she is hardly a parallel to the Blessed Virgin of Christian beliefs, her presence, even in myth, lends credence to the need for a female force (*yin*) to balance the male (*yang*).

Besides, while Chinese religion lacks a formal doctrine of creation, mythology provides enough food for thought, in this story and in others. Another better-known story from the third century A.D. seeks to explain the origin of the universe itself. It brings in the 'cosmic egg' motif, that P'an-ku (literally, Antiquity), a giant born of an egg, was the 'father' of all, since from his death came the universe.[11]

5　Divination: Seeking for Ancestral Advice

Divination may be explained as the search for understanding about the future, by a human being who relies on the wisdom of a spirit, through the mediumship of a diviner. The intent is usually practical: the seeker desires to know the wise way of acting, be that in war, marriage, or treatment of a malady. Presumably the diviner has a special skill, including that of extra-sensory perception, to look into symbols and events and make utterances about certain patterns of action which the person or persons who consult him or her should follow.

It is hard for us to speculate on the effectiveness of divination. Certainly, in today's society, the practice is quite prevalent, even in high places, to mention only Nancy Reagan's efforts to consult an astrologer on behalf of her husband, the former US President Ronald Reagan, in finding proper dates and times for certain actions. Many people believe in the stars underneath which they were born. Many also in the West consult the Chinese *Book of Changes* (*I-ching*), a divination manual that also ranks as a Confucian classic.

It is a widespread and venerable custom to divine the future by the coloration, cracks, and other features of animal shoulder blades. Speaking generally, in Europe, the Near East and North Africa, the natural condition of the bone was read after the flesh had been scraped away. In North and Central Asia as well as North America, however, the diviner created omen cracks by applying fire to the bone.

In Judaism, the place of divination is ambiguous. While Jewish law formally forbade sorcery, divination, the interpretation of signs and necromancy (Dt. 18:10f, Lev. 19:26) it permitted the use of the oracle, the interrogation of God's will through a priest (Dt. 33:8) and approved of prophets (Dt. 18:15; 1 Sam. 28:6) and seers (1 Sam. 9:9). Although King Saul expelled all spirit-mediums and diviners from his realm around 1,000 B.C., he would consult the spirit-medium of Endor when he himself was desperate (1 Sam. 28). During his struggle with Saul, David consulted the sacred lots, kept in the pouch of a priestly garment called the ephod, which gave Yes/No answers to inquiries (1 Sam. 23:6, 9–12).

Court Divination in Shang China

We focus now on divination in ancient China. Indeed, the Neolithic population in northern China (starting from the late fourth millennium B.C.) appears to have been the first people anywhere to use animal shoulder blades for divination, by heating them and interpreting the cracks which ensued. The practice reached its height by Shang times, with the widespread use of turtle shells in addition to shoulder blades, the sophisticated preparation of the animal remains, chiselled to produce hollows and grooves to facilitate the application of fire and also structure the omen cracks. Inscriptions were added afterwards, noting the occasion and result of the particular divinatory act, and also sometimes the coming to pass of the events which proved the efficacy of the oracle. After the

fall of the Shang, the Chou continued divination by shells and bones
for a while before the practice died out.[12]

Later ritual texts and historical records, such as the *Historical Annals* (*Shih-chi*) compiled during the Han dynasty (about 1st
century B.C.), give us information about how the shells and bones
were prepared for divinatory uses. This happened probably after the
animal victims themselves had been offered in sacrificial ritual. The
assumption was that the dead animals would have special power in
contacting others in the spiritual world, especially ancestor figures.
The ritual itself usually took place under the direct supervision of
the king and at his court, perhaps in the ancestral temple; the
questions were usually addressed to ancestral spirits; the fire was
applied, and the cracks appeared. The persons who engraved the
records on the shells and bones were not the same persons as those
who probed or interpreted. But we do not know on what basis the
simple 'yes' or 'no' reply from the spirits was chosen. So far, the
notations in the inscriptions do not offer enough correlation with
the shapes and angles of cracks. Although there is evidence that
divination manuals were followed, these are no longer extant.
Besides, we do not know whether the manuals explain the logic
of prognostication, or whether such was left to a so-called higher
form of reasoning.

Divination and Seance

Between the name of the ancestor and the word for king, a word
which means 'guest' (*pin/bin*) in modern Chinese is often found
on oracle records. There is speculation that it refers to the king
'receiving as guest' a specific ancestor, or God himself, or at least,
to a kind of possibly ecstatic *seance*. How this happened remains
unclear. Apparently, music and dancing were part of the divination ritual, during which alcohol, served from bronze vessels,
was possibly consumed in some quantity – and these could have
contributed to a ritual trance. Perhaps, the 'guest' was the prototype
for the institution of the ancestral impersonator (*shih/shi*), in whom
the spirit allegedly descended and to whom ritual offerings were
made. But another question is: if so, did such take place during the
sacrificial ritual, or also during the divination ritual, frequently a
preamble to an important sacrifice? Unfortunately, available records
do not enlighten us on these points.[13]

In the context of the Old Testament, it is said that all inspired
prophetic speech is based on a 'revelatory trance experience'. In
early Christianity, the Shepherd of Hermas was much influenced

by Graeco-Roman magical divination, which involved divine possession. But divination never became part of the living traditions of the institutional Christian church.[14] What about the diviners of ancient China? Were they mere ritual specialists, or were they *shamans* given to trance-like sessions? According to the shells and bones, and the ritual texts of later ages, the *Institutes of Chou* (*Chou-li*) and especially the *Ceremonials* (*Yi-li*), divinatory functions were divided between the person(s) who posed the question (*chen-jen/zhenren*), the person(s) in charge of the specific ritual itself, including the burning, and the person(s) who interpreted the results. In the case of royal divination, there were also official recorders or archivists. Since royal divination revolved around decisions concerning state matters or the ruler's private life, the assumption was to involve the supernatural order in the human and natural order, to receive blessings from above, and to avoid punishments and calamities. In this sense, it differed little from divination elsewhere, such as in ancient Sumero-Babylonian religion.

In Shang times, divination involved mainly the use of shells and bones, and occasionally yarrow stalks. With the fall of Shang, the tortoises gradually fell into disuse, while the stalks were increasingly used, especially in association with the *Book of Change*. But yarrow plants are perishable materials, and have not survived. Our knowledge about them comes from the texts, and from extant usage. In these cases, the diviner appeared to have the dual responsibility of performing the ritual and of interpreting its outcome with help of divination manuals. These have as their kernel the sixty-four hexagrams (*kua/gua*), which, in turn, are derived from the eight trigrams, composed of broken or unbroken lines. In divining with help of the *Book of Changes*, today's diviners still have recourse to yarrow stalks, acting somewhat like playing with a deck of cards. Since it is a time-consuming process, it is being replaced in many parts of Taiwan and Southeast Asia by the use of coins.

Astrology and Dream Interpretation
Besides divination by oracle, there were related practices such as astrology and divining the future through the interpretation of dreams. This ancient practice is well known to all who have read the Old Testament story of the Hebrew patriarch Joseph, who interpreted the pharaoh's dreams, and predicted seven years of plentiful harvests followed by seven lean years.

In ancient China, there was little difference between astronomy or the study of the heavens, and astrology or analysing the influence of heavenly bodies on human life and society. Indeed, the observation of the heavens was motivated by the belief that heavenly laws and astral bodies have influence on earth as well. Besides, a calendar based on astronomical knowledge was important, as this was to be the basis of the seasonal arrangement of religious rituals and agricultural work. Tradition makes the cultural hero Fu-hsi the maker of the first calendar, and the Yellow Emperor its reformer and the rectifier of intercalation. It appears that the Chinese already knew about the five planets and the twelve zodiacal signs, and carefully determined solstices and equinoxes some four thousand or more years ago. Comets and eclipses were considered warnings from above, so that human beings, especially rulers, might reform their personal conduct as well as their conduct of government.[15]

Oracle bone inscriptions often refer to dreams, which may also carry warnings from the spiritual world. Sometimes the spirits were understood as demanding sacrificial offerings. Thus the interpretation of dreams often involved divination itself. In ancient Egypt, this was done with help from astrology. In China, there was a multitude of methods, by consulting oracle bones or the *Book of Changes*, or with the help of meteorological phenomena. Even more interestingly, the practice was made of divination by dreams which was later subjected to verification by appeal to oracle divination. In Chinese antiquity, there were also officials (*chan-jen/zhanren*), in charge of dream interpretation, who apparently performed their duties with the help of their knowledge of the stars.[16]

The *Book of Poetry* offers various examples of dreams and dream interpretation of good or evil fortune:

> Below, the rush-mats, over them the bamboo-mats.
> Comfortably he sleeps,
> He sleeps and wakes
> And interprets his dreams.
> 'Your lucky dreams, what are they?'
> 'They were of black bears and brown,
> Of serpents and snakes.'
> The diviner thus interprets it:
> 'Black bears and brown
> Mean men-children.
> Snakes and serpents,
> Mean girl-children.'[17]

6 The Decline of Divination

After the fall of the Shang, the practice of divination lost some favour at court but spread widely among the common people. Nevertheless, voices of disbelief were heard from among the more intellectual. From the third century B.C., we have the story of Ch'ü Yüan, the minister exiled from the court of the state of Ch'u, who called upon the Great Diviner Chan Yin to settle the turmoil in his mind. His questions were so phrased as to allow for simple affirmative and negative answers:

> Is it better to be painstakingly honest, simple-hearted and
>   loyal,
> Or to keep out of trouble by welcoming each change as it
>   comes?
>
> . . .
>
> Is it better to risk one's life by speaking truthfully and with-
>   out concealment,
> Or to save one's skin by following the whims of the wealthy
>   and high-placed?
>
> . . .
>
> Is it better to be honest and incorruptible and to keep oneself
>   pure,
> Or to be accommodating and slippery, to be compliant as lard
>   or leather? [18]

It is said that the Great Diviner threw aside the divining stalks, excused himself, and said:

> There are cases in which the instruments [of divination] are
>   of no avail, and knowledge can give no enlightenment.
> There are things to which my calculations cannot attain,
>   over which the divinity has no power.
> My lord, for one with your mind and with resolution such as
>   yours,
> The tortoise and the divining stalks are unable to help. [19]

The answers Ch'ü Yüan sought seemed simple enough, but the questions he asked were obviously not such that the tortoise and the stalks could answer. He was ruminating over ethical decisions, and these were not meant for oracles. The diviner readily admitted impotence, indicating the limits of divination as well as, perhaps, the rise of a new age, when human beings were to rely more upon themselves, their own moral intuitions, rather than upon the 'instruments of divination'. Just as an ethical, prophetic religion in ancient Israel followed upon an earlier stage when divination and ecstasy had played a more important role, so too, in China, a new epoch was on the horizon.[20]

2
Sacrifice and Kingship: the Eclipse of Ancient Religion

1 Of Gods and Spirits

It has sometimes been said that the Chinese knew no gods, and that Chinese civilisation is by nature secular. This assertion, often made in the past, is no longer tenable. The study of archaeology and textual philology has yielded us a hierarchy of gods and spirits worshipped in Chinese antiquity, which rivals that of the ancient Near East and of the Graeco-Roman world.

The Supreme Deity: A Duality of Names
Above all the spirits and deities of ancient beliefs stood a supreme deity. In Chinese, this figure was called Lord (*Ti*) or Lord-on-high (*Shang-ti*), who reigned over a host of nature-deities just as the king below ruled over his court. The exact etymological meaning of the term *Ti* is not clear, and various explanations have been offered, especially those surrounding the sacrificial cult. He is usually understood anthropomorphically, and considered to be the supreme deity. He is also frequently referred to in Western literature as God. In divination, questions regarding eclipses of the sun and the moon were especially posed to him, such natural events being then regarded as manifestations of heavenly displeasure with earthly conduct.

   In Shang times (c. 1766–1122 B.C.), the Lord-on-high was represented as a being remote and impersonal, perhaps a creator God. I am not asserting that the ancient Chinese believed in any clear doctrine of creation. There is scant evidence for this. The speculation is based rather on a comparison between this figure and the later Chou figure called Heaven, which was much closer to the people who worshipped it, and displays more the characteristics of an ancestral deity.

In Chou times (1122–249 B.C.), Heaven became the preferred term for God. According to etymology, the term *T'ien* referred probably to a human with a big head. The word was often found on bronze inscriptions, designating a personal God who was interested in human affairs, and possibly the supreme ancestor figure worshipped by the Chou royal family. The conquest of Shang by Chou was actually the conquest of an eastern people in North China by a western people. It probably led to the confusion and combination of two originally distinct cults, and to the subsequent usage of both *Ti* and *T'ien* to designate the supreme being, regarded as a personal God.

The presence of these two names for God reminds us of early Judaism, where there were also two different names for God, stemming out of Yahwist and Elohist sources for the Pentateuch or the Five Books of Moses. I am referring to the name Yahweh (Hebrew: YHWH) which was explained to Moses in the burning bush as *ehyeh asher ehyeh* (Exod. 6:6f.), that is, 'I am who I am' according to the early translators and their scholastic followers, or 'I shall be what I shall be' according to the Jewish philosopher Martin Buber and more modern exegetes. The other name was Elohim, a plural but used with the singular verb, meaning God or Godhead. These too were later used interchangeably in the Old Testament: 'that you might know the Lord (Yahweh) is God (elohim); there is no other besides him' (Deut. 4:35). In this Jewish case, both terms had personal connotations, whereas, in the Chinese case, the term *T'ien* would later take on pantheistic tones.[1]

Nature Deities and Ancestral Spirits
Besides this supreme deity, there were three other classes of gods or spirits in ancient China.[2] These include the following:

- The nature deities of the Shang oracle bones. These include such heavenly deities as sun, moon, wind, clouds, rain, and snow; earthly deities as the earth (*she*) itself and its produce, grain (*chi/ji*), rivers and mountains; the so-called 'Queen Mothers of the East and West', perhaps goddesses identified with the sun and moon, perhaps also the spouses of the Lord.

    These were all under the direct control of *Ti*. Their ancient cult and the veneration they continued to receive in later ages give witness to the mixed character of Chinese religion: never exclusively an ancestral religion, but rather, a combination of the cult of ancestors with that of other spirits.

- The high ancestors, frequently semi-divine figures to whom the royal lineage was traced, and to whom the later ancestral spirits, both male and female, as well as the spirits of deceased ministers, looked up.

  The Three Dynasties were each allegedly founded by members of a different clan – people who traced their descent from the same mythological ancestor. The Hsia dynasty (3rd millennium B.C.?) goes back to the sage-hero Yü, allegedly born out of a rock. The Shang dynasty had for its principal high ancestor a mythical hero whose mother became pregnant after devouring a dark bird's egg. The Chou dynasty goes back to Chi, the 'Lord Millet', whose mother had allegedly trodden on *Ti's* divine footprint.

- The ancestral spirits of the common people. Their cult was little known until a much later age, as the practice was not meticulously recorded. One might associate with these departed spirits the term for the 'ghost' (*kuei/guei*), the graph for which shows a human being wearing a huge mask, possibly to signify a feeling of strangeness.

2   Sacrifice and Ancient Religion

Like the ancient Hebrews, the ancient Chinese had a three-tiered world view, of heaven above, the abode of the dead below, and earth, the abode of the living, in between. They believed that at death, the upper soul (*hun*) rises up to heaven while the lower soul (*p'o/po*) descends into the earth. While this belief was formulated only in Chou times, it was already implicit in the religious beliefs of Shang times, and in Shang practices of divination and sacrifice. This is not to say that the dead were supposed to be 'imprisoned' down under. The royal ancestors were often represented as somewhere 'on high', in the presence of the Lord, and continued to have power over the living, whether to protect or bless them or to punish and curse them. They were also represented as expecting their descendants to provide sacrificial 'blood' offerings for their nurture and enjoyment.

Sacrifice represents the offering of one's self to the divinity. As such, it is often characterised as *the* holy action, in which the human being finds his or her religion most clearly expressed and realised. And human history offers us evidence of a great diversity of practice, regarding who offered the sacrifice, what was offered, where, when and how, why and for whom it was offered. Yet no unanimous theory has emerged regarding the origin of sacrifice – whether that be a test of endurance or homage, or expression of anxiety or gratitude, or magic, or re-enactment of a primordial event or that of the idea of a scapegoat.

Presumably through a complicated process of development, different forms of sacrifice emerged very early. What was already present in the archaic cultures also evolved in the early high cultures as very complicated rituals, complete with detailed instruction manuals. It is especially in China and Israel that we can observe how offerings, mostly fruit or animal victims, were brought to the altars, sanctified and destroyed, in order to achieve contact with an invisible power and thereby avert evil or invite beneficial influence.

Sacrifice in General
Technically, the Chinese word *chi/ji* (sacrifice) is said to derive from a graph representing the offering of meat, and possibly also wine, to some spirit. Originally, the practice began as a simple act of providing food for the dead. According to the Shang oracle inscriptions, burnt offerings were made also to other than heavenly spirits. But later ritual texts describe an elaborate system of state sacrifices, each with its own name, offered to heavenly and earthly deities as well as to ancestral spirits.

We have ample evidence from both oracle and bronze inscriptions as well as from later classical texts regarding what victims were used and how rituals were carried out. The usual victims were cattle, goats and pigs, with young bulls being preferred for the most important sacrifices. Other objects, like jade and silk, were also offered. In the case of animal victims, the selected animal had to be the best available, perfect in itself. This was led to the site, killed and opened up by the chief priest celebrating the event, with some assistance from the other participants. The fat was burnt to make smoke, inviting the spirits to descend, and the internal organs were prepared and cooked. In the royal ancestral temples, special halls and yards were available for various kinds of sacrificial rituals, with bronze vessels of different sizes and shapes to hold the raw and cooked offerings.

Often implicit in sacrificial action is a sense of sin. Everywhere – not just in China or Japan – an animal or a human victim could, as *pars pro toto*, serve as 'scapegoat' and take upon itself the sins of the community and of the individuals, in order to destroy or expel them. This becomes evident when we examine the case of King T'ang, founder of the Shang dynasty, who sought to offer himself to the supreme being in an effort to save the people from the consequences of long-term drought. We should emphasise at this stage that sin did not necessarily imply moral evil, but simply some offence against God or the ancestors. Indeed, ancient religion showed little interest in questions of moral good or evil. Its ritual practices were aimed at pleasing the spirits, rather than in inculcating moral values.

Human Sacrifice

We cannot avoid discussing the topic of human sacrifice. Since we take for granted the value of human life today, we are often astonished to find evidence to support the practice of sacrificing human victims, be that in Aztec Mexico, or among the ancient Israelites, where God appeared to have approved of this practice, such as in the case of Jephthah offering his daughter as fulfilment of a vow (Judges 11:34–40). Among scholars, human sacrifice is now regarded as a universal religious phenomenon in antiquity. In China's case, even without consulting archaeological finds, there is mention in the *Historical Annals* of the story of Duke Hui of Chin who was nearly offered in a ritual sacrifice to the Lord-on-high by his captors, but was saved after the interventions of the Chou king and his own sister (645 B.C.). Presumably, royal or noble captives were not the usual sacrificial victims. Since the number of victims was often high, even in the hundreds, the unfortunate were often war captives, perhaps sometimes even criminals, and sacrificial rituals resemble thereby civil punishments.

According to other textual evidence, human victims were not always offered on altars of sacrifice. There were those also who accompanied their lords and ladies to the other world, in the burial chambers of ancient Egypt as well as China. Such a practice might not formally rank as ritual sacrifice, but served a purpose that is also based on religious belief in the after-life, as well as the human desire for companionship in the after-life. The chosen victims were from all states of life. Some belonged to the nobility, either as spouses or retinue of the deceased. Others were slaves or captives.

Let us offer here a record of the sorrow of some such noblemen chosen to be burial companions to a deceased duke:

'Kio' sings the oriole
As it lights on the thorn-bush.

Who went with Duke Mu to the grave?
Yen-hsi of the clan Tzu-chu.
Now this Yen-hsi
Was the pick of all our men.
But as he drew near the tomb-hole
His limbs shook with dread.
That blue one, Heaven,
Takes all our good men.
Could we but ransom him
There are a hundred would give their lives![3]

One wonders whether the action is taken not only because the chosen victims were nobles, that is, the best the realm could offer, but also because of political motivation, to remove such valiant men who might become trouble-makers to the duke's heir. While I mention this possibility, I do not assert that I have evidence to support it.

Frequently, burial companions were women, concubines to the deceased or just ladies of the court. The first Ch'in emperor and dynastic founder took with him all those who constructed his underground mausoleum – and with them went the secret of access to the mausoleum. But he took as well all the childless ladies of his harem, presumably because they were not needed by the next generation, and might better serve him underground. Archaeologists have successfully unearthed many things from this vast subterranean hideaway. Thus we have near Xi'an today the impressive life-size terracotta army of men and horses, recovered from their burial place by those who dug them up. These had served as secondary burial companions to the dead emperor.

The classical texts confirm the practice of human sacrifice in antiquity, but without giving it approbation. We know the stories in the *Book of Rites*. One gives the example of a disciple of Confucius, telling his brother's widow that burying the living with the dead was contrary to the rites and should not be followed. Another gave the instance of a son who refuses to follow his father's dying wish to have him buried in the same coffin with two living concubines.[4] It reflects the result of ethical consciousness which came with the evolution of Confucian humanism.

3   Priesthood and Shamanism

The English word 'priest' denotes a religious specialist with a special ability to communicate with the divine, devoted especially to cultic worship, and belonging to both a profession and a class. As such, the priest may occasionally appropriate the function of other specialists, whether medicine men, diviners, or magicians, but functions usually as someone with specialist knowledge of the deity and expert skills permitting the performance of cultic duties. The priest's mediating powers depend upon his ability to influence the supernatural powers or the deity, whereas the magician's powers to manipulate nature rest upon *techniques* properly applied, such as spells and incantations.

Scholars have often remarked on the absence of a powerful priestly caste in the case of China. While we know of Taoist priests, they have not, as a group, possessed much power. Yet the ancient sacrificial cult had its ministers, be these specialists or not. Who were these people called *chu/zhu*, dedicated to the Shang sacrificial cult? Whereas we find a differentiation of sacrifices depending on the people – gods, spirits and ancestors – to whom they were offered, we do not have a term which is exactly parallel to the English word 'priest'. That is why scholars tend to characterise ancient Chinese religion as a religion of 'shamans', known as *wu*, or the combined term *wu-chu*. But then, is it possible to make a meaningful differentiation between the religious specialists of ancient China, between diviners, priests and shamans?

Priesthood

The biblical term for 'priest' is the Hebrew word *kohen*, and Jewish priests are known to have performed multiple functions: cultic, oracular, healing, and others.[5] According to definitions given in the Han dynasty lexicon, the *Shuo-wen chieh-tzu*, the *wu* is a person who serves the invisible spirits and can call these down by dances. The word also refers both to a person who is skilled in dancing, and to someone holding in two hands the instruments of magic or divination. Thus it refers to a person who apparently reaches a state of trance through ritual dance, and is able afterwards to transmit the wishes of the spirits to human beings.

While the *wu* does not so far bear much resemblance to the priest in Judaism or Christianity, the term *wu* is often used in association with another word, *chu*, signifying communication through the mouth with the divine. Indeed, the oracle bone script for *chu* offers the picture of a human being kneeling in front of an altar. But the Han lexicon calls *chu* a female *wu*. The term *wu-chu* can refer to the same individual, or to two persons, or two kinds of persons, with distinct functions – espcially in antiquity. When it is used particularly to refer to the *wu* or shaman, his or her special skills include praying in rain dances, communicating with the spirit world, perhaps also predicting good or evil fortune, healing sicknesses and interpreting dreams. One explanation is that the word *wu* refers to a mediator between the human world and the divine, while the word *chu* refers to the mouthpiece of the Lord who transmits his messages to human beings, an expert in ritual incantations. We come now to a stronger parallel for the priest in Western religions.

Presumably, the *chu* were members of the official clergy, to whom was entrusted especially the worship of ancestors in antiquity, and may be described as the priests and deacons of the state cult, with special responsibility for sacrifices. Their status appears to have risen, at the expense of the *wu*, by the end of the Chou dynasty. Their duties included praying for blessings from on high, especially for a good harvest. To the extent that their incantations were considered effective in themselves, these peoples may also be called magicians. Unlike the *wu*, however, they did not have the gift of ecstasy.

'Shamanism'

There is much that may be described as *ecstatic* in the traditional religion of East Asia in general, and in ancient Chinese religion in particular. I use here the singular for 'religion', which, in turn, has a plurality of forms and expressions. For 'ecstatic religion', I shall borrow the description from I. M. Lewis, who speaks of 'the seizure of man by divinity' in ecstatic encounters.[6] According to him, the Tungus word *shaman* means literally 'one who is excited, moved, or raised', that is, a person of either sex who has mastered spirits and who can at will introduce them into his or her own body, or a person who permanently incarnates these spirits and can control their manifestations, entering into controlled states of trance in appropriate circumstances. He insists on the regular occurrence together of spirit possession and shamanism, particularly in the Arctic *locus classicus*, that is, in today's Siberia, but also beyond, such as among the Inuit or Eskimo people of the North American Arctic.

In my opinion, ancient Chinese religion may be defined as an *ecstatic* religion, to the extent that it had an essentially shamanic character. And even following upon the emergence of ethical humanism and the humanist repudiation of many of the myths and practices of an earlier age, religious Taoism and certain forms of Buddhism, together with that product of their union which is called popular or folk religion, continued to manifest those features that can be identified as shamanic and also ecstatic. We may even say that it continues to persist in today's folk religious tradition, wherever the Chinese live and thrive.

Speaking etymologically, the word 'shaman' comes from a North Asian, specifically Siberian context (Tungusic – *saman*), and denotes a person, male or female, who has a special ability of communing with the gods, or with one of the gods, through knowledge and mastery of a 'technique of ecstasy'. Indeed, they are described as becoming shamans through initiatory ecstatic experiences such as pathological sicknesses, dreams and trances, followed by theoretical and practical instruction at the hands of the old masters. Such is always an ecstatic type of experience, including what resembles a mystical marriage with a god, that determines his or her 'vocation'. They are alleged to have the ability of having visions, of seeing the spirits, whether of deceased humans or of animals, and of being able to communicate with these in a secret language, such as during a seance. They are also described as being able to levitate, to make magical flights into the sky and magical descents into the underworld, to have mastery over fire and to cure sicknesses – all of this, usually in a trance state. And they are alleged to have power over rain.

While the later Old Testament prophets, like Ezekiel and Jeremiah, were associated with priesthood, the earlier prophets, who were wonder-workers and soothsayers, were also ecstatics, and have been called 'shamanistic prophets'.[7] It has even been suggested that Jesus, in his desert experience followed by a career as a miracle-worker, healer and exorcist, demonstrated shamanic features.[8] But on balance, the ecstatic character appears much stronger in the ancient Chinese tradition than it does in the Hebrew.

Arthur Waley has described the *wu* of ancient China as intermediaries in spirit-cults, experts in exorcism, prophecy, fortune-telling, rain-making and the interpretation of dreams, as well as magic healers. 'Indeed the functions of Chinese *wu* were so like those of Siberian and Tunguz shamans that it is convenient . . . to use shaman as a translation of *wu*.'[9]

The *wu*'s special gift is especially described in the collection of poems called the Nine Songs, derived from the 'Songs of the South', that issued from the mid-fourth-century-B.C. kingdom comprising parts of today's provinces of Hunan, Hupei, Anhwei, Honan and Szechuan, which together included about a third of the then-known China. There, the relationship between the shaman and the deity (either that between a female deity and a male shaman, or between a male deity and a female shaman) was described as a fleeting love affair, and the mood is often wistful:

> I have washed in brew of orchid, bathed in sweet scents,
> Many-colored are my garments; I am like a flower . . . .
> The Spirit in great majesty came down;
> Now he soars up swiftly amid the clouds . . . .
> Longing for that Lord I heave a deep sigh;
> My heart is greatly troubled; I am very sad.[10]

The shamans also served their clients by 'summoning back' the soul of a sick or deceased person. At one time, the soul was summoned wherever death had occurred, when a relative would climb onto the roof, holding the deceased's garments and crying out for the person to return.[11] In a poem entitled 'Summoning the Soul', we have the following dramatic plea on the part of the shaman, arguing the inhospitality of the other regions as reasons for returning:

> O soul, come back! In the east you cannot abide.
> There are giants there a thousand fathoms tall,
> who seek only for souls to catch,
> And ten suns that come out together,
> melting metal, dissolving stone . . . .
> O soul, come back! In the south you cannot stay.
> There the people have tattooed faces and blackened teeth;
> They sacrifice flesh of men,
> and pound their bones to paste . . . .
> O soul, come back! For the west holds many perils:
> The Moving Sands stretch on for a hundred leagues . . . ,
> And you will drift there for ever,
> with nowhere to go in that vastness . . . .
> O soul, come back! In the north you may not stay.
> There the layered ice rises high,
> and the snowflakes fly
> for a hundred leagues and more . . . .
> O soul, come back! Climb not to the heaven above.
> For tigers and leopards guard the gates . . . ,
> O soul, come back! Go not down to the Land of Darkness,
> Where the Earth-God lies, nine-coiled,
> with dreadful horns . . . .
> O soul, come back! Return to your old abode.[12]

Spirit-mediumship

Besides shamans and prayer-men, there was also another category of spiritual professionals (or semi-professionals), today called spirit-mediums, who continue to serve an important role in surviving folk religion.

Is there a clear difference between a shaman and a spirit-medium? The question is relevant, as we are now concluding the presentation by repeating the suggestion of ecstatic behavior and possible shamanic influences in ancient Chinese religion. Here, let me recall that Arthur Waley has made a distinction between a shaman dancing and a medium in motionless trance. I agree that such a distinction can be made, that is, between the charismatic shaman and the impersonator (*shih/shi*) serving as medium, who was not always a professional. I also perceive a possible distinction in behaviour, such as between a private individual absorbed in meditation, reaching perhaps a transformed state of consciousness, rendering him or her somewhat 'motionless', which I shall consider as a kind of 'personal religion', and the professional shaman or spirit-medium engaged in a public or semi-public performance including so-called magical feats, which is what I understand by 'shamanic religion'. Perhaps this distinction is better discerned today than in antiquity, and is in part derived from the difference between the semi-amateur medium, unable to control the trance state completely, and the professional shaman who does so at will. Besides, accounts given today of the trance behaviour of spirit-mediums in public include a whole *spectrum* of ecstatic behavior, ranging from motionless passivity to violent acts of self-injury and what may appear much more 'shamanic' in Waley's terms. All this we shall resume for description and discussion later in this book.

4 Kingship and Ancient Religion

The king was ultimately in charge of divination and diviners. He was similarly, in his capacity as chief priest, in charge of sacrifice and the priesthood. And he has also been described as the chief of shamans, in charge of the *wu* in his kingdom. Accepting that the king was a religious as well as a political leader, should we also consider his office to be not only a charismatic one, with reference to his purported claims of divine or semi-divine ancestry, but also a *shamanic* one? Was the first king of each dynasty, so to speak, a powerful shaman in his own right? And were his descendants considered as having inherited his shamanic powers as well? Here we are led to probe into an examination of kingship itself.

Shamanic Kingship in Ancient China

The Chinese word *wang* (king) is found frequently on oracle bones. The graph is sometimes supposed to represent a fire in the earth, other times an axe, but in any case designates without doubt the political ruler and his royal ancestors. The French scholar Léon Vandermeersch sees a relation between this word and another term, originally denoting 'male', and explains it as the virile 'king', father of the ethnic group, heir of the founder-ancestor's power. Thus he places kingship in a familial and patriarchal context.[13] As already explained, the ancient kings also claimed some kind of divine descent, whether we are to understand it totemically or otherwise. Divine descent symbolises without doubt a direct access to the supernatural, and the kings of antiquity were already called *t'ien-tzu/tianzi*, literally, the sons of Heaven, even if the kings and other rulers of historical China, unlike the emperors of Japan, never claimed for themselves any personal divinity. This is like the contrast between Mesopotamian and Egyptian concepts of kingship. Whereas in Egypt the king was a god descended among men, the Babylonian king was not a god but a human being charged with maintaining harmonious relations between society and the supernatural powers.

Were the ancient kings also shamans (*wu*)? One way of answering this question is to look at the stories concerning the early dynastic founders. The mythical Yü the flood-controller, of the Hsia dynasty, has been characterised as walking in a particular gait, described as the shaman's dance step. The information about King T'ang, the founder of the Shang dynasty, that we find in classical texts is much more rational. According to several accounts, T'ang's conquest of Hsia was followed by many years of drought, during which he was told by the diviners that Heaven could be placated only by a human sacrifice. Thereupon he purified himself, placed himself on the firewood, and prepared to offer himself to the Lord-on-high. But no sooner was the fire lit than rain came and quenched it.

T'ang's prayer is cited in the terse language of the *Analects* (20:1):

> I, the child Li, presume . . . to announce to thee, O most great and sovereign God. . . . If in my person, I committed offenses, they are not to be attributed to . . . the people of the myriad regions. If

[the people in the myriad regions commit offenses, these offenses must rest on me alone, the one man . . . . [14]

This gesture of self-sacrifice is a supreme example of a king's acting as both priest (*chu*) and victim while serving a shamanic (*wu*) role for the sake of getting rain. And he did so after divination, as would have been expected. The sense of expiation for sins, committed either by himself or the people, should especially be noted.

The story of King T'ang bears some resemblance to Jesus' offering of himself on the cross. It also recalls to mind the account of Abraham's offering of his son Isaac, in a sacrificial ritual which was commanded by God and which was also interrupted by God, who asked for the substitution of the human victim by an animal one. Abraham's story is all the more relevant as it points to the practice of human sacrifice in ancient Israel as something demanded by an apparently bloodthirsty God. It is usually said that what happened was the testing of the patriarch's faith, but it can also be said that the final outcome showed divine disapproval of the institution of human sacrifice.

Kingship in China and Israel

In comparing the role of kingship in China and in ancient Israel, we should assert that neither the Chinese ruler, called the 'Son of Heaven', nor the ancient King of Israel, known as 'Son of God', had divine natures. We are rather speaking of rulers who exercised authority in the name of a higher power, the stewards of God rather than god-kings.

In ancient Israel the king was and remained, in spite of the title Son of God, wholly human, never divinised. As such, he was quite different from Egyptian and other ancient Near Eastern god-kings, and his power never extended over the forces of nature. According to the Jewish conception,

the king was not the son of God by nature, neither did he enter the divine sphere of his own accord at his accession. He was instead recognized as son by an express declaration of Yahweh's will, and in this fashion received a portion in Yahweh's dominion, property and heritage.[15]

In the case of ancient China, the ruling power was to evolve a theory called the 'Mandate of Heaven'. According to this, Heaven gives the mandate to the deserving man, who keeps it provided he and his descendants govern wisely and humanely. This theory developed with the emergence of the classical texts and of Confucian humanism. Flowing from it was the recognition that the evil ruler or tyrant could be overthrown. This gave justification to the rise and fall of many dynasties in Chinese history, an event unknown, for example, in Japan, where the emperors were themselves considered divine.

But since there was no separation between kingship and priesthood in ancient China, the king functioned at the same time as the Chief Diviner, the Chief Priest, and the Chief Shaman, and possessed all-embracing power. Among China's neighbours, we find the same kind of sacred kingship and early shaman-rulers. There was no difference between 'church' and 'state' in these traditional East Asian countries. If, in thirteenth-century Europe, pope and emperor fought repeatedly over power, in traditional China, political power was absolute, and only limited by circumstances such as the ruler's age or personality, and the power and personality of those who surrounded him.

5   Revisiting the Role of Women in Antiquity

It is interesting that the word *wu* originally referred to a female shaman, but was extended to include all shamans, long after their status had declined. It is also interesting that we should dwell so much on the shamanic character of rulership while we have only been able to speak of male rulers as kings in ancient China. Surely, female shamanic figures are abundant, especially in mythology. But the shaman-queen in ancient Japan appears as an exception to the historical rule established in China of male kingship.

My hypothesis is that the decline of the role of the professional shaman led as well to the decline of the role of women in society. Female shamans were increasingly assigned to one area of responsibility: that of rain-making. It remained an important responsibility, indeed, the official responsibility of the ruler. But as the ruler's secular duties took up increasing importance, kingship or rulership itself became more and more secularised. Also, in the patriarchal clan-family system, the practice of the ancestral cult rested very much on the shoulders of the male heirs. As the cult developed, female ancestors also received veneration in association with their spouses, and women could participate in certain auxiliary aspects of the cult, but sons, or in their absence, sons-in-law, were the chief priests in the family.

In the *Book of Poetry*, we find a song describing the differing ritual receptions of sons and daughters in the early Chou times:

> So he bears a son,
> And puts him to sleep upon a bed,
> Clothes him in robes,
> Gives him a jade sceptre to play with.
>
> . . .
>
> Then he bears a daughter,
> And puts her on the ground,
> Clothes her in swaddling clothes,
> Gives her a loom-whorl to play with.[16]

The gender roles were clearly determined at birth, with the male as a future ruler, to be honoured and pampered, and the female as educated to be subservient and destined for the work-force.

Shamanic Queenship in Ancient Japan
Unlike in China, the ruler in Japan was very early considered to be divine, by virtue of the shamanic powers that were associated with this position. Interestingly, the position was not reserved for men, and very early records disclose the existence of women rulers. We shall dwell briefly on this to offer a comparative context to our exploration of kingship in ancient China.

Indeed, the 'divine' character of the Japanese emperor already reveals something of its shamanic origin. And the shamanic character is also evident in the Shinto enthronement rituals surrounding the accession of the Heisei emperor in 1990. Actually, many of the early rulers were women, that is, shamanesses. The best known example is the charismatic Queen Himiko of the Yamato state, who reigned during the late second and early third centuries. Her story is described in the Chinese chronicle, *Wei-chi*:

> [The people of Wo] elected a young girl as their queen who was then named Himiko [literally, 'child of the Sun']. She attended and rendered service to the gods or spirits [literally, the way of the ghosts] and had a special power that bewitched the people. She never married even in her youth and her brother helped her administer the affairs of the Kingdom. After she was enthroned only a few persons were able to see her. Only one man always

attended her, served her meals, transmitted her words, and had access to her dwelling . . . . [17]

This charismatic queen appears to have been enthroned when she was only fourteen or fifteen, and her reign continued for sixty-eight years. Her personality and character appear typical of a shamanic queen. Some historians have even identified her with Amaterasu-O-mikami, that is, the Great Sun Goddess, and the mythical ancestress of the imperial family.

6　The Ecstatic Character of Ancient Religion

The religions of China, like Judaism, Christianity and Islam, did not simply arise out of intellectual reflections, especially the strictly rational demonstrations of a higher reality. After all, no religion is only a doctrine of God, or a theory about God. On the other hand, religions do not arise, as earlier historians of religions had suggested, in an oversimplified manner, from the purely irrational and unintellectual strata of the human psyche. Rather, today's specialists overwhelmingly agree that religions are grounded in an experiential unity of knowing, willing and feeling. And religion is also the pristine response to an encounter with or experience of the Holy, of Heaven, of the divine, of God, or whatever this may be called, an encounter or experience which is of a different nature from other encounters or experiences.

In a society like that of ancient China, life was dominated by the belief in ancestral spirits. The bond between the human and the divine was especially assured by communication between the ancestral spirits and their living descendants, or communication between the human and the divine through the mediumship of diviners or shamans. The heart of all rituals was that by which such communication was maintained, and the formal celebration of the ritual reveals its ecstatically shamanic character. I emphasise this point, because I assert that the bond between the human and the divine, the natural and the spiritual, was especially experienced in moments of ecstasy, such as through the shamans' experience of trances or spirit possession. This primordial 'Oneness of Heaven and Man' can be described as the model for the philosophical statement of the continuum between Heaven and Man – *T'ien-jen ho-yi*. Indeed, the latter may well represent a philosophical transformation of a primordial ecstatic experience.

To hear the voice of the gods and to act as their mouthpiece: was this not basically the function of the *wu-chu*, the shamans and priests of antiquity? Perhaps not all the historic kings in China – or in Japan – had the special gift of communicating with the divine, but they appeared to have descended from ancestors with such shamanic and ecstatic powers. It was a case of the institutionalisation of shamanic (and ecstatic) charisma. In this charismatic role, the king served as the chief diviner, the chief priest, and the chief shaman – at least in name. If certain later kings lost their powers, they continued to make use of those religious professionals who did possess and exercise the gift of ecstasy, of calling down the deity at will. All religion in ancient China, whether divination, sacrifice, rain-dance, and so-called magical healing, were predicated upon this special relationship between certain gifted people and the deities. All ritual pointed symbolically, and sometimes also actually to a primeval union between the human being and the gods, a union that was shamanic and ecstatic, a union that would be celebrated in a different way in later philosophical humanism.

7 The Emergence of Chinese Humanism

There is a palpable difference between the Shang and the Chou reigns. Where the Shang kings led the people in the service of 'ghosts and spirits', the Chou rulers made use of ritual and music to educate the people, keeping a 'respectful distance' from spirits and ghosts. The early Chou kings are represented as wise, even inspired leaders, conscientious in their performance of duties toward Heaven, the ancestors, and the people. But the later successors to the Chou mandate lacked their ancestors' political wisdom. History repeated itself at the end of the Shang dynasty. The royal domain was shaken by barbarian intrusions, while feudal lords grew impatient with the decline of central authority and began competing for hegemony among themselves.

The following poems, coming from the period following the eighth century B.C., express a sense of questioning of religion and of Heaven, in a time of disorder and uncertainty:

> Alas for my father and mother
> Alas for all their toil in bringing me up!
> Their good deeds I would requite
> It is Heaven, not I, that is bad.

. . .

Other people all prosper;
Why am I alone destroyed?[18]

Here is the voice of a man suffering from natural or man-
made calamities. Here are also echoes of Job complaining about
God's silence during his own sufferings. The Book of Job concludes
with Job's renewed faith and the return of God's blessings. In the
Chinese case, the questioning of religious belief is also reflected
in the philosophical thinking of the times. During a period of
unrest, in the sixth century B.C. and afterwards, a series of great
minds made up the Golden Age of Chinese philosophy. Confucius,
Mo-tzu, and Mencius, and possibly also Lao-tzu and Chuang-tzu,
further contributed to the rationalist atmosphere of philosophical
reflection, focusing upon the place of the human in the universe,
and the need of finding social and natural harmony. These men
had different ideas on many points regarding religion and morality,
but their common impact was to strengthen the sense of human
autonomy and rationality. Increasingly, human destiny – fortune
and misfortune – was associated with the activities of human beings
themselves rather than with the authority of the ghosts and spirits.
The system of religious orthodoxy, in belief as well as in ritual order,
was not discarded, although its importance was relativised.

3

Morality and Rituals: Confucianism as Religious Humanism

1 Confucianism as Religious Humanism

In the West, people are accustomed to an image of Confucius as a wise man or a sage, propounding a teaching about how to live a virtuous life, much as did Socrates in ancient Greece. Socrates is regarded as a humanist; in fact, he was condemned by the state for misleading youth, for turning them away from the gods of their fathers. Confucius had his own struggles with the state, but died a natural death. As a teacher, he too instructed the young in ideals different from those of the world around them. And extant records indicate that he seldom touched on religious matters. He is known as a humanist, and today's secular society tends to understand all humanists as secularists or at least religious agnostics.

Many Western philosophers are not sure that Confucius was even a philosopher, if by that word one is referring to a 'professional' philosopher, who analyses language and concepts or offers a systematic teaching about the world or human existence. Many would see him simply as propounding a practical wisdom without much speculative content. But then, many of these people have hardly ever read Confucius. They might even say that they have attempted some reading, and found it unattractive, since works like the *Analects* of Confucius, which gives the conversations between the master and the disciple, have at first sight too much of an *ad hoc* character without any challenging profundity.

But there are also exceptions. The American philosopher Herbert Fingarette is known for his work, *Confucius: The Secular as Sacred*

51

(1972). He singles out Confucius' love of ritual and discovers in this a sacred or religious dimension. Fingarette acknowledges philosophical value in Confucius, although he refrains from delving into the more metaphysical side of Confucius' teachings.

The German philosopher Karl Jaspers counts Confucius among the Great Philosophers, the 'paradigmatic individuals', together with Socrates, Jesus of Nazareth and the Buddha Gautama. In each case, we have a man who lived in a time of a social crisis, and sought to respond to this through special teachings aimed at all people. In each case as well, disciples were gathered, without regard to social backgrounds. In all cases, the teachings were not of abstract metaphysics but concern with the higher order of things (the 'Rites' or *li*, the Law or Torah, or the Dharma). These individuals offered their own critical interpretation of this higher order in opposition to external conformism and hypocrisy and in favour of an interior disposition. All lived what they preached, and represented a very high personal *ethic*, which expressed itself in clear moral demands.[1]

Within China itself, debates have also taken place in our own times about how to evaluate or categorise Confucius and his teachings. We are not speaking here of the diatribes that raged during the Anti-Confucius Campaign (1973–74) that have been discredited as politically motivated. We are referring to differences of opinion regarding how to view Confucius, and whether Confucianism should be considered a philosophy or a religion. The presupposition in Communist China is that Karl Marx was the greatest philosopher the world ever produced and that philosophy is superior to religion. To call a tradition a religion is therefore to put it in a place that is lower than that of philosophy, but higher than that of 'superstition'. Thus those scholars (including Fung Yu-lan and Kuang Yaming) who have more respect for Confucianism prefer to see it as a philosophy, while others who have less respect for it (especially Ren Jiyu) prefer to call it a religion.

In our own case, removed from ideological considerations, and also from any presumed superiority of philosophy over religion or vice versa, we shall regard Confucius mainly as a seminal thinker, and describe Confucianism as a humanism that is open to religious values. Here we are using the term Confucianism broadly, to include not merely the Master's original teachings, but also those teachings of later disciples that became integrated into the school of Confucius or the doctrinal and ritual system called Confucianism.

2   The Origins of Confucianism

What do I mean by 'Confucianism'? A Western designation of a
Chinese tradition, the term itself is ambiguous, representing an
ideology developed by a man of the name Confucius (552?–479 B.C.).
The Chinese themselves have usually preferred *Ju-chia/Rujia* or *Ju-
chiao/Rujiao*, the school or teachings of the scholars. Etymologically,
it has been claimed that the word *ju/ru* is related to the word for
'weaklings' or 'cowards', and referred originally to those dispos-
sessed aristocrats of antiquity who were no longer warriors, but
lived off their knowledge of rituals or history, music, numbers
or archery. It is a case of a pejorative term becoming eventually
a designation of honour, as also with the Christians. Eventually,
the school of *Ju* came to refer to the ethical wisdom of the past
that Confucius transmitted to later ages, as well as the entire
development of the tradition after his time.[2]

Confucius and the school named after him offered a moral or
ethical answer to the question regarding life's meaning and order
in society, an answer that would dominate Chinese philosophical thinking for about two millennia. But how did this answer
arise in the classical period? Obviously it was not produced in
a vacuum. And yet, the search for its genesis in the society of
its times is beset with problems. Many of the sources for the
period in which Confucius and his followers lived are coloured
by Confucian ideas, and either come from a later age or have been
edited at a later period. But then, must we accept Confucius as a
kind of Melchizedek figure, emerging in time, without immediate
intellectual predecessors, a lone voice that eventually won a hearing
for two thousand or more years? And what can we say about his life,
given the paucity of solid historical evidence, and the abundance of
legendary materials?

The Historical Confucius

In recent history, the *questioning* into Chinese tradition as such
and Confucianism in particular involved also a *quest* – that for
the historical Confucius, as distinct from the Confucius-image of
popular veneration. The development in the 1920s and 1930s of
a more scientifically critical historical method facilitated this task
to a certain extent. It might be studied in terms parallel to the
quest for the historical Jesus. But it is a much more difficult quest,
since the oldest extant source, the *Analects*, was compiled at least
a century after the Master's death, whereas the oldest document

in the New Testament came from within a generation of Jesus' death.[3]

First of all, *Confucius* is the Latin rendering by seventeenth-century Jesuit missionaries of K'ung Fu-tzu, or Master K'ung, whose name was K'ung Ch'iu, also styled K'ung Chung-ni. He was a native of the small state of Lu, whose birthplace is near modern Ch'ü-fu (Qufu, Shantung). As with the life of Jesus or even more, little can be established about his life, including the exact year of birth, and about his forebears and immediate family. However, legends (including very early ones) are abundant. He is sometimes said to be a direct descendant of the Shang royal house. However, at the time of his parents, the family's circumstances were far from comfortable. The highest public office he occupied at the age of fifty was as a kind of police commissioner in his home state, and only for about a year. In over ten years of travel, K'ung visited many feudal states, seeking, but never finding, a ruler who would use his advice. In old age, he devoted more time to teaching disciples, while also occupying himself with music and poetry, occasionally conversing with rulers or ministers.[4]

Were we to judge him on the basis of his attainments in public office, we would not even give him a footnote in history. This is despite the praises sung about the good order he set up for the state of Lu, where the people allegedly could go to sleep without locking their house doors, and also despite the allegation from some sources that he had his deputy executed on dubious grounds – an allegation that fuelled the Anti-Confucius campaign in 1973–74. Like many great personages, K'ung was to be remembered for reasons other than those goals to which he had oriented his life. Without doubt, he had a correct sense of his own mission to regenerate the culture of his time, without fully realising how that was to come about. Like Jesus, K'ung became historically influential only after his death, which was at around the age of seventy, from natural causes. Like Jesus, K'ung did not develop any systematic doctrinal structure in which manners, morals, law, philosophy and theology were clearly separated. In K'ung's case, the teachings were systematised only with Mencius (c. 371–289) and Hsün-tzu (c. 298–238).

The following passage gives us some insight into K'ung's own self-consciousness. His profound sense of reverence for the will of Heaven should help us appreciate the basically religious orientation of his life and character.

At fifteen I set my heart on learning [to be a sage].
At thirty I became firm.
At forty I had no more doubts.
At fifty I understood Heaven's Will.
At sixty my ears were attuned [to this Will].
At seventy I could follow my heart's desires, without
overstepping the line.

(Analects 2:4)

It is interesting to dwell on how his ears were attuned, presumably to Heaven's will. After all, the word *sage* was originally the graph for a large ear and a small mouth. But K'ung was a modest man who said, 'How dare I rank myself with sages . . . ? I prefer to say of myself, that I strive without cease [for sageliness] and teach others without weariness.' But then, what is sagehood, if not this constant striving – as his disciples recognised? They responded: 'This is just what we, your disciples, have been unable to learn from you' *(Analects* 7:33).

It might also be inferred that K'ung was a believer in Heaven as personal deity, as higher power, order and law, displacing the many 'gestalts' of the old gods. 'He who sins against Heaven, has no one to whom he can pray' *(Analects* 3:13). K'ung lived in an age of turmoil, during which the ancient religious beliefs were questioned, and he contributed to the rationalist atmosphere of philosophical reflection. But why shouldn't he question them, knowing what we do of ancient religion, with its emphasis on divination and sacrifice, including human sacrifice? Understandably, K'ung distanced himself from this. Interestingly, he heralded in a new age of ethical wisdom, by appealing to the legacy of the ancients. Was he a conservative or a reformer, or perhaps a revolutionary? We may already have some clues to answering this question.

The Confucian Classics

While Confucius' teachings are best found in the *Analects* – the record of his conversations with his disciples – early Confucianism regards as its special texts the Five Classics. This group of books includes various genres. Let us take another look at this text and the others in proper focus:[5]

- The *Book of Changes* or the *I-ching* probably existed at the time of Confucius, and was attributed to the sages of old. The manual centres upon short oracles arranged under sixty-four hexa-grams, symbols made up of combinations of broken and unbro-ken lines in groups of six. Commentaries were later added to the oracles. The longest one is the *Hsi-tz'u* or Appended Remarks, which offer early cosmological and metaphysical speculation in a cryptic language. The text is reaching a wide audience in our own times, especially since the psychoanalyst Carl Jung introduced the notion of 'synchronicity' to replace that of chance in evaluating the validity of divination.[6]

- The *Book of History*, also called the *Book of Documents* (*Shang-shu*, literally, ancient documents), is allegedly a collection organised and introduced by Confucius. It is mainly an assortment of speeches from royalty and chief ministers, as well as cer-tain narrative accounts of royal achievements and principles of government, arranged chronologically. While the materials describing early Chou times are more credible, some of the allegedly older chapters have been called forgeries.

- The *Book of Poetry*, also called the *Book of Songs*, or the *Odes* (*Shih-ching*) is basically a collection of three hundred and five songs. Probably compiled around 600 B.C., even if the materials could be much older, it includes four sections, with various genres, such as folk songs of love, courtship and desertion, as well as about hunts and dances. There are also banquet songs, or state hymns. Allegedly, Confucius compiled them from an ancient repertory of three thousand.

- The Classic of *Rites* is an entire corpus. This includes the *Ceremonials* (*I-li*), an early manual of etiquette for the nobil-ity, detailing such occasions as marriages and funerals, sac-rifices and archery contests. There is also the *Book of Rites* (*Li-chi*), with its forty-nine sections of ritual and government regulations, as well as treatises on education, the rites, music and philosophy. Then there is the *Institutes of Chou* (*Chou-li*), apparently an idealised description of offices of government in early Chou times. It is believed that these texts were compiled in the early first century B.C., on the basis of somewhat earlier materials.

- The *Spring-Autumn Annals* (*Ch'un-ch'iu*) is basically a didacti-cally and laconically written chronicle of the state of Lu, the Master's native state, which purports to explain the decline of the ancient political and moral order. The Annals cover the period dating from 722 to 481 B.C., and from this we have derived the 'Spring-Autumn Period'. It was attributed to

Confucius as author, but this is no longer acceptable. It is usually associated with three commentaries, or rather appendages: the vividly narrative *Tso-chuan* or Tso Commentary, the catechetical (question-and-answer) Kung-yang Commentary and Ku-liang Commentary.

A sixth classic, the *Book of Music*, is no longer extant.

In the past, Confucius has been considered the author of the classics, or at least, as their editor. Contemporary scholarship no longer takes this seriously. True, the core of many of these classical texts goes back to Confucius, and even to the time preceding him, which shows the ancient lineage of the school of *Ju*. But each of them underwent a long period of evolution, receiving accretions postdating Confucius.

The textual situation was complicated by the fact of the burning of books under the Ch'in emperor (213 B.C.). He also unified the writing system, making it difficult for later scholars to read more ancient scripts even when certain hidden texts were unearthed. The later restoration of the texts in the Han dynasty was a long process, complicated by the diversity of schools of transmission and forgeries. In 125 B.C., the state made these classics the basis of examinations in the imperial college, obliging aspiring scholar-officials to master their contents, and thus establishing the supremacy of the Confucian school. To assure proper transmission, these texts were, more than once, *literally* inscribed in stone. About them there eventually grew a corpus of commentaries and sub-commentaries, establishing various traditions of textual exegesis.

The Morality of Human Relationships

It has sometimes been said that Confucius' great merit is his discovery of the moral character of human relationships. He taught a doctrine of reciprocity and neighbourliness:

> To regard every one as a very important guest, to manage the people as one would assist at a sacrifice, *not to do to others what you would not have them do to you*. (*Analects* 15:23)

For its resemblance to Christian teachings, the last part of this quotation (my italics) has come to be called the *negative* Golden Rule.

Within Confucianism, the well-known 'Five Relationships' include the ruler–minister, father–son, husband–wife, elder and younger brother, and friend and friend. Three of these are family relationships, while the other two are usually conceived in terms of the family models. For example, the ruler–minister relationship resembles the father–son, while friendship resembles brotherliness. For this reason, the Confucian society regards itself as a large family: 'Within the four seas all men are brothers' (*Analects* 12:5).

The responsibilities ensuing from these relationships are mutual and reciprocal. A minister owes loyalty to his ruler, and a child filial respect to the parent. But the ruler must also care for his subjects, and the parent for the child. All the same, the Five Relationships emphasise the vertical sense of hierarchy. Even with the horizontal relationship between friends, seniority of age demands a certain respect; and if the conjugal relationship bears more natural resemblance to that between older and younger brothers, it is more usually compared to the ruler–minister relationship. Indeed, the duty of filial piety, the need for procuring progeny for the sake of assuring the continuance of the ancestral cult, has been for centuries the ethical justification for polygamy.

Confucius' main legacy is the teaching on *jen/ren*. Etymologically, it is written with the radical 'human' and the word for 'two', or, if one wishes, for a sign that might also be interpreted as 'above'. It is pronounced the same as the word for human being. Understandably, *jen* is always concerned with human relationship, with relating to others. It may also be explained as the virtue of the 'superior man', the gentleman. It is associated with loyalty (*chung/zhong*) – referring basically to loyalty to one's own heart and conscience, rather than to a narrower political loyalty – and reciprocity (*shu*) – respect of, and consideration for others (*Analects* 4:15).

Jen is also related to *li* (propriety or ritual). But the latter refers more to social behavior, and the former, to the inner orientation of the person. *Jen* is translated variously as goodness, benevolence, humanity and human-heartedness. It was formerly a particular virtue, the kindness which distinguished the gentleman in his behaviour toward his inferiors. He transformed it into a universal virtue, that which *makes* the perfect human being, the sage. The later importance of his teachings gave this a social importance – that moral character and merit should replace birth as the criterion for a gentleman.

Jen offers certain parallels to the Christian virtue of love or charity (Greek: *agape*). But it does not offer explicitly Heaven's love for human beings as a reason and model for imitation. It is rather based on human nature itself, and is rooted in human sentiment as well as in a fundamental orientation of life. *Jen* means affection and love: 'The human being of *jen* loves others.' This is the interpretation of a great Confucian thinker, Mencius (371–289?) (Mencius 4B:28). Indeed, such a person loves *all* and *everyone* (Mencius 7A:46). In somewhat contradictory language, such a person 'extends love from those he loves to those he does not love' (Mencius 7B:1). Hsün-tzu (c. 298–238), another Confucian thinker, concurs with this definition of *jen* as love. So does the *Book of Rites*. But the Confucian interpretation of *jen* as universal love differs from that of Mo-tzu (5th century B.C.), who advocates a love of all without distinction and who became the darling of Western missionaries in China. The followers of Confucius emphasise the need of discernment, even of making distinctions. They reserve for parents and kin a special love.

If the natural feelings underlying kinship call for special consideration, the natural feelings aroused by the neighbour's – *any* neighbour's – need for help are also recognised. This is especially underlined by Mencius, who gives the example of a man witnessing a child falling into a well (Mencius 2A:6). The *natural* first impulse is to rescue the child, and this comes before any desire for praise or fear of blame. The following of this impulse is an act of commiseration, or love of neighbour. This example serves as a kind of Confucian parable of the Good Samaritan, illustrating the meaning of universal love. And natural feelings serve also as an experiential guide. For the follower of Confucius, parental love for children can be extended to cover other people's children, just as filial respect for the aged can be extended to cover other people's parents and elders, so that the natural order serves as a starting point and an experiential guide in achieving universal love.

Familial relations provide a model for social behaviour. Respect your own elders, as well as others' elders; be kind to your own children and juniors, as well as those of others. These are the instructions of Mencius (1A:7), and have provided inspiration for generations of Confucians. They have been the reason for the strong sense of solidarity not only in the Chinese family, but also in Confucian social organisations even among overseas communities.[7]

3   Confucianism as Ritual Religion

Rituals are an essential dimension of religious life, giving expression to communal beliefs. They are closely related to prayer, meditation and even mysticism, whether in Christianity or any other religion. The Chinese word for ritual (*li*) is related etymologically to the words 'worship' and 'sacrificial vessel' with a definite religious overtone. But, in fact, the term has a much broader range of meanings in the Chinese context, straddling the sacred and the profane spheres. Somewhat like the contemporary English term, it came to include social practices, partaking even of the nature of law, as a means of training in virtue and of avoiding evil. And going beyond the English term, it refers also to propriety, that is, proper behaviour.

Ritual is a very important part of Confucius' teachings, and has been understood as such by his disciples, who were also teachers of rituals. Thus, Confucianism also became known as the ritual religion *li-chiao/lijiao*, with its emphases upon the doctrinal as well as ritual prescriptions for 'proper behaviour' in family and society. Confucian teachings helped to keep alive the older cult of veneration for ancestors, and the worship of Heaven, a formal cult practised by China's imperial rulers, who regarded themselves as the keepers of Heaven's Mandate of government, a kind of High Priest, a mediator figure between the human order and the divine order. With the official establishment of Confucianism, its classical texts were inscribed in stone, and collected a corpus of commentaries and sub-commentaries, establishing various traditions of textual exegesis. This took place during the period of time spanning the Han (B.C. 206–220 A.D.) and the T'ang (618–906 A.D.) dynasties. Among these texts, the *Spring-Autumn Annals* in particular gave rise to allegorical interpretations that drew in *yin-yang* metaphysics offering a new cosmological and historical vision, while the *Book of Rites*, with its elaborate instructions for correct deportment, especially regarding mourning and funerals, became the backbone of Chinese society.

Confucius also emphasised the need to have the right inner dispositions, without which ritual propriety becomes hypocrisy (*Analects* 15:17). He insisted that sacrifice is to be performed, with the consciousness of the presence of the spirits (3:12). Besides, 'what can rites do for a person lacking in the virtue of humanity (*jen*)? What can music do for a person lacking in humanity?' (3:3)

Speaking of sacrificial rites, we should give attention to Confucius' announced distaste for an item of ritual usage: the human effigies or wooden burial figures (*yung*). These were made with moving limbs, to better represent human beings capable of serving their lords and ladies in the world of the dead. Confucius is reported to have said that those who made such figures did not deserve to have posterity (Mencius 1A:4). It was an unequivocal condemnation of human sacrifice, even when performed symbolically.

The Cult of Heaven

We made mention of the worship of Heaven. The phrase refers to the annual sacrifices offered by the emperor to heaven and earth. Today we may still visit the sites on which these rituals took place in Peking (Beijing). The Temple of Heaven, which goes back to the Ming dynasty (1368–1661), is situated in a wide park outside the former 'forbidden city'. There are several old structures there, including the well-known circular prayer hall for good harvests, with its blue tiles (blue being the colour of Heaven). What is even more impressive are the three circular open-air marble terraces, under the sky itself. Here is the altar for the cult of Heaven. The middle of the topmost terrace is the place where the emperor used to make sacrifices to the Lord-on-high at the time of the winter solstice.

To what religion does the Temple of Heaven belong? This is a question often posed by visitors. The correct answer is: to Chinese religion. But exactly what is Chinese religion? Tradition has transmitted a plurality including Confucianism and Taoism. We would have to say more specifically: that Chinese religion includes a dimension of nature worship which was transformed by Confucianism and Taoism and incorporated into each system in a different way. And, to the extent that the cult of Heaven has been approved by the Confucian tradition, one might even designate the Temple of Heaven as a *Confucian* temple. Indeed, the *Book of Rites* contains precise instructions for the performance of this cult to Heaven. This ritual surrounding the cult of Heaven developed very early, existing already at the time of Confucius, and remaining in many respects the main feature of Chinese religion until the twentieth century.

The cult to Heaven was a sacrifice of burnt offerings. It resembles the Jewish Temple sacrifice more than it does the Christian Eucharist, occurring as it did only once a year. Attendance was strictly limited, as the population in general was not admitted, and individual citizens would be guilty of high treason should they attempt to perform it. Rather, the performance was the privilege as well as sacred duty of the Son of Heaven, the emperor. This itself was not only proof that there was no separation between political and religious powers, between the *imperium* and the *sacerdotium*, but also that the office of the emperor was basically a continuation of the ancient office of the priest-shaman-king.

Within the temple compound, the annual sacrifice took place at the winter solstice. The emperor prepared himself for this high-priestly function by a three-day fast and vigil, in which his assistants, princes and officials, also took part. The offering was an animal victim, a bullock of one colour, without blemish. The ritual was accompanied by other oblations and invocations as well as by solemn music. And the keynote was *thanksgiving*, as with the Christian Eucharist. 'The whole service was a *thanksgiving* to the Lord-on-high and to the great dynastic ancestors, and to the hosts of heaven, for the blessings bestowed from above during the year.'[8]

In speaking of the cult to Heaven, one should not neglect the other cult, offered to Earth. The dual cults give an impression that Heaven and Earth are equals, each accepting a sacrifice. But the reality is not quite so. While the sacrifices of Heaven and Earth both belonged to the category of 'great' sacrifices, performed by the emperor himself as Son of Heaven, Heaven takes on greater importance and is addressed as Lord-on-high. It would appear that these cults represented a mixture of beliefs, which came down with the interaction of Shang and Chou religions. Sacrifices were thus offered both to Heaven and Earth as cosmic forces, and to Heaven in particular as a supreme deity.[9]

The Other State Cults

Starting from the time of the Han dynasty, an elaborate state cult was evolved, which has been, rightly or wrongly, attributed to Confucian teachings. They include expressions of very ancient beliefs, not just in a supreme deity, and in natural powers as deity symbols, as well as in the intercessory powers of deceased worthies or heroes. We mentioned the great rituals performed by the emperor himself, not only for the worship of Heaven but also for that of Earth, and of his imperial ancestors. There were also intermediate rituals, for the worship of the sun and the moon, and numerous spirits of earth and sky. There were the lesser sacrifices to minor gods, including those of mountains, lakes, and rivers as well as those well-known historical figures – in particular wise and incorrupt magistrates – honoured as 'city gods'. Besides, surrounded by his disciples, and also by later worthies, Confucius himself became the centre of an elaborate cult which possibly would have been most repugnant to him.[10] While not deified, he received official sacrifices as the teacher *par excellence*, and was especially venerated by the scholarly class. The Confucian emphasis on rituals assured a continuity with the past, and offered also a ritual as well as a moral education for the would-be gentleman.

With the establishment of a republic in China (1912) the cult of Heaven, as well as the other state cults, came to an end. But their memory remains as witness to a theistic belief (be this monotheism or polytheism, depending on one's interpretations) present at the heart of traditional Chinese religion, and persisting throughout the ages, in spite of the changes in the philosophical interpretation of this belief.

The Cult of Ancestors
Any religion that focuses so much on ancestors presupposes some belief in the hereafter. The Confucian belief was that the human being is compounded of two 'souls', an upper, or intellectual soul, called the *hun*, which becomes the spirit (*shen*), and ascends to the world above, and a lower, or animal soul, called the *p'o/po*, which becomes the ghost (*kuei*) and descends with the body into the grave. These ideas are especially found in the *Tso Commentary* (*Tso-chuan*), in a recording of a conversation dated 534 B.C., where these 'souls' are also presumed to be possessed by everyone, not just nobility. Such ideas are confirmed by archaeological findings of tomb paintings of a heavenly realm, as in Ma-wang-tui, the Han site. They were also accepted by the Taoist religion, which greatly elaborated them. The Taoist cult of immortality, involving physical immortality or the ascent to Heaven as immortals, developed from these beliefs, especially regarding the *hun*.[11]

The ancestral cult was a memorial service, held previously at ancestral temples, and after that at gravesides or at home. Wine and food libations were usually offered, with silent prostrations in front of the tablets. The ancestors were alleged to have tasted the food, before the whole family partook of the meal. Conversion to Christianity frequently represented a rupture with this tradition, since the converts were either forbidden, or no longer expected, to continue the cult.

Much better known than the cult of Heaven, the cult of ancestors goes back to the dawn of Chinese history, although originally it was the exclusive privilege of the nobility. It became associated with the state orthodoxy, while remaining very much a family practice – an expression of a community of both the living and the beloved deceased. While the ancestral cult may be regarded as a religion in itself, its persistence has also been considered as another indication of the religious character of Confucianism. Until today, in many Chinese houses in Hong Kong, Taiwan and Southeast Asia – as well as in Korea and Japan – the ancestral shrine is maintained.

Until very recent times, memorial services were held, either at ancestral temples (which became impossible in Communist China), or at ancestral graves, or at home, where tablets, engraved with the names of the ancestors, used to be kept. Wine and food libations were usually offered; silent prostrations would be made in front of the tablets. And then, the whole family partook of the meal, which the ancestors allegedly had already tasted. In this sense, then, the memorial dinner also resembles the Christian Eucharist as a religious celebration of a common meal, in which both living and dead take part.

The Family Rituals

There are, of course, other rituals as well, recorded in the *Book of Rites* and practised during many centuries. I am referring especially to those ceremonies surrounding a person's growth and maturity, the affirmation of the family principle by marriage, and the mourning and funerary rites. These are the so-called Family Rituals, and they have been singled out for special attention by the great Neo-Confucian thinker Chu Hsi (1130–1200), who has helped to promote their influence not only in China itself, but also in traditional Korea and beyond. While many of these rituals are no longer observed, they offer useful evidence of the religious character of Confucianism.

The rituals include the male adolescent's 'Capping', some time between the ages of fifteen and twenty, when he receives his formal hat and ceremonial gown, as well as his formal name. In addition, a wine libation is made and the young man is presented formally to his ancestors. It has its parallel in the Christian sacrament of confirmation, and in the Jewish Bar Mitzvah. After that comes marriage, also a union of families, which begins with the announcement of the event to the ancestors in the temple, accompanied by a wine libation. To quote from the *Book of Rites*:

> The respect, the caution, the importance, the attention to secure correctness in all the details, and then [the pledge of] mutual affection – these were the great points in the ceremony, and served to establish the distinction to be observed between husband and wife . . . . From that righteousness came the affection between father and son; and from that affection, the rectitude

between ruler and minister. Whence it is said, 'The ceremony of marriage is the root of the other ceremonial observances.'[12]

The fundamental importance of marriage and the family is well emphasised. Together with this, we find the enumeration of three of the five pivotal relationships: between husbands and wives, parents and children (especially father–son), rulers and ministers. The other two, it will be recalled, are between siblings and between friends.

The family rituals are obviously part and parcel of an ancestral cult. The invisible ancestors receive reports from the living members of the family regarding births and weddings, as well as during those occasions that mark the adolescent's entry into adult society. There are also other rituals dedicated more directly to the deceased, such as mourning and funerary rites, and the anniversaries attached to the memories of the deceased members of the family. These occupy much attention in the *Book of Rites*; one might say the entire classical text is preoccupied especially with these occasions and how such rituals should be enacted.

In his chapter on 'Human Community as Holy Rite', Herbert Fingarette speaks thus of the Confucian rites:

> It is in this beautiful and dignified, shared and open participation with others who are ultimately like oneself (12:2) that a man realizes himself. This perfect community of men – the Confucian analogue to Christian brotherhood – becomes an inextricable part, the chief aspect, of Divine worship – again an analogy with the Central Law taught by Jesus.[13]

4   Confucius as Prophet?

What kind of figure was Confucius – a conservative, a reformer, or a revolutionary? Here we pose the question once more not just to reassert his historicity, but to understand better his contributions to religion and society.

'I am a transmitter, not an innovator; I believe in antiquity and love the ancients' (7:1). Thus said Master K'ung. Here we find that his rhetoric was conservative. And yet, with all his love of the rites, he also asserted that human beings are to respect the gods and spirits, but to keep a distance from them. Thus, if we focus on his attention to the rituals, we might decide that he was basically a traditionalist. But knowing of his own ideological preferences, we might also see him as a *selective* heir to the legacy of the past which he transmitted to the future.

In actual beliefs and actions, Confucius often showed reformist or even revolutionary preferences. His teachings on *jen*, for example, contributed to a social revolution by putting ahead of nobility by birth the nobility of virtue. And his general preference for education and philosophy over a military career eventually conditioned the entire society. It is interesting that Confucius should use the term for a nobleman or gentleman (*chün-tzu/junzi*, literally: the ruler's son, to denote a person of high moral character). Today, this is the meaning the term still retains. Another word, that for scholar (*shih/shi*), originally meant a warrior – as with the Japanese *samurai*. In historical China, however, the scholars became the top class, ahead of farmers, artisans and merchants, while soldiers were nearly social outcasts.[14] Confucius, it would seem, was a traditionalist by avocation, a reformer by choice, and a revolutionary in some of the consequences that his teachings produced.

In this context, could he be called a prophet figure, like the Hebrew prophets of old? H. H. Rowley has said Yes.[15] He describes Confucius as both reformer and statesman, as were the great Hebrew prophets like Amos, Isaiah, Jeremiah, and so on. But he acknowledges that Master K'ung does not have what most distinguishes the great prophets of Israel: a very personal vocation from God as his direct messenger:

> His confidence in the power of Heaven to preserve him, and his sense of a mission to men appointed by Heaven, is as strong as that of the prophets of Israel. Where he falls short of them is in the remoteness of God, and in the small place that God had in his teaching. While for him God was real and His purpose clear, his unwillingness to talk about Him meant that he did little to make Him real for his followers. There might be a will of God for him, but he said nothing to make men feel that there was a will of God for them, and worship was but the offering of reverence and not the receiving of grace. Hence, in effect, his teaching was reduced to ethics, instead of the communication of the religion which he himself had.[16]

Hans Küng disagrees with Rowley's perspective, claiming that Confucius represents a different religious type, that of the 'wise man', of the 'sage', with the literary genre of wisdom literature, which is also found in the later strata of the Hebrew tradition.

This position presupposes the necessity of a revealed religion for a prophet figure, as it places emphasis on the prophet's intimacy with God.[17]

I should like to raise the question of whether Confucius might be at least regarded as prophet-like, if not a prophet himself. This is not because of any added stature an answer in the positive might bring him, but rather to help us in understanding Confucius' historical achievements. My understanding of 'prophet' is precisely in ethical terms – as a messenger with ethical teachings. I do not feel necessarily that Confucius can only belong to one type, i.e., either as wise man or as prophet. Rather, I have in mind Max Weber's assertions. According to Weber, in China 'there had never been an ethical prophecy of a supra-mundane God who raised ethical demands'.[18] He asserts that the Chinese tendency toward harmony with nature and society reduces all tension between religion and the world to an absolute minimum, and that no prophet ever arose to revolutionise the Chinese soul.

Thus the subject of whether Confucius was a prophet depends very much upon our definition of a prophet. Those who favour an answer in the positive emphasise the ethical message of Confucius as analogous to that of the great ethical prophets of the Jews. Those who answer in the negative often place West Asian prophets and prophetic religions ahead of others, emphasising their distinctiveness as a religious type. In my opinion, Confucius can certainly be described as someone who *'revolutionised* [my italics] the Chinese soul', and he did it in the name of the ancients rather than his own, but with the consciousness of a mandate given by Heaven. Our discussions of Gods and spirits, of transcendence and immanence, in this book should help to respond to the other question regarding a supra-mundane God.

In the next chapter, we shall place Confucius in a comparative context with certain later thinkers like Mo-tzu and the Legalists. This should help us locate his teachings on a middle ground. Whether in religious beliefs, in discussions of human nature, and in discussions on politics, Confucius and his school tend to mediate between excesses of zeal, between Mo-tzu the believer in ancient religion and the agnostic and cynical Legalists. Thus, the fact that the Chinese people chose to prefer Confucianism was also a choice of moderation over fanaticism – a choice of the middle ground and the middle way.

4

Love or the Law: Confucianism and its Rivals: Mohism and Legalism

1 Religious and Anti-Religious Humanisms

Ancient Greek humanism emerged at a time of intense questioning of religious beliefs, producing Socrates, Plato and Aristotle. So did Chinese humanism, with its many voices belonging to outstanding individuals. But tradition speaks more of schools of thought than of the individuals as such. These grappled with problems which also preoccupied religious thinkers in the West, problems like: 'Why are we in this world, and what is the meaning of life?' In this context, we can discern in the schools of Confucianism, Taoism and Legalism, three distinct vantage points: what I call the moralist, the naturalist, and the political positions.

The Confucian school represents the moralist answer to both these questions. The meaning of life is to be found in the existential quest for wisdom or moral perfection, and this, in turn, is especially discovered in those social virtues that govern family relationships (between parents and children, between husbands and wives, between older and younger brothers), as well as relationships outside the family (between rulers and ministers, and between friends). These relationships constitute the warp and woof of East Asian society – not only in China itself, but also in Korea, Japan, and Vietnam.

This does not mean that there is nothing in life beyond these horizontal relationships. While these relationships define the parameters for the striving for human perfection, they also represent a structure of existence comprehending that which transcends the relationships themselves. By this I refer to the Confucian inclination to find the absolute in the relative, to discover transcendence in immanence. Filial piety, for example, is the virtue by which the child is not only serving the parents, but also the ancestral spirits, and even Heaven, from whom all life comes. After all, the Confucian school has never demanded a denial of the belief in a supreme being, or Heaven. Confucianism is defined on moral grounds, but Confucians themselves may be theists, agnostics, or atheists. In fact, the mainstream tradition has always preserved a vertical dimension, through the belief in the Lord-on-high or Heaven, even if Heaven has been variously interpreted as supreme being, moral force, or nature.

The moralist answer to the big questions of life became the 'mainstream' answer, with the eventual triumph of Confucianism as state orthodoxy. Moral earnestness would characterise the Chinese preference for good just as intellectual curiosity characterised the Greek love for truth, and the sensitivity to nature characterised the Japanese proclivity for the beautiful. While this brought an important sense of orientation to the entire Chinese culture, it also, unfortunately, led to a lip service of moral values among some people which is nothing less than hypocrisy. Still, I would assert that Confucianism offers many parallels to biblical prophetic religion as well as to the wisdom tradition of the Hebrews.

2   A Rival Religious Philosophy: Mo-tzu on Love

We have mentioned Confucianism, Taoism and Legalism. But there was another ancient school of philosophy with strong moral and religious overtones. This was Mohism, the school of Master Mo. A thinker whose dates of birth and death are not known (470–391 B.C.?), Mo Ti, known as Master Mo (Mo-tzu) lived some time after Confucius and died in the early fourth century B.C. He was first a student of the Confucian school. But Mo-tzu was a commoner, whereas Confucius had come from a humbled yet minor aristocracy. And he tended to extremes, where Confucius was a moderate. Indeed, in later life, Mo-tzu became a severe critic of the Confucian school as he knew it. His own thinking is found in the work *Mo-tzu*, consisting of fifty-one extant sections, presumably composed by disciples of his school.

Generally speaking, *Mo-tzu* is organised around specific topics, sometimes with tripartite elucidations coming from the diverse schools of transmission. Its later chapters have to do more with logic and military strategy, and are presumed to have come from later hands. The style is lucid, if dull and repetitious. But the teachings are exceptional. Some are traditional, like the belief in ghosts and spirits, derived from ancient religion, and others, like non-aggression and even militant pacifism, sound modern.

As a believer in God and spirits, Mo-tzu placed importance on certain rituals, those devoted to heaven and the higher spirits, including sacrificial rituals, for which he would spare no expense. But he was critical of the extravagances shown by followers of Confucius in ritual practices surrounding the cult of *human ancestors*. He ridicules the Confucians for lavishing attention on funerals in particular. Some of these criticisms reflect the Confucian practices of his time, actually re-enactments of ancient practices, such as in searching for the spirits of the deceased before preparing for burial, presumably with the aim of calling for the spirits to return to life.

> When a parent dies, the Confucians lay out the corpse for a long time before dressing it for burial while they climb up onto the roof, peer down the well, poke in the ratholes, and search in the washbasins, looking for the dead man. If they suppose that they will really find the dead man there, then they must be stupid indeed, while if they know that he is not there but still search for him, then they are guilty of the greatest hypocrisy.[1]

Where Confucius taught the virtue of humanity (*jen*), which has sometimes been called graded love, since it begins with the family, and extends outward, Mo-tzu taught universal and equal love (*chien-ai/jian-ai*), on the basis that Heaven loves all equally. He follows an unstinting, if boring, logic:

> How do we know that Heaven loves the people of the wold? Because it enlightens them universally. How do we know that it enlightens them universally? Because it possesses them universally. How do we know that it possesses them universally? Because it accepts sacrifices from them universally.[2]

Mo-tzu has been hailed by Christian missionaries for his theism and for teaching universal love. Marxist scholars have also applauded the doctrine of universal love for its egalitarian assumptions. The German Sinologist Wolfgang Bauer characterises the Mohist school as teaching the 'fundaments of socialism'. Acknowledging the risks in graded love, especially 'the love of relatives', he explains nevertheless:

The gulf separating the Mohists from the Confucians was a wholly different concept of love. Having been made more comprehensive, it lost its intimate warmth.[3]

On politics, Mo-tzu believed in authority even more fervently than did Confucius, and certainly much more so than the later Mencius. He not only considered it a duty for persons like himself to offer advice to the rulers of the time (as did Confucius and Mencius), but actively devoted himself to the cause of maintaining peace and opposing war. In other words, he was a militant pacifist. He even became a specialist in weaponry and military strategy, in order to use these skills to bring about peace. When Mo-tzu heard, for example, that the state Ch'u was planning an attack on a smaller state Sung, he walked for ten days and ten nights to the capital of Ch'u, where he convinced the ruler to call off the expedition, but only because he had organised disciples with better weapons to help protect the threatened state.

This anecdote indicates Mo-tzu's tireless devotion to his causes. It also reflects the good organisation of his band of disciples, sometimes described as a kind of knights, religiously devoted to their leader as almost to a pope-figure.

It is significant that the Chinese people over time preferred as a teacher Confucius, a man of the middle, to Mo-tzu, an extreme pacifist, who carried things to excess and expected others to do the same. Important in his own time, Mo-tzu and his teachings were overshadowed by Confucianism as well as by Taoism and Buddhism. Very much later, Mohism enjoyed some revival of interest, possibly because of the introduction of Christianity by the missionaries and the parallels discovered in his teaching on Heaven and on universal love, as well as in his defence of pacifism. In attacking Confucianism, certain scholars in mainland China also tried to exalt Mohism, although they were unable to approve his religious teachings.

Mo-tzu was a great man, and his teachings leave us much for reflection. But he has been criticised for his excesses in virtue:

Mo-tzu wrote a piece 'Against Music', and another entitled 'Moderation in Expenditure', declaring that there was to be no singing in life, no mourning after death. With a boundless love and a desire to insure universal benefit, he condemned warfare . . . . His views, however, were not always in accordance with those of the former kings, for he denounced the rites and music of antiquity . . . . A life that is all toil, a death shoddily disposed of – it is a way that goes too much against us.[4]

3   Human Nature and the Rites: Mencius and Hsün-tzu

As we have described it, Confucianism was an ancient teaching, which Confucius himself preferred to attribute to the sages of old, even if we find in it facets that are new and distinct against the perspective of ancient religion. With time, the disciples of the school, called *Ju* or scholars, achieved greater social recognition. Etymologically, as we have mentioned, the word refers to a coward or weakling, and it became associated with these people probably because they preferred attention to ritual matters and the learning of the ancients rather than to the sword at a time when aristocrats were mostly fighting men. Eventually, the term would also achieve respectability, and the entire culture became tilted to scholarly rather than military virtues, even if conquests continued to be made by the sword.

The Confucian school was further developed by its later followers, including Mencius and Hsün-tzu. These differed not merely with Confucius himself on certain issues, but even more among themselves. Yet they share enough to contribute together to the building up of the Confucian tradition. On the other hand, Mo-tzu, who was once a follower of the Confucian school, moved away from it to begin a distinctive school of thought, and was much criticised, especially by Mencius, for ideas like universal love, as being subversive of family values.

The word Mencius, like the word Confucius, is the Latinised form for Master Meng (Meng-tzu), whose name was Meng Ko (372–289 B.C.), a native of a small state adjacent to Confucius' Lu. From the stories that have come down to us, Meng is described as having been an orphan boy, quite difficult when very young, and brought up by a wise and virtuous mother. Like Confucius, he travelled from one feudal state to another, looking for a ruler who would accept his advice. Unlike Confucius, his advice was often given bluntly, and of course, his time (the 'Warring States') was in much greater turmoil than the earlier times (the 'Spring and Autumn period'). It appears that the feuding lords regarded him as hopelessly impractical for preaching benevolence and righteousness when might was making right in the struggle for political survival. More than the *Analects*, the *Book of Mencius* possesses real eloquence, with passages of lofty idealism and even mysticism.

Hsün-tzu was no contemporary of Mencius. Master Hsün, called Hsün K'uang or Hsün Ch'ing (312?–238 B.C.), a native of the state of Chao, also in North China, from which came virtually all early Confucians and even Mohists. He was appointed magistrate of Lan-ling, in the powerful state of Ch'i, and served as such for a short period. He left behind a work of the same name (*Hsün-tzu*) with thirty-two sections. The extant version appears to include sections coming from his own hand as well as from his disciples. The work is organised around definite topics, such as the nature of Heaven, and the wickedness of human nature. The thinking is developed much more logically than in the other Confucian works.

Some of Hsün-tzu's teachings were diametrically opposed to those of Mencius. Besides, by career as well as by orientation of thinking, he has been associated with some Legalists. He is said to have had as disciples both Li Ssu, the chief minister of Ch'in who helped to propel the state to pre-eminence and became prime minister of the First Emperor of the Ch'in dynasty, and Han Fei, the aristocrat whose teachings on political power have come down in the work, *Han Fei Tzu*.

The Rites: Sacred or Secular?

In the *Book of Mencius*, we find a clear evolution in the meaning of the term Heaven. Where Confucius only makes infrequent mention of the personal deity, Mencius speaks much more of Heaven – but not always as personal deity. According to Mencius, Heaven is present within man's heart, so that he who knows his own heart and nature, knows Heaven (*Mencius* 7A:1). It represents, therefore, a greater immanence. It also refers more and more to the source and principle of ethical laws and values. Nevertheless, Mencius continues to hold in esteem the practice of offering sacrifices to the Lord-on-high and to ancestors: 'Though a man may be wicked, if he adjusts his thoughts, fasts and bathes, he may sacrifice to the Lord-on-high' (*Mencius* 4B:25).[5]

Hsün-tzu sees a difference between a *gentleman* of education, who uses his rationality, and the common people, who believe in fortune and misfortune. Where we had earlier found divination in the royal ancestral temples of the Shang dynasty, and rain dances sponsored by the state, we find in *Hsün-tzu* the movement away from such religious practices, on the part of the higher classes, and the identification of such with the 'superstitious' commoners. It is the beginning of the separation between Confucianism as an élite tradition, and so-called popular religion, at a grass-roots level.

You pray for rain and it rains. Why? For no particular reason, I say. It is just as though you had not prayed for rain and it rained anyway . . . . You consult the arts of divination before making a decision on some important matter. But it is not as though you could hope to accomplish anything by such ceremonies. They are done merely for ornament. Hence the gentleman regards them as ornaments, but the common people regard them as supernatural.[6]

And again:

Heaven does not suspend the winter because men dislike cold; earth does not cease being wide because men dislike great distances; the gentleman does not stop acting because petty men carp and clamor.[7]

While apparently reducing Heaven's ways to the laws of nature, he maintains the importance of rituals:

. . . rites serve Heaven above and earth below; honor the ancestors, and exalt rulers and teachers. These are the three bases of rites.[8]

As an education, the rites are supported by music. In the *Book of Rites*, a text which manifests Hsün-tzu's influence, the chapter on music also extols it as a help in gaining inner equilibrium and tranquillity – the equilibrium is the reflection of the harmony of elegant music. Together, music and the rites maintain or restore an inner harmony, which is or ought to be, a reflection of the harmony between Heaven and earth. This reflects the teachings of the Doctrine of the Mean, also a chapter from the same ritual text. The philosophical assumption here is the correlation between the microcosm and the macrocosm, between the inner workings of man's mind and heart and the creative processes of the universe. Here, we touch upon the heart of the Chinese meaning of harmony, with its obvious mystical dimension.

The idea that the human being is a universe in miniature, a microcosm, can be traced back in Western thought to the pre-Socratics. The fourth-century Greek Father and mystic, Gregory of Nyssa, had this to say of the analogy:

If the arrangement of the whole [universe] is some kind of a musical harmony, whose . . . maker is God, . . . and if man is a small-scale universe . . . then man himself is also a copy of the harmonious universe . . . . I mean in human nature, the whole music of the universe can be discerned, the whole being proportionately reflected in each part.[9]

Gregory of Nyssa belongs to the Byzantine tradition, where the tradition of Greek thought and the insights of mystical experience have been better regarded than in the Latin tradition. We shall develop this comparative perspective further on.

Human Nature: Good or Evil?

The Chinese word for human nature is *hsing/xing*, a compound including the term for mind or heart, and life or offspring. Philological scholarship demonstrates the association between etymology and early religious worship. The human being is he or she who has received from Heaven the gift of life and all the innate endowments of human nature, especially the shared faculty of moral discernment. Thus the meaning of *hsin* as mind and heart is closer to the biblical Hebrew notion of *lev*, the seat of both reason and emotions, than it is to the somewhat more intellectual Greek *nous* or Latin *mens*, to which English 'mind' is related. Mencius says that the sense of right and wrong is common to all (2A:6), distinguishing the human from the beast. From this flows another belief, that of the natural equality of all, which exists in spite of social hierarchy, or any distinction between the 'civilised' and the 'barbarian'.

The Confucian tradition has sometimes been criticised for its inability to explain the place of evil in human existence. While the Shang dynasty's King T'ang publicly begged the Lord-on-high for forgiveness for his sins (as we have already described in an earlier chapter), Confucian philosophy was not to develop a theory of sin as offence against God. Rather, it affirms the presence of evil, explaining this as either the product of contact between an originally good nature and its wicked environment, as Mencius tends to say, or as inherent in human nature itself, which is the position of Hsün-tzu.

Until our own days, Western Christian thinkers have usually emphasised man's fall from grace rather than the original state of goodness. In representing sin as a transition from 'essence' to 'existence', however, Paul Tillich comes close to Mencius' line of original human goodness from which human beings have deviated:

Creation is good in its essential character. If actualized, it falls into universal estrangement through freedom and destiny.[10]

The Jewish philosopher Martin Buber has also commented upon the Chinese nostalgia for original goodness, as manifest in Mencius. He considers this to be a notion alien to Western mentality. According to Buber:

> This [Chinese] trust in the primal being is missing in the Western man . . . . Even Christianity was not able to alter this situation . . . . Of the biblical story of the first man, only the Fall is present in a living way in the reality of the personal life of the Western Christian man, not the life before the Fall.[11]

Buber considers Chinese beliefs to be excessively supernatural (!) when compared to Western consciousness, which is aware only of the fallen state. Obviously, he would have found Hsün-tzu more congenial for teaching the original wickedness of human nature.

But the two Chinese thinkers concur in assenting to human perfectibility. Mencius declares that all have the potential of becoming sages. Hsün-tzu explains that the *evil* in human nature desires its opposite, and that education can train nature to seek goodness:

> Man's nature is evil; goodness is the result of conscious activity. The nature of man is such that he is born with a fondness for profit . . . . Therefore man must first be transformed by the instructions of a teacher and guided by ritual principles . . . . It is obvious . . . that man's nature is evil, and that his goodness is the result of conscious activity.[12]

Hsün-tzu was more influential than Mencius in the Han dynasty and, generally, in early Confucianism. The situation changed with the development of Neo-Confucianism. At the time that Christian missionaries entered China, they found Confucian scholars usually upholding the basic goodness of human nature, explaining evil as a deflection from the good, a perversion of the natural. Besides, the Chinese language lacked a clear equivalent for 'sin' – the term *tsui/zui* has a double significance: of crime as well as of sin. The resultant ambiguity has led some people to the incorrect assertion that the Chinese (and the Japanese) had no guilt-oriented morality, with its internalisation of the consciousness of moral evil, but only a shame-oriented one, which is external and superficial, being based on mere human respect. Certainly, Confucian education sought to instil a strong sense of moral responsibility, inseparable from guilt consciousness.

So, where Confucius stands as a kind of prophet, offering an ethical teaching grounded in the religious consciousness, Mencius proclaims an inner doctrine, alluding to the presence within the heart of that which is greater than itself. The Chinese word for this is *hsin/xin*, derived from a graph for fire. The heart comes to us from Heaven (*Mencius* 6A:15) and leads us back to Heaven. It represents both the symbol and reality of man's oneness with Heaven. It is the ground of innate virtues which require cultivation in order to blossom and bear fruit. Mencius' teaching was to become mainstream Confucian teaching, with the later emergence of Neo-Confucian thinkers, who reinforced the belief that all can become sages. And this is similar to the teaching of Gregory of Nyssa. Instead of a presumed dogmatic chasm of 'original sin' between the two men, we find a certain convergence. For the Greek Fathers preferred to focus upon an 'incarnational theory of Redemption' in their struggle against the pessimism and determinism of Gnosticism and Manichaeism.

We are referring here to the Byzantine tradition which was not marked by St. Augustine's sense of human depravity, that so influenced Latin Christianity and all that came from it, including Calvinism and Lutheranism. Instead, the great Byzantine mystics preferred to see the soul as God's image, inclined toward the good, not simply a creature but a co-creator, a co-worker with God in creating himself and the universe.[13]

Thus differences in human nature gave Confucian philosophy two schools, one emphasising original wickedness and the other focusing on original goodness. While both agreed on human perfectibility, Mencius' position was much more positive in that regard, and became accepted as true teaching by roughly the twelfth or thirteenth century. On the other hand, there have also been two schools of opinion in Christian thought, of which Augustine's position became influential in the West, while Eastern Christianity has maintained the possibility that a life of faith must achieve consummation in an ecstatic vision and love of God on earth. Only very recently have Pierre Teilhard de Chardin and Henri de Lubac in the West voiced opinions that were more like those of Gregory of Nyssa.[14]

4   Politics: Confucianism as 'Civil Religion'

The term 'civil religion' comes from the American sociologist Robert Bellah, who is also a Japan specialist. It refers to the religious or quasi-religious regard for civic values and traditions marked by feasts, rituals, dogmas and creeds. He applied the term especially to the American situation, with the coexistence of several faiths like Protestant and Roman Catholic Christianity and Judaism, sharing a common belief in one God and in a set of religious values, as well as in a religion of nationalism with its creed, catechism and dogma reflected in symbols of civil unity like the flag, and in documents like the Declaration of Independence and the Constitution. Certain addresses like Washington's Farewell and Lincoln's Second Inaugural took on religious overtones, while the Pledge of Allegiance became a standard rite for school children much as morning prayers had been.[15]

We make use of the term here in the Chinese context, because we find certain parallels in the cases of a modern society like that of the United States and traditional Chinese society. Although not usually regarded as a high priest, the American President is expected to adhere to, and articulate, certain common tenets of the religious beliefs of the people, and does this in a near-ritual form on certain state occasions. In the Chinese case, state religion, which overlaps with Confucianism as the state ideology, actually embraces the tenets and practices of Taoism. Aside from the sacrifice to Heaven and the ancestral cult, which are not found in American civil religion, traditional China adhered to certain political principles with implicit religious sanctions. These bear similarity to some of the principles enshrined in the American Declaration of Independence, which offers the justification for the people's revolution against British rule. We refer here to the Chinese belief in Heaven's bestowing a mandate to govern to the rulers, who forfeit it if they become tyrants.

The Politics of Heaven's Mandate

Much more than Christianity, Confucian teachings are oriented to improving the political order, as a means of achieving human-heartedness. The teaching of *jen* is extended to the political order, where it is defined as benevolent government, a government of moral persuasion, in which the leader gives the example of personal integrity, and selfless devotion to the people. Confucian teaching prompted generations of scholars to strive for participation in government. For the human is never regarded as dualistic, as matter and mind, body and soul. It is always accepted as *one*, as existing in society, as striving as well for physical well-being, for social harmony, and for moral and spiritual perfection. The Confucian sage has been described as possessing the qualities of 'sageliness within and kingliness without'. In other words, he should have the heart of the sage, and the wisdom of the king. We have here what may be called 'philosopher kings' as in Plato's *Republic*.

But while Confucian teachings were originally aimed at advising the rulers, they became increasingly applied to the training of those who would act as the rulers' advisors. The problem for the minister or would-be minister is: what should one do were the ruler not only less than sage, as most rulers turned out to be, but even despotic and tyrannical, as some of them definitely were? Confucius himself offers a doctrine of Rectification of Names, which has sometimes been misunderstood. In eight cryptic words, he says: 'Ruler, ruler; minister, minister; father, father; son, son' (*Analects* 13:3). These have been misinterpreted as representing a caste system where the ruler is always ruler, the minister always minister. However, this is obviously a mistake, since every son is expected to become a father. The correct interpretation is that the ruler should be a *good* ruler, the minister a *good* minister, the father a *good* father, and the son a *good* son. Names should represent realities, but in Plato's sense of ideal forms.

Mencius teaches how political power is legitimated by a Mandate bestowed by the supreme Lord, Heaven. He is only articulating a theory that is implicit in the accounts of dynastic changes given in the classical *Book of History* and reflected also in the *Book of Poetry*. And Mencius also offered a clear formulation of the doctrine of rebellion or revolution, known popularly as the 'removal of the Mandate' (*ko-ming/geming*). It was Mencius who said that killing a tyrant was not regicide, since the tyrant no longer deserved to rule (1B:8); it was Mencius who declared: 'The people come first; the altars of the earth and grain come afterwards; the ruler comes last' (7B:14).[16]

Thus Confucian China shares with Christian Europe the idea of vicarious authority in kingship. According to the Confucian classics, the king is the 'one man' (a term made famous by the German philosopher G. W. F. Hegel). He is Son of Heaven, governing by a Mandate from above, mediator between the powers above and the people below. His exalted position and awesome responsibilities make him a *solitary* man, the title by which he referred to himself. In another sense, he is the *collective* man, alone guilty of fault whenever his people offend Heaven (as in the case of King T'ang).

The very idea of a justified rebellion is incipient in the notion of delegated authority. And the theory of tyrannicide, developed so early in China, would only emerge much later in Christian Europe, and then only in the midst of controversy. Treatises by an anonymous Huguenot author and by the Spanish Jesuit Luis Mariana were either publicly burnt or condemned, although they were to wield tremendous influence.[17] In this light, we need not be surprised that the fourteenth-century founder of the Ming dynasty sought to delete from the *Book of Mencius* those passages that approved of tyrannicide.

The Confucian tradition was to include political conservatives as well as moderate and radical reformers; there were those whose priority was to serve the state; there were also those who remained independent of the state, while seeking to change or transform it. Confucian scholars were usually activists, either serving the government, advising and admonishing the ruler or engaging in reforms, or even protesting against tyranny through passive or active resistance.

5 Political Opposition to Religion: The School of Law

The term 'Legalism' (*Fa-chia/Fajia*) should not be confused with a rule of law. It refers rather to an ancient school of thought that advocates the use of harsh penal law to deter political opposition and enhance and maintain power. Thus, it is no surprise that Legalism should have been the favourite of despots. Legalism is an age-old teaching, almost as old as Confucianism. Some of its ideas and policies are said to go back to the seventh-century-B.C. statesman Kuan Chung (d. 645 B.C.) whose teachings are allegedly given in the *Kuan-tzu*. Other ideas might have come from the *Book of Lord Shang* (*Shang-chün shu*), attributed to Kung-sun Yang (d. 338 B.C.), who served as high minister in the feudal state of Ch'in, where he developed agriculture and strengthened the military, preparing it to conquer the entire country. Other Legalist thinkers include Kung-sun's contemporary Shen Pu-hai (d. 337 B.C.) who served in the state of Han. But the best-known thinker is a prince from that state, a man who allegedly had a speech defect. He is known to posterity as Han Fei Tzu, the title also of a work attributed to himself and his school. It has been compared to Machiavelli's Renaissance work, *The Prince* (1512–13). Both manifest a cold and calculating rationality which reckons with only one concern: that of the ruler in power.

True, all the early Chinese schools of thought dealt with the problem of finding or creating order in society. After all, they arose in a time of social disorder and political disunity, with the gradual crumbling of late Chou state and the competition for power among the various feudal domains. But Confucianism, Mohism and Taoism had much to say about human existence and relationship to nature. And both Confucianism and Mohism especially exhorted rulers to exercise benevolence and righteousness in government. Legalism, in contrast, dealt exclusively with the problem of political power, and presumes always that the end justifies all means. Legalist writings tend to be handbooks for rulers, teaching them how to manipulate people and circumstances to keep themselves in power.

Legalists are great cynics who put no faith in any power higher than that of the state or ruler. Incidentally, the biographies of several Legalist thinkers demonstrate their cynicism and their distrust of others. For example, Han Fei Tzu tasted the bitterness of human betrayal. Invited to the state of Ch'in by its ruler, he was prevented from meeting the ruler by Li Ssu, a jealous high minister who had been his own fellow student. In fact, Li threw him into prison, where Han's speech defect did not help him to defend himself against trumped-up charges.

Legalism can hardly be described as a response to the big questions of life, since it does not address these. It is essentially a response to the problem of finding order in a time of social and political chaos, during the disintegration of feudal society. It offers a *political* answer – that of despotism and power politics. It is utterly devoid of any religious belief, moral sense or sensitivity to nature. Where the Confucians and the Taoists address themselves to both rulers and the ruled, Legalists speak only to the actual or would-be rulers. They had no belief in God and no reverence for nature. They usurp the term *Tao*, referring it to the mysterious way of power politics in a kind of pseudo-metaphysics. They subordinate all human relations to that between ruler and minister, divest this of any moral significance, and recommend that the ruler ascertain the loyalty of his subjects by using the 'two handles' of rewards and punishments.

Legalism uses a metaphysical language borrowed from Taoism to describe the sage in its own descriptions of the ruler and his mysterious might. Where the sage had absolute wisdom, the ruler possessed absolute power. Where the sage, according to Taoism, was above right and wrong, the ruler, according to Legalism, was a law unto himself. Hidden from the multitude in the depths of the palace, the Legalist ruler was to set in motion a machinery of government which could then run by itself.

In contrast to Confucianism and Mohism, Legalists have a low opinion of the past and of history, and also of human nature. The ruler was to be guided by enlightened self-interest, which bade him to keep at arm's length his own wife and children, never pouring out his heart to anyone, in case that anyone, including members of his immediate family, might become his foes.

> The Way lies in what cannot be seen, its function in what cannot be known. Be empty, still, and idle, and from your place of darkness observe the defects of others. See but do not appear to see; listen but do not seem to listen; know but do not let it be known that you know . . . . Hide your tracks, conceal your sources, so that your subordinates cannot trace the springs of your action . . . . Destroy all hope, smash all intention of wresting them from you; allow no man to covet them.[18]

Legalism was the official ideology of China's first emperor, who founded the Ch'in dynasty and is known to posterity among other things for having burnt books and buried scholars – alleged actions that have been supported by historical evidence. Following the downfall of his short-lived dynasty (207 B.C.), many Legalist ideas infiltrated Confucianism as the latter philosophy gained prominence in the Han dynasty. As the erstwhile Communist Eastern Europe and the Soviet Union unravelled, our world has learnt more and more about a ruthless political system that was run according to 'Legalist' principles. To the extent that Chinese Marxism has been mainly an ideology of power, it made conscious use of Legalist tenets. That is why we can say that Legalism is still alive and well in Communist China, where punishments are usually severe, and human rights are often disregarded.[19]

6 Confucian Humanism Today

In the recent past, Confucianism has been attracting increasing attention in the world, its 'work ethic' being applauded for the rapid economic development of the Asia-Pacific Rim. Even in Communist China, signs of respect were shown for the man and the teaching that had been so much maligned during the Cultural Revolution (1966–76). In August 1987, an international scholarly conference on Confucius and Confucianism was held in Qufu, Shantung, the birthplace of Confucius. It was jointly organised by the Confucius Foundation of China and the Institute for East Asian Philosophies in Singapore. Taiwan, the seat of a rival Chinese (Nationalist) government, has never disowned Confucianism and was the venue in November 1987 for another international scholarly conference on Confucius and Confucianism. Even after the Tiananmen debacle of June 1989, China's rulers have expressed approval of Confucius and Confucian ideas. There is speculation that they are imitating the erstwhile authoritarian régimes in pre-war Japan, in post-war South Korea and Taiwan, as well as in Singapore. But is Confucianism really experiencing a revival in China today? Has it a future tomorrow? Are its values useful also for the world outside China?

The French Sinologist Léon Vandermeersch has analysed the political, economic, and cultural dimensions of this Asia-Pacific region in a book that deserves to be much better known.[20] However different countries like China, Japan and Korea may be, they are bound together by the same Chinese writing system: the characters, which can be understood in all the different languages, even when these are pronounced altogether differently. These written characters, unlike the letters of the alphabet, possess a content of meaning as 'ideograms', and present certain basically common attitudes and world views which are essentially conditioned by the age-old system of Confucianism. He claims that typically Confucian virtues are exactly what appear to be so important in our own age of high technology – virtues like sobriety, impartiality, adaptability, flexibility, creativity and foresight, which can easily be blended with Taoist and Buddhist beliefs. And if institutions like family, rites, and bureaucracy are facing a serious crisis, the spirit of Confucianism is expected to remain intact.

According to Vandermeersch, such a Confucian legacy differs from Western individualism especially by adhering to traditional family values that remain intact, with a 'communitarian' style and a ritualised way of life that is mindful of the old ritual order. And if the old officialdom is no longer extant, the old concept of the state remains functional.[21]

The Transcendent Dimension

I agree with many of the things Vandermeersch has said, but I have to disagree with his assertion that Chinese religion had already lost its transcendent and God-dimension at the time of Confucius, allegedly dissolving it in purely cosmological discussions.[22] We have described the ancient and long-enduring ancestral cult, still present today in many places, as a witness to a belief in a life after death. We have also described the cult of Heaven, which long preceded the time of Confucius, and which, in many respects, remains the principal hallmark of Chinese religion. Even if this cult is no longer practised, there remains evidence of a certain belief in God, present even today in the widespread popular belief in Heaven as a 'higher power', and in folk religious consciousness and practice in Taiwan and elsewhere.

All this helps us to understand why the Jesuit missionaries to China in the sixteenth and seventeenth centuries saw in ancient Confucianism, so much more than in Buddhism, something of a natural religion on a philosophical level. They compared Confucian humanism to Greek humanism, especially to Stoicism, with its pantheist inclinations and its emphasis on ethics, as a *praeparatio evangelii*, a preparation for the Christian gospel.

Confucianism: Philosophy or Religion?

Is Confucianism a philosophy or a religion? I resume here a discussion that was started in the previous chapter. My definition of religion in this book focuses on a consciousness of a transcendent dimension, and I perceive it as present in Confucianism from the very beginning, without always expressing itself in a personal theism. I recognise also the tendency in the tradition to identify the transcendent with what is immanent, to acknowledge the presence of the 'way of Heaven' in the 'way of man', to an extent that the issues have often become ambiguous. But the very insistence upon the priority of the 'way of Heaven', and the quest itself for the discovery and fulfilment of such within the 'way of man', point to a movement toward self-transcendence that has always given the tradition an unusual inner vitality and dynamism.

True, Confucianism has served a secular as well as a religious (and ritual) function throughout history. With the end of the cult of Heaven and the gradual disappearance of an ancestral cult, Confucianism has little more to offer in ritual terms. But it remains religious at its core, on account of its spiritual teachings of sagehood or self-transcendence, so strongly re-affirmed and developed by the Neo-Confucian thinkers, whom we shall discuss in a later chapter.

Undeniably, the influence of Confucianism is growing more and more diffuse, and at times, almost elusive. With the gradual disappearance of the ancestral cult, today – but only today – Confucianism has become more a philosophy than a religion. Yet to the extent that it is not only a philosophy of life, but also a *living* one, that exerts a real influence, and directs those who hear its call to the goal of self-transcendence, it may still be called a diffused religion.

5

Freedom and the Natural: Taoism as Religious Philosophy

1 What is Taoism?

In the West religion is presumed to include a belief in theism, as we mentioned in the Introduction. It is also understood in an exclusive sense, and the Judaeo-Christian-Islamic God is characterised as a *jealous* God. One is either a Christian or a Jew or a Muslim, but one cannot be more than one of these at the same time. In East Asia this is not so. It is often assumed that many Chinese are Confucians in action, and Taoists in contemplation. We have said quite a lot about Confucianism. But what is Taoism?

Indeed, many scholars have asked this question, and found the answer elusive. *What Is Taoism?* asked Herrlee G. Creel in the book (1970) that bears this as a title. He explains that it is foolish to try to propound a single, sovereign definition of what Taoism is, since the term denotes not one school but a whole congeries of doctrines. The problem is all the more complex as the word *Tao/Dao* ('the Way') is used by every school of Chinese thought or religion, and because the English word 'Taoism' is used to refer to both the so-called Taoist philosophy (*Tao-chia/Daojia*) and Taoist religion (*Tao-chiao/Daojiao*). And then, Taoism has contributed much to traditional science and medicine, as well as to *ch'i-kung/qigong* (sometimes written as *'chigong'*) or breathing techniques, including martial arts, and this whole world of discoveries and inventions might also be placed under the umbrella term. Taoism, indeed, may designate anything and everything.

Besides, there has always been a certain shroud of secrecy surrounding Taoism. Starting as a philosophy of recluses and for recluses, it has preferred anonymity and chosen to articulate its teachings in riddles. Then too, as an esoteric religion, it tends to disclose many of its secrets only to the initiated. Only recently has this shroud of secrecy been penetrated, as some of the initiates have begun to publish their knowledge and expertise, sharing it with a wider audience.

Today, we are able to appreciate better the Taoist *intentionality*. We can recognise as religious the *desire* of transcending the limitations of this life, a quest known since Adam and Eve had wanted to be god-like. We can better understand the religious striving for the immortality of the whole person, as well as the active *and* contemplative practices associated with the quest. In Western Christianity, we may discern a similar concern for the final resurrection of the entire human being, body and soul. However, Aristotelian separation between matter and spirit made its impact on Christian thinking. Besides, the monastic movement subordinated the material to the spiritual, to the extent that asceticism became mortification. In Taoism, on the other hand, although asceticism did turn at times into mortification, even this was done in the name of preserving life.[1]

Historical parallels may also help to understand early Taoism. With its recluse tradition, its superior message of the Tao, and its close relationship to early Confucianism, Taoism may be compared to early Gnosticism, which stood in close relationship to early Christianity. The developments are parallel, but apparently several centuries apart. Like Gnosticism, Taoism is a wisdom tradition (as also is Confucianism). The Gnostic motif of mankind's fall and eventual redemption is not clearly reflected in Taoist philosophy, but finds a stronger echo in Taoist religion, where a divinised Lao-tzu became a 'divine man' with Messianic qualities. Like Gnosticism, Taoism also harbours a strong mystical urge, much more than may be found in official Christianity or Confucianism. However, while Taoist philosophers might retreat from the world, they did so more for the sake of freedom and protest than in the name of rejecting the material world as evil.[2]

2 Taoism as Philosophy

Classical Taoist philosophy is especially found in the two texts of *Lao-tzu* (also called *Tao-te-ching*) and *Chuang-tzu*, bearing the names of their alleged authors, of whom we possess only fragmented and uncertain information. So today's scholars cannot ascertain whether Lao-tzu ever lived and what the dates would be if he had lived. But veneration of him remains, as a wise man and as the patriarch of the Taoist school. Also, little that is historically verifiable can be said of Chuang-tzu or the connection between such a man and the text of the same name, which some would attribute to composite authorship.

If these men did live at the times assigned to them by tradition, they must have witnessed a lot of suffering. It was an age of turmoil, first during the Spring-Autumn Period and then during the Warring States Period. There were man-made sufferings of war, poverty and injustice, together with natural sufferings like disease and death. Many of these are recorded, especially in *Chuang-tzu*. However, if Confucius and Mencius sought to solve the social problems by appealing to human beings to become better and more benevolent people, Lao-tzu and Chuang-tzu tend to awaken their readers to an inner, spiritual liberation, freeing them from the bondage of conventional ways of seeing things and putting values on things.

The Quest for a Historical Lao-tzu

Lao-tzu has been named by Karl Jaspers as an original thinker, in the company of several pre-Socratic Greek philosophers, of Plotinus and Nicholas of Cusa, as well as of the Indian Buddhist Nagarjuna.[3] But we know little that is historically verifiable about either Lao-tzu or Chuang-tzu, including the information as to the authorship of the texts that happen to bear their names. Traditionally, it has been held that Lao-tzu (literally, 'old master') was an older contemporary of Confucius, to whom Confucius went for advice (6th century B.C.). But scholars tend to place him, if he was a historical person, in a later period. Among other problems, the best biography we have of him, coming from the second-to-first-century-B.C. historian Ssu-ma Ch'ien's *Historical Annals* (*Shih-chi*), is a composite life of three people. We are not even certain of the actual name of this legendary figure, and whether his surname was Lao (Lao Tan) or Li (Li Erh, Li Tan). He was allegedly a native of Ch'u, a large state in South China, and a court archivist for the Chou house before he retired from the civilised world that was China, by going west. The small book he has supposedly left behind at the border at the request of the keeper of the pass contains unmistakably political statements.[4]

The Way and Its Power: Lao-tzu's Philosophy

The text *Lao-tzu* is also called *Tao-te-ching* or the 'Classic of the Way and Its Power'. It is a brief but cryptic text, containing little more than five thousand words, presented in parallel verses and poetic stanzas. In spite of the difficulties of dating and authorship, as well as of interpretation, it is certainly one of the most translated texts of the world. Some scholars would prefer to treat it simply as a secular text, with no religious content or dimension. But this is not a position accepted by all. Indeed, as we maintain, religion means many things, and *Lao-tzu* offers a vision that may be called religious, which is for humans to return to nature, to be reconciled with themselves and with nature. It is a vision that carries with it a mystical impulse for communication and union with nature, a vision that has also been described as 'salvific'. Thus the word 'sage' in the text, usually referring to the sage ruler, has even been translated as 'saint' with all the religious aura of the term, 'because it gives more emphasis to the magical power, which is proper to a saint'.[5]

The concept of the Tao is what has given the school its name, Taoism. *Lao-tzu* begins with the famous line: 'The Way (Tao) that can be spoken of, is not the constant Way (Tao).' There is a double play of words here, since the term *tao* is also a verb, *to speak*. It is really saying: 'The Tao that can be articulated (*tao-ed*), is not the constant Tao.' I mention this because the Chinese word Tao is an equivalent of *both* the Greek word *logos*, the Word, and the other Greek word *hodos*, the Way. It has been used in translations of St. John's Prologue: 'In the beginning was the Tao' and echoes the other line: 'I am the Way, the Truth and the Life.'

The above quotation serves also to show the dialectical method in Taoist thinking and the effort to point to the nameless Tao as the first principle, itself indeterminate, from which all things proceed to become determinate. Moreover,

> Deep, it is like the ancestor of the myriad creatures. (4:11)

> It images the forefather of the Lord (*Ti*). (4:13)

And also:

> There is a thing confusedly formed,
> Born before Heaven and Earth.
> Silent and void
> It stands alone and does not change,
> Goes round and does not weary.
>
> (25:56)

Here, the Tao is described as existing before the universe came to be, an unchanging first principle, the ancestor of all things, by which all come to be. We discern a philosophical attempt to conceptualise an earlier, religious belief. In the Confucian classics, the 'Lord-on-high' has referred to a supreme deity, while 'Heaven' has at least the great ancestor's role, as that which gives birth to all things. The term Heaven did not completely disappear from Taoist philosophical writings, appearing especially in *Chuang-tzu* alongside the term Tao, but *Tao* has obviously taken over 'Heaven' in *Lao-tzu*, as the natural Way as well as the human way, even the political way. And while the Tao is no longer a personal deity, it remains as a model for human behaviour.

Contemplation of the universe has led Taoists to the discovery of the nameless first principle, of the disposition that should accompany such contemplation, and of the whole of life. This is expressed by the term *wu-wei*, literally, non-action. It does not signify the absence of action, but rather, acting without artificiality, also without over-action, without attachment to action itself. We now come to the practical part of *Lao-tzu*, to the *way* of living according to the Way. I refer here to its 'power' (*te*), that by which the universal Tao becomes particular. It is the power of *the natural*, of simplicity, even of weakness. Yet it teaches the lesson of survival, of how to keep one's own integrity in a time of disorder. Possibly the most important practical lesson of Taoist philosophy, this has had immense importance in the development of Taoist religion.

Lao-tzu suggests a measure of asceticism, of withdrawal from the world – its pleasures, and even its cherished values. For the person seeking the knowledge of the Tao, the senses and passions are in need of purification or moderation, since

> The five colours blind man's eyes.
> The five notes deafen his ears.
> The five tastes deaden his palate.
> Riding and hunting make his mind go wild.
>
> (ch. 12)[6]

Civilisation marks a departure from the Tao. The virtues preached by the Confucians, such as benevolence (humanity) and righteousness, are also relativised; instead, one is to follow nature, and nature only.

Lao-tzu also offers political teachings, ostensibly to the ruler, and these are the most controversial. It appears to advocate a small, pacifist village state, where the sage-ruler seeks to undo the cause of troubles coming from too many prohibitions and prescriptions, too many philosophical contentions, especially those coming from the ethical teachings of Confucianism. Rather, by a government of non-action, he is to keep the people healthy but ignorant, protecting them from the excesses of knowledge. These lines evoke a sense of 'back to nature' romanticism, but have also given rise to political authoritarianism.

Archaeological discoveries (1973) have confirmed the greater political importance of the text *Lao-tzu* in early history. At the site Ma-wang-tui, near today's Changsha (Hunan), archaeologists have unearthed two manuscript versions of what has become the oldest extant text of the *Tao-te-ching*, handwritten on silk and dating back to the second century B.C. The difference is that, unlike the text to which we have become accustomed, it places Part Two (more concerned with the *te*) before Part One (more concerned with the Tao). In other words, it gives greater priority to the specific applications of the Tao in politics. This Han version, while very useful to the scholarly world, is not regarded as the original text, which is presumed to have the same order of Tao before Te, as we have previously been used to. Scholars now associate the use of the Han text with the early school of Huang-Lao (i.e., the Yellow Emperor and Lao-tzu), tracing it back to the Warring States period and seeing it as associated with Legalism.

The Quest for a Historical Chuang-tzu

According to Ssu-ma Ch'ien, Chuang-tzu's name was Chuang Chou, a contemporary of Mencius and a native of Meng. Scholars are not certain where Meng is; some would place it in Honan, south of the Yellow River, possibly in the former feudal state of Sung which was given by Chou to the descendants of the Shang kings. But then, scholars are not sure of any of the other facts alleged of Chuang-tzu: the dates, for example. It is often speculated that Chuang-tzu, like Lao-tzu, came from a different part of China than that of Confucius and Mencius, and that this explains their different perspectives from the classical Confucian thinkers. Usually, the Confucian thinkers are regarded as northerners, more rationalistic and systematic, whereas the classical Taoist thinkers are regarded as southerners, quite non-conformist, and preferring imagination and fantasy to strict reason and moderation.

Taoist masters are known historically to have resisted and combated both Confucianism and Buddhism, and Taoist alchemists have won political favour at court. However, the reclusive character of many Taoists has led to their remaining basically mysterious and anonymous – which is probably what they preferred.

Freedom and the Natural: Chuang-tzu's Philosophy
Chuang-tzu shares with *Lao-tzu* the central concept of the Tao as the principle underlying and governing the universe, while showing a complete eremitical distaste for politics. The text, which is ascribed to a thinker presumably of the fourth or third century B.C., resembles a collection of essays which make abundant use of parable and allegory, of paradox and fanciful imagery. It makes an ardent plea for spiritual freedom: not merely the freedom of the individual from social conventions and restraints, but rather a self-transcending liberation from the limitations of one's own mind – from one's self-interested inclinations and prejudices. According to the text, such freedom can only be discovered in embracing nature itself, in the Tao.

To live according to nature is to respect its laws, including that of dying. By a superior wisdom, the sage is no longer affected emotionally by the vicissitudes of life and the world. He has not lost his sensibility, but he has risen above it. This acceptance of the natural indicates an attitude of equanimity regarding life and death, rather than a sole desire to prolong one's life. Nevertheless, there are other passages in *Chuang-tzu* that could be interpreted otherwise. For example, *Chuang-tzu*'s lyrical descriptions of the perfect man, the sage, has especially led to the development of the religious belief that there are 'Immortals' who are no longer dependent on a diet of grains, have conquered death, and are able to help others to overcome sickness and other evils.

The reference to immortals is important on account of the development of an immortality cult within Taoist religion. With help from archaeological findings, scholarly opinion today tends to date the immortality cult to a much earlier age. Such cult is associated with the use of mercury and sulphur. And, according to Ssu-ma Ch'ien, 'mercury rivers' were designed and installed in the tomb of the founder of the Ch'in dynasty (2nd century B.C.) to assure the preservation of his body. This fact has been confirmed by archaeologists.

3 Religious Meaning in Taoist Philosophy

We wish now to ask: 'What is the religious meaning of the Tao?' The word, of course, is omnipresent. Everyone uses it, whether Confucian, Taoist, or Legalist, and their meanings definitely diverge. For Confucians, it refers to the fundamental principle(s) of moral philosophy; for the Legalists, it refers to the way of power. Today, the word is used even more broadly. We hear of a Tao of physics, among other things. We have already discussed briefly its meaning in philosophical Taoism. We are referring also to a universal Tao, the *all*-inclusive Way.

Is this Tao also God? Such a question should be tackled in a book like this one. An obvious answer is: it is not a personal or anthropomorphic deity, at least not in the context of philosophical Taoism. This answer is given in the language of negation. In this respect, even Thomas Aquinas affirms what the mystic Pseudo-Dionysius says:

> Wherefore man reaches the highest point of his knowledge about God when he knows that he knows him not, inasmuch as he knows that that which is God transcends whatever he conceives of him.[7]

We may also see more resonance of the Tao in the negative theology of the mystics, including Meister Eckhart and his philosophical heirs – the great German philosophers like Hegel and others who incorporated the mystics' insights into their own thinking. Even Martin Heidegger was fascinated with the concept of the Tao, and speaks of it as 'the way that gives all ways, the very source of our power to think . . . . Perhaps the mystery of mysteries of thoughtful Saying conceals itself in the word "way," Tao'.[8]

4   Mystical Taoism and Magico-Ecstatic Behaviour

Both Lao-tzu and Chuang-tzu have been called mystics. The text *Lao-tzu* was addressed to rulers and contains also political teachings. The text *Chuang-tzu* is in this sense quite different. It defines happiness and freedom as being found in a mystical union with nature that presupposes withdrawal from politics and society. In examining the latter text, we find blissful descriptions of a trance state that is akin to the quietist mysticism known in Western Christianity, especially in seventeenth-century France and Flanders. In the Chinese case, more meditative techniques have been developed, and the trances are usually described as self-induced.

Mysticism in Chuang-tzu
The author of *Chuang-tzu* believes that absolute happiness comes with transcending the distinctions between one's self and the universe, by perfect union with the Tao. It involves a higher level of

knowledge, that of wisdom, which goes beyond the distinctions of things, including that of life and death. This may be called mystical knowledge, since it is not acquired by ordinary means. Indeed, it comes only with 'forgetting' the knowledge of all things – especially that of the self. The text mentions 'sitting in oblivion' (*tso-wang*), as well as of a 'fasting of the mind', which is different from fasting of the body. This requires the emptying of the senses and of the mind itself. But such a preparatory, purgative state leads to the presence of the suprahuman and divine: 'Let your ears and your eyes communicate with what is inside . . . . Then even gods and spirits will come to dwell . . . . ' (ch. 4)

Occasionally, *Chuang-tzu* puts words into Confucius' mouth to give expression to Taoist teachings and ideals. The practice of 'sitting in oblivion', or of freeing the mind, is explained in a feigned conversation between Confucius and his favourite disciple, Yen Hui:

> [Yen Hui said:] 'May I ask what the fasting of the mind is?'
>
> Confucius said: 'Make your will one! Don't listen with your ears, listen with your mind. No, don't listen with your mind, but listen with your spirit. Listening stops with the ears, the mind stops with recognition, but spirit is empty and waits on all things. The Way gathers in emptiness alone. Emptiness is the fasting of the mind.' (ch. 4)[9]

Another time, Yen Hui and Confucius had the following conversation in this book:

> Yen Hui said, 'I'm improving!'
> Confucius said, 'What do you mean by that?'
> 'I've forgotten benevolence and righteousness.'
> 'That's good. But you still haven't got it.'
> Another day, the two met again and Yen Hui said, 'I'm improving!'
> 'What do you mean by that?'
> 'I've forgotten rites and music!'
> 'That's good. But you still haven't got it!'
> Another day, the two met again and Yen Hui said, 'I'm improving!'
> 'What do you mean by that?'
> 'I can sit down and forget everything!'

Confucius looked very startled and said, 'What do you mean, sit down and forget everything?'

Yen Hui said, 'I smash up my limbs and body, drive out perception and intellect, cast off form, do away with understanding, and make myself identical with the Great Thoroughfare. This is what I mean by sitting down and forgetting everything.'

Confucius said, ' . . . So you really are a worthy man after all! With your permission, I'd like to become your follower.'[10]

Ecstasy and Shamanism in Chuang-tzu

But there is still another dimension in *Chuang-tzu* which goes beyond nature mysticism, with its self-effacing and quietist connotations. We are referring to those passages which evoke the memory of more ancient customs, involving ecstasy and shamanism.

These 'shamanic' passages in *Chuang-tzu* include the lyrical description of the holy or perfect man, who has also been called an immortal:

There is a Holy Man living on the distant Ku-she Mountain, with skin like ice or snow . . . . He does not eat the five grains, but sucks the wind, drinks the dew, mounts the clouds and mist, rides a flying dragon, and wanders beyond the four seas. By concentrating his spirit, he can protect creatures from sickness and plague and make the harvest plentiful.[11]

Chuang-tzu could very well have been referring to a shaman of traditional antiquity, his dietary habits, his shamanic 'flights', and his healing and other magical powers. From these lines, it would seem that the shamanic tradition has become something of a legend, peripheral to the society in which it was born, and yet, appropriating in the meantime a prestige coming from being a rarity.

Eventually, the texts of *Lao-tzu* and *Chuang-tzu* also served a later generation of religious zealots, anxious to transcend the limited conditions of human existence. They revived belief in personal deities, practising rituals of prayer and propitiation. They fostered the art of alchemy – both the external alchemy which sought the elixir of life, and the internal alchemy which internalised this elixir through meditation. This popular Taoist tradition developed its own mystical traditions, embellished with stories of wondrous drugs and wonder-working immortals, of levitations and bodily ascensions to Heaven. It even evolved a kind of 'nuptial' mysticism, manifested in bridal piety and in the fruit of marital union. All this, *and more*, exceeds what we know of Christian miracle-workers and mystics, and brings us back sometimes to the ecstatic experience of the shamans.[12]

5   The Role of the Feminine in Philosophical Taoism

We may associate Confucianism and its emphasis on action with the *yang* force, and Taoism and its preference for peace and quiet with the *yin* force. This has been done before. And it has also been asserted that Taoism, both philosophy and religion, gives a higher place to women than Confucianism. The claim may be supported by an examination of *Lao-tzu*. This classic refers to the Tao as the mother of all things, and shows preference for images of the weak (water, valley, emptiness, etc.) over their opposites. Even more explicitly, it says:

> Know the male,
> But keep to the role of the female
> And be a ravine to the empire. (ch. 28)[13]

and also:

> The world had a beginning
> And this beginning could be the mother of the world.
> When you know the mother
> Go on to know the child.
> After you have known the child
> Go back to holding fast to the mother,
> And to the end of your days you will not meet with danger.[14]

While the image of mother and child suggests a cycle, a movement from the Tao back to the Tao, the choice of the mother–child relationship is indicative. Besides, the passage begins with the implicit recognition of the Tao as the mother of the world.

In chapter 67, *Lao-tzu* also speaks of three treasures, and lists them as compassion (*tz'u/ci*), frugality (*chien/jian*) and 'not daring to take the lead', that is, not exposing oneself to unnecessary risks and dangers. The term used for compassion (*tz'u*) has been translated by Ellen M. Chen as 'motherly love'. True, the same term is used for motherly love, although it also translates the Buddhist concept of compassion. In the context of Mahayana Buddhism, one might also argue that this same compassion is the special characteristic of those great and unselfish beings, the Bodhisattvas, who forgo their own Nirvana in order to save more people. Interestingly, Chinese religious art has tended to portray Bodhisattvas in female forms. I mention it to offer some support to Ellen M. Chen's argument that *tz'u* signifies a mother's protective and nurturing love. And of course, not taking the lead, a Taoist tenet for survival is also a feminine characteristic.[15] As we shall see, Taoism will further contribute to an increasing role for the feminine in popular religion as this is active today.

6   Neo-Taoism as Exegetical Tradition

Taoist philosophy has left behind an interesting if ambiguous legacy. This may be discerned if we look at the commentaries on *Lao-tzu* and *Chuang-tzu*. Few books, indeed, have received so much attention as these two. Like the Confucian classics, they have each developed a tradition of commentaries, some of which are very important, not only for understanding the original text, but also for what the commentators themselves have to say. After all, remembering the example of Confucius, there is much that has been said by creative thinkers who attribute their ideas to the ancients. There are also important questions asked about the original texts. For example, is *Chuang-tzu's* Tao the same as *Lao-tzu's*? The answers can be diametrically opposite, depending on whether one focuses on some or other of the chapters of the book, and also on whether one agrees or disagrees with some of the chief commentators.

For our purposes, Neo-Taoism was a multi-faceted movement, including exegesis, philosophical discussions, as well as poetry and art. It was also an iconoclastic movement, which may be compared with that of the modern 'hippies'. The age-old respect for authority, and for the Five Relationships, was collapsing. Children were calling their parents by their personal names, while poets and philosophers found solace in drink and conversation.

A Religious Tao: Ho-shang Kung on Lao-tzu

For the Taoist religion, the Ho-shang Kung commentary is second only in importance to the text *Lao-tzu* itself, because of its discussion of divine beings, and because it emphasises a type of self-cultivation oriented toward personal immortality. The work itself may be dated to the later Han period (A.D. 25–220), even if it reflects ideas that came down much earlier, associated with what we have called the

Huang-Lao Tradition – the school of the Yellow Emperor and of Lao-tzu.[16] The figure of Ho-shang Kung is as enigmatic as that of Lao-tzu. Literally, the name means 'Old Man by the River'. Traditionally, the authorship of the commentary bearing this name has been ascribed to the third-century-A.D. scholar Ko Hsüan. But this too is uncertain. The later and more famous Ko Hung (c. A.D. 284–364) has also been considered as a possible author.

In content, the Ho-shang Kung commentary shows a political as well as a religious concern. This is understandable, given the concerns of *Lao-tzu* itself. The Tao is described in terms of formlessness and nothingness (*wu*). Another key term, not found in *Lao-tzu* but prominent in other texts as the late second-century-B.C. eclectic work *Huai-nan-tzu*, is *ch'i/qi*, literally 'breath' or 'air', referring to the basic stuff of life that constitutes all beings and pervades the universe. Good government is presented as operative when the ruler has no desires, and educates the people to be the same. Such a government of non-action (*wu-wei*) does not entail doing nothing, but rather doing little by force. Thus a firm and awe-inspiring ruler need not rely on excessive punishments to have his orders obeyed.

The text regards the body as a microcosm, mirroring heaven and earth. It is the home of the spirits, who can be happy when material desires are overcome. This note of the indwelling of the spirits and of asceticism is very important for its later influence, and reflects – polytheism aside – the Pauline motif of the body as temple of the Spirit (2 Cor. 14:15; Eph. 2:22).

A Metaphysical Tao: Wang Pi on Lao-tzu

Wang Pi (A.D. 226–49) is known to be an historical figure, a genius who died young. Interested in both philosophy and politics, he left behind the image of an abstract thinker, associated with the movement called *Hsüan-hsüeh/Xuanxue*, mysterious or dark learning, with the kind of 'pure conversation' (*ch'ing-t'an/qingtan*) it generated, that is, discussions of pure philosophy. This was an activity current among many intellectuals tired of politics. They belonged to the Neo-Taoist movement, with its two faces, a 'rationalist' or philosophical one, and a 'sentimentalist' or literary-artistic one.[17]

Wang Pi also left behind commentaries on the *Analects* of Confucius and the *Book of Changes*. He is associated with a debate on whether the sage can have emotions. His position is that the sage differs from ordinary people only in spirituality and wisdom, but possesses all the emotions without becoming ensnared by them. This is no abstruse question. It concerns sagehood as a universally accessible ideal, at a time when society itself was rigidly structured. It influenced the later Chinese Buddhist doctrine of universal Buddhahood, and was reaffirmed in the Neo-Confucian teaching that everyone is potentially a sage. And it is evidence that the problem of 'universal salvation' has always occupied many minds throughout Chinese history.

Wang Pi's *Lao-tzu* commentary is our main concern here. It brought out certain key ideas, especially the concept of *wu* (nothingness). This word is difficult to understand on account of its apparent negative connotation. Actually, the Tao is described in terms of *wu* because it is indeterminate, the source of all things and not identified with any *one*:

> All beings originated from *wu*. Thus before there were form and names, [the Tao] then is 'the beginning of the ten thousand things'. When there are form and names, [the Tao] then 'brings them up, nourishes them, makes them secure and stable;' it is their 'mother'. This means that Tao in its formlessness and namelessness originates and completes the ten thousand things.[18]

A Nominalist Tao: Kuo Hsiang on Chuang-tzu

The *Chuang-tzu* Commentary ascribed to Kuo Hsiang (d. A.D. 312) is allegedly done with the collaboration of another scholar, Hsiang Hsiu. It has become the standard commentary on the text. However, its interpretation of the Tao as nothingness remains controversial. It is also diametrically opposed to Wang Pi's interpretation in *Lao-tzu*. For Kuo Hsiang claims that *Chuang-tzu's* Tao is really 'nothing', that is, non-existent, since he gives to the term *wu* a negative meaning. In Western terms and recalling medieval scholastic arguments, his teaching is 'nominalistic'. For the sake of a pun, we may say that the unnamed Tao is then understood as a name only, representing nothing in reality. But this interpretation has not remained unchallenged. According to Kuo's understanding, there is no creator, not even an impersonal or transpersonal one, but all things produce themselves according to a law of natural 'self-transformation' (*tu-hua/duhua*). In this light, the universe is in a state of constant flux, as are social and moral institutions.

7 Neo-Taoism as a Protest Movement

Neo-Taoists often voiced their protest in a world of disunity and chaos. Wang Pi himself had iconoclastic attitudes toward the authority of the past. Others included Hsiang Hsiu and Hsi K'ang, who belonged to a group called 'The Seven Worthies of the Bamboo Grove'. Many of these were adherents of a school called 'Doctrine of Names' (*ming-chiao/mingjiao*). The term recalls to mind an ancient school of logic (*ming-chia/mingjia*), and some of the Neo-Taoists did revive this interest. Speaking generally, theirs was a kind of Taoist-influenced Confucianism, which reinterpreted Confucius as a sage united with the Tao – but giving him a place higher than Lao-tzu.

Individualism and Hedonism

A product of those days was the chapter entitled 'Yang Chu' in the text *Lieh-tzu*, attributed to a fifth-century-B.C. Taoist. It uses the figure Yang Chu, denounced by Mencius as an egoist, to articulate a pessimistic view of life and an approval of hedonism. In direct contradiction to Lao-tzu and Chuang-tzu, it advocated the satisfaction of the senses:

> . . . whether we are clever or foolish . . . we all die . . . . Make haste to enjoy your life while you have it; why care what happens when you are dead?[19]

And then, in a language pitted directly against that of *Lao-tzu*, it says:

> Give yourself up to whatever your ears wish to listen to, your eyes to look on, your nostrils to turn to, your mouth to say, your body to find ease in, your will to achieve.[20]

Lieh-tzu also gives voice to scepticism, especially regarding the existence of a higher power, and to fatalism. In it, the Taoist idea of non-action degenerates into 'doing nothing' and living according to one's impulse. And the text has exerted real influence among a circle of Chinese Epicureans, some of whom were intentionally anti-establishment. For example, the 'Seven Worthies of the Bamboo Grove' were also known for their nonconformist behaviour, evocative of the 'hippie' movement of the 1960s. Several were known as great drinkers. Liu Ling, for example, asked for more wine from his wife while suffering from a hangover. When she resisted, he promised to take an oath in the presence of the spirits, and asked her to make the preparations. Liu then knelt down and prayed:

Heaven produced Liu Ling
[Who] took wine for his name.

. . . .

As for his wife's complaint,
Be careful not to listen.

Whereupon he drained the wine and ate up the meat, and before
he knew it was already drunk again.[21]

There are also stories about Juan Chi and drinks. The seventh-
century poet Wang Chi would claim that Juan Chi eventually
travelled to an earthly paradise which he calls the 'Land of the
Drunk', where the inhabitants

sip the wind and drink the dew, and abstain from the Five
Cereals. Their sleep is dreamless, their walk leisurely. They live
among fishes, crabs, birds and animals, and have no idea what
ships and chariots, weapons and implements are good for.[22]

Such are the examples of the *romantic spirit* of spontaneity, as
expressed by the term *feng-liu* ('wind and stream'). In traditional
China, this term represents an *aesthetic* attitude toward life and
the universe much more than a sexual one. Taoist philosophy has
exercised a profound influence on many aspects of culture, inspiring
creativity in art and poetry, and eventually contributing to a Chinese
appropriation of Indian Buddhism.

Protest, Freedom and Anarchy
Neo-Taoism is true to original Taoism in its individualistic bent.
Juan Chi was a political anarchist, for whom Utopia is a land
without a ruler, and certainly without the need for the ruler–subject
relationship. In his fictitious biography of 'Master Great Man', he
has this to say:

When rulers are set up, tyranny arises; when officials are established, thieves are born . . . . Now if there were no honors, those
in low position would bear no grudges; if there were no riches,
the poor would not struggle [to obtain them]. Each would be
satisfied within himself . . . there are no superior persons, the
inferior need not worry. When there are no rich people, the poor

need not quarrel with each other, and everyone finds a sufficiency within himself.[23]

More associated with alchemy than with philosophy, Ko Hung was opposed to such ideas of anarchy. In his work *Pao-p'u tzu* (The Master Who Embraces Simplicity), his antagonist is made to say that rulers are tyrannical only because they have the power to do so:

But when princes and ministers have established themselves, the anger of the masses grows day by day. They feel the urge to shake their fists, tied down and chained though they be, and to bemoan their labor in dirt and misery, until the prince finally seeks refuge in the hall of the temple of the ancestors, trembling with fear.[24]

To seek solace in intoxication is an artist's privilege. But while philosophers, poets and artists have always looked for freedom, they have never found enough of it in political society. With some difference, we may see their parallels in those persons in the West who are anti-establishment, and look for greater self-expression. Perhaps this explains why Taoism is attractive today to many young people in the West.

Are we, however, to consider Taoist philosophy only in the historical past, or is it still a living philosophy? For many, this will seem a strange question, as Taoist philosophy appears to have been absorbed into Buddhist and Neo-Confucian thought centuries ago, and no longer enjoys an independent existence. The facts actually are not so simple. For the intellectuals living under Communist rule in mainland China, Taoist philosophy has once more become an important guide, offering its teachings of inner freedom, and of survival in difficult circumstances.[25]

6

Immortality and Mysticism: Taoism as Salvation Religion

1 The Origins of Taoist Religion

As a religious tradition, Taoism came down from very early times indeed, from the times of oracle bones and divination. Taoist priests are heirs to a past society where the diviners and shamans (*wu*) were venerated for their ability to communicate with the spiritual world – the world of the Lord-on-high, and of the other gods and spirits – to bring down rain to the dry earth and to heal the sick. This does not mean Taoism is identical to ancient religion, but it does highlight its difference from the philosophical Taoism of *Lao-tzu* and *Chuang-tzu*, through which the ancient religion was partially eclipsed by a process of rationalisation and philosophical speculation.

Taoist Philosophy and Taoist Religion
Philosophical Taoism is only one of several strands that converged to make up religious Taoism. The others include ideas from the Yin-Yang school, which understands the natural order under the two complementary yet antithetical aspects of the Tao, and the Five Agents school. Although Taoist religion revered Lao-tzu (both the man and the text), it radically reinterpreted his teachings as well as those of *Chuang-tzu*. And it accumulated a huge body of scriptures called the *Tao-tsang/Daozang* (Taoist Canon) with over a thousand volumes compiled over fifteen centuries. The principal books are alleged to be divine revelations made to Taoist adepts during a state of trance. None bears the name of the author or the date of composition; many are written in a coded, esoteric language which can only be understood by the initiated. Only in our own days are scholars beginning to gain mastery over many texts which were not previously accessible.

Before it became a formally organised religion, Taoism was known, in the early Han times, as the cult of the Yellow Emperor and Lao-tzu, that is, as 'Huang-Lao'. By this name, we understand a combination of esoteric magical teachings about immortality and of political teachings associated with non-action (*wu-wei*), enjoining a government policy of non-interference in the people's lives. As it developed, religious Taoism showed itself to be a salvation religion. It instructs its faithful in healthy living, and also seeks to guide its believers beyond this transitory life, to a happy eternity. It professes a belief in an original state of bliss, followed by the fallen state. And it relies on supernatural powers for help and protection. Some of these features might, of course, represent later Buddhist influence.[1]

2   Taoism as Institutional Religion: The Heavenly Masters Sect

The formal beginning of the Taoist religion as an institution is often identified with the founding of the Heavenly Masters Sect. In later Han times (2nd century A.D.), a significant religious movement developed in Szechuan under Chang Lin (also called Chang Tao-lin). Allegedly, Lao-tzu appeared to this hermit in a mountain cave in A.D. 142 complaining of the world's lack of respect for the true and the correct, and of people's honouring pernicious demons. In this alleged revelation, Chang was made the Heavenly Master, with the order to abolish the things of the demons, and to install true orthodoxy. He would become founder and first pope of a religion that parallels in many ways Catholic Christianity.[2]

This new sect opposed the bloody sacrifices that were being offered to the spirits of the deceased at that time, substituting offerings of cooked vegetables. In healing sicknesses, it instituted the confession of sins in 'secluded rooms', where the priests prayed for the sick, who wrote down their sins. The document was then offered to heaven (on mountain tops), to earth (by burial) and to the rivers (by drowning). For services rendered, the sect levied and collected a tax of five pecks of rice from the members of its congregation, for which reason it was called the Five Pecks of Rice Sect.

Chang organised his followers into 'parishes', with male and female priests or 'libationers', who served as representatives of the Tao on earth and, as such, were opposed to the numerous spirit-mediums and shamans of the folk religion of the time. Through the teachings of this sect, the invisible world beyond this life came to be represented as that of a systematic spiritual bureaucracy, with officials to whom prayers were made for cures of specific sicknesses. In other ways as well, the Taoist religion represented by this sect gradually served as a superstructure to the many local cults which it had sought in vain to replace, but ended up by supervising and perhaps incorporating them.

The Heavenly Master became a hereditary institution. The line eventually moved its traditional base from Szechuan to the Dragon-Tiger Mountain of Kiangsi. The sect has been especially popular in southern China. After the Communist takeover (1949), the headquarters was moved to Taiwan. It continues to have hereditary instructors, assisted by what resemble parish councils of Taoist notables, including men and women who take part in various ceremonies, as well as secular patrons of the organisation.

Rituals have always been the soul of the Taoist religion. But its liturgy was further transformed after the alleged revelations received by a family in Mao-shan (Kiangsu) especially in the later fourth century. Visions and inspired writings crystallised in a Buddhist-influenced ecstatic literature which gives assurances of salvation to the initiated during coming cataclysms. New hymns were introduced, together with Buddhist customs like circumambulation and the chanting of sacred texts called *ling-pao/lingbao* ('sacred treasures'). We find here the beginning of the *Tao-tsang* as a response of the religion to Buddhist challenges and stimulus, and giving expression to eschatological hopes based on Lao-tzu's new advent, which would establish a reign of peace and equality for the elect, the very 'pure'.[3]

3 The Quest for Immortality

Religions are usually concerned with the life hereafter. But Taoists do not conceive of eternal life in terms of spiritual immortality alone. As there is no strict separation of spirit and matter in Chinese thought, they look forward to the survival of the whole person, including the body. This is not enunciated in any doctrine resembling the Christian one regarding the final resurrection of the body. Taoists talk rather of the doctrine of the three life-principles, of breath (*ch'i/qi*), vital essence or semen (*ching/jing*), and spirit (*shen*), each of which has two dimensions, being present at the same time in the human being as microcosm, as well as in the cosmos as macrocosm. The Taoist trinity (a pantheon of deities) is therefore represented as a manifestation of these cosmic principles.

For the proper cultivation of life, techniques are developed: of healing and breath circulation, of meditative exercises and sexual hygiene (a blending of sex and yoga). Much of this teaching is transmitted in secret from master to disciple, as is Tantric Buddhism, the religion of the Mongols and Tibetans. Out of such, often as a by-product, we have today what are called Chinese healing techniques, and what are called 'martial arts', as well as herbal medicine. We refer here to a truly 'holistic' healing system, based especially on an age-old text, the *Inner Classic of the Yellow Emperor* (*Huang-ti Nei-ching*) which goes back to the sixth century B.C. It gives a clear list of priorities for maintaining health: that before healing comes proper nutrition, before proper nutrition comes the treatment of the spirit.[4]

Taoist meditation practices include a standing form with the knees slightly bent, which is considered as contributing to the proper balance of energy or *ch'i* within the body. Allegedly, this *ch'i* travels along 'meridians' in the body. The proper exercise of Chinese yoga or *ch'i-kung*, as well as the application of acupuncture, depends on these meridians with their various 'acupuncture points'. These physiological underpinnings are still considered as speculative by Western scientists. But there has been undeniable therapeutic success: in acupuncture for pain relief as well as for anaesthesia, in yoga-like practices and in massages and physiotherapy, to preserve as well as to restore health.

The belief in Immortals is an ancient one, going back at least to the third century B.C., and was elaborated after the founding of an institutional religion. We hear of 'heavenly immortals' who have ascended to the celestial regions, and of 'earthly immortals' who roam about in the sacred forests and mountains. After these come those human beings who appear to die, but actually only leave behind their physical frames (*shih-chieh/shijie*). Such fanciful ideas about deathlessness have left their imprint on literature as well as religion. We can discern this even in a poem written by Mao Zedong (1957), and addressed to a woman who had lost her husband, surnamed Liu (literally, 'willow') in battle. Mao mentions his own earlier loss, as his wife, née Yang (literally, 'poplar') had been killed by the Nationalist government in 1933:

> Long have I lost my Yang, the brave poplar tree
> And Liu, your spreading willow, is now cut down.
> But silken haired poplar seeds and willow wisps
> Float up, as did they, to the ninth heaven.
> Passing the moon, they tarried, and . . .

Were given to drink of gold cassia wine.
And the goddess of the moon honoured these
Loyal souls, with her sleeves spread, dancing for them
All through the boundless spaces of the sky.[5]

The poem's wistful allusions to drinks of immortality disclose the fundamental human desire to imagine one's deceased beloved as continuing to live somehow in the hereafter. It is interesting to note that the beginning of the Cultural Revolution (1966) was marked by Mao's displeasure with a play which he considered to have criticised him, among other things, for seeking to 'live forever'.[6]

Looking for Elixirs: Outer Alchemy
Alchemy has always been associated with esoteric or 'mystical' traditions, whether with *gnosis* in Hellenistic Egypt or with Taoism in China. The names of popes and theologians are connected with alchemy: the tenth-century Gerbert, who became Pope Sylvester, the fourteenth-century John XXII, as well as the thirteenth-century teacher and disciple – Albertus Magnus and Thomas Aquinas. But whereas Europeans were more interested in transmuting base metal into gold, the Chinese focused on finding or making the elixir of life. Their belief that men and women could become Immortals (*hsien/xian*) led historically to the practice of alchemical experiments, like that of transmuting the mercury ore cinnabar. This is especially given in early treatises, as the *Ts'an-t'ung-ch'i* of Wei Po-yang (2nd century A.D.) and the *Pao-p'u-tzu*, written by Ko Hung. Taoists have described this effort as the attempt to 'steal the secret of Heaven and Earth', that is, to wrest from nature the mystery of life. In so doing, they might not have found the elixir of immortality, but did become, like the medieval European alchemists, the pioneers of scientific experimentation, and made certain discoveries of lasting value to various fields, including chemistry, medicine and pharmacology.

Elixir mixtures frequently contained dangerous compounds derived from mercury, lead, sulphur and the like; some were certain to cause arsenic poisoning and death. But there was hope that such death was temporary, followed by eternal life. A story in another Taoist text helps to explain the faith and perseverance of Taoist adepts in the face of disturbing symptoms and common-sense evidence. I am referring here to the well-known tale in the fourth-century *Shen-hsien chuan* (Biographies of Immortals), recounting the legend of Wei Po-yang.

Allegedly, Wei Po-yang had made an elixir in the mountains, and decided to try it first on his dog, which died instantly. He turned then to his disciples, and said: 'I have abandoned worldly ways and forsaken family and friends . . . I should be ashamed to return without having found the Tao of the Immortals. To die of the elixir is no worse than living without having found it.' And so he too, took the elixir and fell dead. On seeing this, one disciple commented: 'Our teacher is no ordinary person. He must have done this with some reason.' So he followed the master's example, and also died. The other two disciples said to each other: 'People prepare elixirs for the sake of gaining longevity. But this elixir has brought on death. It would be better not to take it, but live a few more decades in the world.' So they left the mountains to procure coffins for the burial of their master and fellow disciple. After they were gone, however, both Wei Po-yang and the loyal disciple, together with their dog, revived, became real immortals, and went away! They left behind a message for the other two, who were then filled with remorse.

Ironically, alchemical information and experimentation did contribute to the preservation of the physical body. While metallic components like mercury and lead can be fatal when swallowed, they are also known to have preservative powers, and bodies from Ming times and earlier have been discovered well preserved, with perfumed mercury in the abdomen. Perhaps the knowledge of such was also taken by the Taoists as evidence of an 'apparent', rather than real, death. Possibly also, Chinese aristocrats made sure that their physical bodies would be protected from corruption, so that their 'souls' would remain with their bodies, and eventually attain immortality together. In 1972, archaeologists discovered in Ma-wang-tui, near Changsha, Hunan (where Taoist texts were also unearthed), the uncorrupted body of an approximately fifty-year-old noblewoman from the second century B.C., in a state like that of someone who had died only a week or two before. The body had been immersed in a liquid containing mercuric sulphide. Could it be that she had died of elixir poisoning as well, in an effort to gain immortality? Also, together with the body, archaeologists found various talismans designed to conduct the deceased to her eternal destination after burial, into the presence of the Lord-on-high, and these offer evidence of the beliefs of the time.[7]

Immortality and Transcendence of Life?
While some Taoists searched for an elixir that might permit physical longevity or even immortality, other Taoists (or perhaps the same

ones) believed, like Christians and Muslims, that true immortality can only be attained upon physical death. At that moment, the 'spirit-self' allegedly ascends to heaven and takes up its place in the otherworldly bureaucracy. While on earth, however, an aspiring immortal should strive to make progress in meditation and moral striving. One is to detach oneself from sensual attractions, and eliminate all feelings of enmity and hatred which do injury to oneself. Thus death is to be regarded as a change of residence: the ageing body is like a house with rotten walls, and must be exchanged for a better one. 'Desiring eternal life in this body', the T'ang dynasty Taoist mystic Ssu-ma Ch'eng-chen says, 'how is it possible?'[8]

Often, people have remarked that the quest for physical immortality was opposed to the ideal of the natural in philosophical Taoism. But the attitude expressed above implies an utter equanimity toward life and death, sickness and health, gain and loss, wealth and poverty, that is, going beyond all the values usually held by most people. It reflects once more the ideas and values found in the philosophical text *Chuang-tzu*. If it contributes to the creation of the immortal embryo: that truly immortal body, the production of which is the goal of 'inner alchemy', it is also more. It represents the ideals of a mystical tradition, where all the symbolic images of the alchemical transformation are abandoned. We speak here of a gradual process toward union with the mystical Tao, leading to the emptying of body and mind, and enabling an improved practice of inner visualisation, of self-forgetfulness in meditation and of the indwelling of the Tao.[9]

Taoist Meditation and Inner Alchemy

We shall quote here from a text by the fourth-century Ko Hung which speaks of visualisation in a meditation entitled, 'Guarding the One' (*shou-yi*). The term 'the One' reminds us of the Han worship of the Great One (*T'ai-yi*) as the highest God, presumed to reside in the Polar Star above, but capable of descending into our own selves.

> Visualize the One in the center of the Northern Culmen and in the deepest abyss of yourself:
> In front – the hall of light (in the head); behind – the scarlet palace (in the heart).
> Imposing: the Flowery Canopy (the lungs); lofty: the Golden Pavilion (the kidneys?)

Left – the *Gang* Star; right – the *Kui* (of the Northern Dipper).
Rising like a wave, sinking like the void itself.

. . .

Guard the One and visualize the True One; then the spirit
world will be yours to peruse!
Lessen desires, restrain your appetite – the One will remain
at rest!
Like a bare blade coming toward your neck – realise you
live through the One alone!
Knowing the One is easy – keeping it forever is hard.
Guard the One and never lose it – the limitations of man will
not be for you!
On land you will be free from beasts, in water from fierce
dragons.
No fear of evil spirits or phantoms,
No demon will approach, nor blade attain![10]

Taoist meditation involved experiments with one's self, including
the body. This was also a kind of 'furnace' in which to make the
inner elixir of immortality, sometimes called the Golden Elixir or
the Golden Flower. Possibly, such was the natural development
associated with a recognition of the dangers associated with outer
alchemy, and the failure to find a 'final' elixir. We are referring to
methods of inner alchemy, associated with yoga and meditation.
According to the theory behind these methods, the human body
is divided into three 'cinnabar fields' – head, chest and abdomen – each of which is inhabited by a large number of gods,
who keep it in life and sustenance, but under the supervision of
each of the members of the Taoist trinity. Methods of meditation
include the visualisation of light, representing energy or *ch'i*, and
conducting it through the three cinnabar fields in a 'microcosmic
orbit' or extending this circulation to the extremities of the limbs in
a 'macrocosmic orbit'.

Information about meditation techniques used to be scanty, as
transmission was only to the initiated. But more and more is being
known today. Already, several decades ago, a meditation treatise
was translated that attracted the attention of the Swiss psychologist
C. G. Jung. While very wary of a Westerner's steeping himself in
Eastern traditions, Jung suggests that human beings possess a common psychic substratum, the 'collective unconscious'. Supposedly,
all conscious imagination and action grow out of these unconscious

prototypes. He quotes a Western mystic, Hildegarde von Bingen, who speaks of an inner light:

> I cannot recognize any sort of form in this light, although I sometimes see in it another light that is known to me as the living light . . . . While I am enjoying the spectacle of this light, all sadness and sorrow disappear from my memory.[11]

Through *ch'i-kung* exercises and meditation, especially by emptying the heart of all distractions and attachments, and by meditation and visualisation, the Taoist practitioner seeks an interior, ecstatic vision which would enable a vision of and a visit to the gods within the body – and there are thousands of them. Through such contact, the adept may obtain help to cure sicknesses by driving away toxins or 'evil spirits' in the body, and even acquire an inner elixir through spiritual illumination, eventually to produce within oneself an ethereal and immortal body. We are speaking here of traditional practices, but we may emphasise that similar exercises, sometimes without the specific religious trappings, are being taught today by the successors to the Taoist healers, not only in China itself, but also in Japan and in the West.

Modelling their lives on nature, Taoists claim to have discovered their various techniques by the observation of natural processes, including animal, and also foetal behaviour. An advanced stage of Taoist practice involved what is called 'embryonic respiration' through the conscious imitation of the life of the foetus in the mother's womb. Scientifically, it was a recognition of important metabolic processes within the human organism. Psychologically, it also involved the quest for inner peace and the integration of the human personality. Besides, in the many methods associated with 'inner alchemy', which developed especially in the T'ang and Sung times, the theory behind outer alchemy is reinterpreted in the light of the nourishing of the *yin* and the *yang* of the human body, the fusing and uniting of the two in an effort to recover the primordial energy, *ch'i*, which permeates and sustains all life. The Taoist speaks also of finding the 'True Self' within, and by doing so, of achieving greater harmony with the rhythm of the cosmos outside. This 'True Self' is sometimes envisaged in terms of a new birth within, of the gestation of a new life coming to be.[12]

While placing some emphasis on physical and spiritual techniques, Taoists do not neglect ethical behaviour, but incorporate it into their practices. They speak of the need of a moral life, of good works as well as of ritual penance for wrongdoing. This shows the continual interaction between Taoism and Confucianism. Buddhist influence also followed, and with it, more advanced doctrines of spirituality as well as meditative exercises. For these reasons, and on account of the belief in the gods, Taoism is more than an immortality cult, more than the sum of magical and ecstatic techniques, and really a religion of salvation.

4   Taoist Scriptures

Taoism is also a scriptural religion. It claims thousands of texts as having scriptural value, incorporating them in a corpus which resembles more a treasury of books (*Tao-tsang*) than a normative 'canon', even if that word is often used by Western scholars.

The structure of the Taoist canon, which came down from the fifth century A.D., can actually shed light on its sectarian character. This is composed of seven sections, placed under the tripartite division of the so-called Three Caverns, each of which originally grew up around a particular scripture or group of scriptures:

The Three Caverns
(each of which is divided into twelve subsections):

1.   The first Cavern (Tung-chen), having as its nucleus the Shang-ch'ing scriptures, surrounding a liturgical poem with secret names of gods and spirits, associated with the Mao-shan movement, originating near Nanking in southern China
2.   The second (Tung-hsüan), having as its nucleus the Ling-pao scriptures, emanating also from the south, with talismans and added texts, disclosing a strong Buddhist flavor, and have been associated with the Ling-pao sect.
3.   The third (Tung-shen), having as its nucleus the San-huang (Three Sovereigns) scriptures. Their origins are less clear; they might have come from the circles of Taoist masters serving at court, and contain at their core talismans and ancillary exorcism texts. They have been connected with the Heavenly Masters sect.

The Four Supplements:

1.   The T'ai-hsüan is ancillary to the First Cavern. Its central text is actually *Lao-tzu* itself (which shows the curiously subordinate place of this treatise).

2. The T'ai-p'ing is ancillary to the Second Cavern. Its central text is the well-known *T'ai-p'ing ching* (Classic of the Great Peace), a Utopian and Messianic text.
3. The T'ai-ch'ing is ancillary to the Third Cavern. Its central texts deal more directly with alchemy.
4. The Cheng-yi is a supplement to all three. Its texts are made up of the canonical texts of the Heavenly Masters sect.

The term 'cavern' (*tung/dong*) is used, presumably because of the claim that the principal texts were allegedly revealed, or discovered in caves by hermits. Each of the Three Caverns is placed under the protection of one of the three members of the Taoist trinity. However, *all* of the central texts in the Supplements are older than the texts around which the Three Caverns are created. Perhaps the Four Supplements were added to the Three Caverns in a reform movement seeking to resist Buddhist infiltrations into Taoism.

5 Monastic Taoism: The Perfect Truth Sect

The Taoist religious movement produced many sects and subsects. But sectarian differences were not doctrinal, but practical. The sects and subsects placed varying emphases on outer and inner alchemy, sexual hygiene and meditative exercises. For example, the Ling-pao tradition gave special attention to rituals at court, while the Mao-shan tradition is better known for its meditative preferences. Although the appearance of the Taoist canon itself signifies the union of these groups into one large eclectic tradition, sectarian distinctions have persisted until today, on the basis of style and performance of rituals.

Since the seventeenth century and in more recent times, Taoism has known a steady decline. The two sects that have survived well are its southern school, as represented by the Heavenly Masters sect, sometimes called the Cheng-yi (Zhengyi), and its northern school, known under the name of the Perfect Truth (Ch'üan-chen / Quanzhen) sect, which developed especially during the Yüan (Mongol) dynasty. The Perfect Truth sect discloses the most Buddhist influence, with monasteries of celibate monks who are required to practise frequent fasts, abstain from alcohol, and pursue the techniques of inner alchemy and meditation. Its best-known monastery is the White Cloud Monastery in Peking, which has been restored, with visits permitted by the public, since 1981. The headquarters of the Chinese Taoist Association is located there.

The Heavenly Masters sect has kept a married and often hereditary priesthood and few food taboos. It is active in the use of charms and talismans, and in healing and exorcism.

6 Taoism as a Salvation Religion

The word 'salvation' is derived from Greek. The Greek word *soter* refers to a saviour or healer. Salvation implies a kind of 'fallen state' from which condition one is to 'become whole' again, with the help of a saviour, or, in the case of some non-Western religions, through one's own striving. True, the quest for physical immortality may seem rather earthly. It appears naïve, and even smacks of *hubris*. Yet the wish for deathlessness hides within itself a quest for transcendence. *Eritis sicut deus: to be godlike* has always been the deepest of human longings. In this perspective, the Taoist religion may well be called a religion of salvation.

Salvation also refers to 'wholeness'. As we have seen, religious Taoism tends to associate human weakness and sickness with sin, that is, offence against both the conscience and the deity. Taoists associate the healing of such ills with the confession of sin, and the forgiveness and help of higher powers. On the other hand, their attention to physiology as well as to pharmacology has led to many contributions in the area of Chinese medicine.

Unlike Confucianism, Taoism is a salvation religion which seeks to guide its believers beyond this transitory life to a happy eternity. There is a belief in an original state of bliss, followed by the fallen state. And there is reliance on supernatural powers for help and protection. Here we come to the subject of the Taoist pantheon.

The Taoist Pantheon
Taoists believe in the supernatural, not only as *powers*, but also as *beings*. I refer to their belief in a hierarchy of gods – including mythical figures, and many divinised human beings, under the supremacy of the highest deity. During the second century B.C., the supreme being was called the T'ai-yi / Taiyi (Great One). Soon afterwards, a triad of gods was worshipped, which assumed different names in different periods. In early Han times, these were known as the T'ien-yi / Tianyi (Heavenly One), the Ti-yi / Diyi (Earthly One), and the T'ai-yi / Taiyi (Great One). They are sometimes interpreted as: the supreme deity (a direct emanation of the Tao itself), his disciple, the Lord Tao (the Tao personified), and *his* disciple, the Lord Lao (Lao-tzu deified). While Lao-tzu appears in this way only

the third in a hierarchy of gods, the cult honouring him is very old, and many in the T'ang dynasty and later considered him as having revealed all the principal texts in the Taoist canon.

Still later, the Taoist trinity would receive other names, including especially that of the 'Three Pure Ones' (*San-ch'ing/Sanqing*), who were the lords of the Three Life-principles or 'Breaths' (*ch'i*). Their names were the Primal Celestial One (*Yüan-shih t'ien-tsun/Yuanshi tianzun*), the Precious Celestial One (*Ling-pao t'ien-tsun/Lingbao tianzun*), and the Way-and-Its-Power Celestial One (*Tao-te t'ien-tsun/Daode tianzun*). Metaphysically, they each represented some aspect of the ineffable Tao, transcendent and yet capable of becoming 'incarnate' especially through Lao-tzu's revelation.[13] In the more recent period, the supreme deity has often been called the Jade Emperor, or, in today's Taiwan, *T'ien-kung/Tiangong* (colloquial for 'Lord of Heaven').

Why is deity worshipped as a trinity? Has there been any Western influence? A Gnostic connection has been suggested; but the very ancient origin (2nd century B.C.) of the Taoist trinity has made this hypothesis difficult to accept. Perhaps, some light may be found in chapter 42 of the *Tao-te ching* itself:

> The Tao gives birth to One;
> One gives birth to Two;
> Two gives birth to Three;
> Three gives birth to the myriad things.

The Taoist trinity had become well established by T'ang times. At that time, Nestorian Christianity was also active and well known in China. There was contact and interaction between the two religions. Scholars have also compared the Three Pure Ones to the Christian trinity: the Primal Celestial One, controlling the past, has been likened to God the Father; the Precious Celestial One, controlling the present, has been compared to God the Son, and the Way-and-Its-Power Celestial One, controlling the future, has been compared to God the Holy Spirit.[14]

Taoist extravagance is manifest in the evolution of a pantheon of innumerable spiritual beings, gods or celestials and immortals, as well as deified heroes and forces of nature. They make up a divine hierarchy, resembling in its functions a state bureaucracy. There are books devoted to establishing the ranks in this hierarchy of transcendent beings, but these efforts actually augment the confusion.

Taoist Messianism

As a salvation religion, Taoism gives special importance to a Messiah figure. This is found especially in the *T'ai-p'ing ching* (Classic of the Great Peace), which looks forward to a future epoch of Great Peace. Even in an incomplete and partially restored version (7th century A.D.), it is sometimes regarded as the most important text after the *Lao-tzu*. It offers a doctrine of salvation, with a saviour or 'divine man', in possession of a 'celestial book', which teaches the return to ideal government while awaiting the arrival of the fullness of time, the Great Peace. The divine man has the mandate of passing the revealed words on to the 'true man' (*chen-jen*/*zhenren*), a prophet figure who is to transmit the texts to a ruler of high virtue. This prince is to rule by the Tao and its power; specifically, he is to govern with the help of his ministers and the people at large, careful to maintain harmony within the realm but slow to exercise coercion or punishment.

Possibly, this text originated in those circles that attempted to influence the ruler in the direction of reform during the Han dynasty. Their lack of success led then to the Yellow Turbans revolt (A.D. 184–215), involving hundreds of thousands of Taoists (wearing yellow kerchiefs). While the revolt failed, Taoist Messianism, with its millenarian overtones, became the inspiration for successive movements of political protest, organised by secret societies throughout history.[15] They resemble similar movements in Western history, started by religious groups peripheral to mainstream Christianity, such as that around the twelfth-century Joachim of Fiore or the later Anabaptists. In the latter case, their Peasants' Revolt in sixteenth- century Germany was supported by Thomas Müntzer (d. 1525), called 'theologian of revolution' by the highly influential Marxist philosopher Ernst Bloch.[16] This is a reason why the Taoist religion has always been regarded with suspicion, even until today, by various governments. It has been severely persecuted in Communist China and carefully supervised in Taiwan.

Rituals and Priesthood

Much attention is given by the Taoist religion to ritual or liturgical expressions. Its complex systems include a quasi-sacramental regard for ritual initiation, for purification and renewal in the life-cycle and development of the human person. Taoist priests are actually *licensed* to carry out rituals of particular traditions, even though, since the Sung dynasty, and in return for a fee, the authorisation comes usually from the Heavenly Master, with a decision made after examination of the individual's ritual knowledge. Exorcism rituals are often carried out in cases of sickness, with the exorcist struggling for a victory over the evil spirits. Many other rituals are regularly performed around the lunar year and its festivals, especially New Year. There is, besides, the rite of cosmic renewal, celebrated at the time of the winter solstice, and symbolising cosmic rebirth.

Incense is indeed central to Taoist ritual, together with the sacrificial offering of sacred writings, such as the burning of paper talismans. Sometimes, the papers sacrificed bear the prayers of the faithful, giving their names and the intentions for which the service is being performed. While ritual expertise on the part of the religious leaders is important, the faithful participating in such rituals are usually urged to prepare for them by fasting and by a spirit of forgiveness and reconciliation. Some of the priests who lead the rituals and recite the prayers are also shamans, soothsayers, or spirit-mediums, who can assist the faithful with their counsels and fortune-telling, explain the baleful influence of the stars, and assist communication with the spirits of the beloved dead. Within the religion itself, those priests who practise ritual as an expression of meditation or inner alchemy usually earn more respect than others who do 'external' exercises of exorcisms and healing for the sake of making a living.

7   Taoism in Korea and Japan

Probably the most visible heir to ancient Chinese religion, the Taoist religion is still alive and vibrant today after all the historical vicissitudes, in those regions where the Chinese live (Taiwan, Hong Kong, Singapore), and has re-emerged even in mainland China during the recent liberalisation. It also has many parallels in popular religion which is dominated by shamanistic beliefs and practices, not only among the Chinese but also in Korea and Japan.

Since the seventh century, Taoism has been known in each of the three medieval kingdoms of Koguryo, Paekche and Silla on the Korean peninsula, with the use of talismans, the practice of exorcism, as well as the quest for immortality. It spread also to seventh-century Japan. The united Korea under the Yi dynasty (14th century) preferred Confucianism, but Taoism suffered less than Buddhism, and its deities continued to receive worship, retaining influence especially among the common people. Korean Taoism tends to have more in common with the Heavenly Masters sect, with a married clergy wearing white where their Chinese counterparts prefer dark blue. Taoism continues its presence in Korea today, exercising an influence on many newer cults that emerged during the past two centuries.

Many scholars prefer to believe in a Japan with an uncontaminated native Shinto tradition. However, Chinese ideas of *yin* and *yang* and the Five Agents are already reflected in such early Japanese works as the *Kojiki* and the *Nihongi*, with their myths and legends. Taoist influences can be discerned in the Shinto veneration of such sacred objects in its temples as the sword and the bronze mirror, both used in Taoist rituals. In comparison with Korea, Taoist influences appear more diffused in Japan, and less distinguishable from native shamanism. In comparison with Confucian influences, Taoist influences are more implicit than explicit, and are usually not recognised by the Japanese as having an alien origin. This does not mean that Japanese scholars have escaped from its influences. Among others, the Neo-Confucian thinker Nakae Tōju (1608–48) is known to have worshipped a personal deity whom he named the *Daiotsu sonshin*, and who was no other than the T'ai-yi of early Chinese religion – or, we may say, Taoism.[17]

8 Taoism Today

As a tradition, Taoism rivals Christianity in many ways, with its belief in a supreme being governing over a spiritual universe of deities and immortals, many of whom were historical persons. Its pantheon offers certain resemblances, especially to the Catholic religious universe, peopled as it is by God, the Virgin Mary and a multitude of saints. For those who desire more theological sophistication, the Taoist religion offers its doctrine of the cosmos and of cosmic process and harmony, tracing all back to the Great Ultimate (*T'ai-chi/Taiji*), and the interactions of the two modes of *yin* and *yang*. But the T'ai-chi is not just an abstract principle, as it is in Taoist or Neo-Confucian philosophy. The famous T'ai-chi emblem, in a circle with a curved line in the middle, separating a darker side from a brighter side, representing *yin* and *yang*, surrounded by the trigrams of the *Book of Changes*, can be found over house doors in Taiwan and elsewhere, and it is also on the South Korean national flag. It is alleged to have the power of protecting people from evil spirits.

Taoism possesses formally religious features. It has a clearly enunciated belief in a hierarchy of gods; it accepts the human condition as sinful; it seeks to bridge the gap between the human and the divine through ritual practices of prayer and penance. In many ways, it is quite different from Confucianism.

Taoist philosophy has contributed to the transformation of Buddhism, while Taoist religion has actually been transformed by Buddhism, accepting such doctrinal presuppositions as rebirth or transmigration, and a system of heavens and hells where the deceased find retribution, and incorporating into its pantheon various Buddhist deities and bodhisattvas. But the Taoists never accepted the basic Buddhist starting point: that all existence is suffering. Indeed, the quest for physical immortality presupposes a contentment with life in this world. Taoism has no universal response to suffering, although it deals with it on a piecemeal basis, through its healing arts, including faith-healing practices.

Today's Taoism is losing its adherents among the more educated and urbane. Not that a scientifically educated individual would automatically abandon his or her religious tradition. There are many, even among the greatest scientists, who are content with a few simple, religious answers to life in this world and perhaps even the beyond. Not only has science failed to answer many important questions of life, but science itself has its bonds with the occult. It is in a sense the child of alchemy and 'magic'; it offers possibilities that were once associated only with the magical. In mainland China, Taoism suffered because of its presumed association with 'superstitions'. With the more recent policy of religious tolerance, the Taoist religion has once more re-emerged. The *forms* of Taoism may be, to some extent, different, depending on the geographic regions, but its strength and tenacity are the same. And this is tribute enough to a tradition which has evolved over centuries, even millennia, to respond to and fulfil the human need to relate not only to nature, but also to the spirits. Taoism offers consolation to those who pray to higher powers for temporary as well as eternal blessings. It offers them the possibility of communicating with the gods, as well as that of *becoming* gods, either experientially in a brief trance, or in the hereafter. It affirms mystical experience, while encouraging a moral life. With all its theoretical defects, Taoism has served generations of followers well, and may continue to do so for many more generations to come.

Part Two
Foreign Religions and
Chinese Response

7

Scripture and Hermeneutics: Buddhism's Entry to China

1 Buddhism as a Missionary Religion

Historical China represents a cultural, and, most of the time as well, a political unity. But the country was not completely ignorant of, or entirely untouched by, outside influences. There had always been contact with Central Asia and with India, the centre of another great civilisation. And this happened especially through the spread of the Buddhist religion. But India, in contrast to China, had been more often politically fragmented than unified. For this reason India never posed a real threat to China and her sense of self-importance.

In discussing the topic of Buddhism as a religion of foreign origin in China, I wish to make a distinction, in the Chinese context, between Islam and Judaism (and, to an extent, Nestorian Christianity) on the one side, as *ethnic* religions, and Buddhism and Western Christianity, on the other side, as *missionary* religions. Here I am proposing a distinction between religions entering and remaining in China as the cultural heritage of ethnic minorities, and religions that went with missionary and proselytising intent. Although a proselytising religion by nature, Islam entered China as the religion of certain ethnic groups, from Persia and other parts of Central Asia and beyond. However, Buddhism and Christianity acted differently, arousing much more attention as well as controversy, as each attempted to make its impact upon the larger society.

Buddhism: An Introduction

The Buddha was considered by Karl Jaspers to be a figure of what he called the Axial Age, as were also Confucius and Lao-tzu. But we possess even less verifiable historical knowledge about the Buddha than we have of Confucius, except that both lived in the sixth century B.C. Tradition makes him Prince Siddhartha Gautama, the son of Suddhodana and his wife Maya, born (c. 560 B.C.) in that part of the Himalayan foothills that is today's Lumbini, in Nepal, and into the warrior caste, which is just beneath the priestly brahmins. Tradition also describes the shattering experience he had as a young man when he first confronted the facts of old age, sickness and death, and was much impressed with a wandering ascetic. At the age of about twenty-nine, he exchanged worldly life for that of a homeless ascetic wandering in the forests. Eventually, at age thirty-five, he attained enlightenment under a moonlit banyan tree near today's Bodh Gaya. It was the culmination of four stages of trance (*dhyāna*). His insights were especially formulated as the doctrine of dependent co-arising or co-origination (Sanskrit, *pratitya-samutpada*). Briefly stated, that existence is mutually conditioned, starting from ignorance conditioning our will, and ending with birth, death and rebirth. And he became the Buddha, i.e., the 'enlightened one'.

The Buddha's first sermon was given at Benares, and is usually summarised as the Four Noble Truths and the Eightfold Noble Path. The Truths included that of suffering being universal and pervasive; that its origin is selfish craving; that the cessation of such craving would be the only breakthrough to the cause and effect that make up life, death and rebirth; and that this can be done through the Path, including (i) right views, (ii) right intentions, (iii) right speech, (iv) right action, (v) right livelihood, (vi) right effort, (vii) right mindfulness and (viii) right concentration. The rest of his life was spent teaching disciples and multitudes until he had reached about eighty, when, through a series of meditative trances, he expired into *nirvāna*.[1]

According to the Indian world view, all animate existence is conditioned by transmigration, i.e., the migration of souls through various levels of existence, both animal and human. The Greek philosopher Pythagoras shared this belief, and some would say Plato also did. The Buddhists accept this but call it rebirth, since they reject the existence of souls and speak only of rebirth through the transmission of *karma*, one's good and evil deeds, through the cycle of existence. Hence Buddhist transmigration is without 'souls'. *Nirvāna* serves as a breakthrough out of such a cycle of *Samsāra*.

With these shifts in doctrine, Buddhism emerged out of the Indian religious landscape as a distinct religion, much as Christianity came out of the matrix of Judaism.

Differing perspectives on history characterised Buddhist India on the one side and Confucian China (and the Christian West) on the other. For Buddhists, the Buddha, also called Śakyamuni, that is, the holy man of the Śakya clan, is only one of a series of many Buddhas, but *the* Buddha of our epoch, which, in turn, is only one in a series of innumerable epochs. These also include, for example, Amitābha, the Buddha of the Pure Land. Besides the Buddha-figure, Buddhism also holds as most important its own teachings, or the *dharma*, and the community of believers called the *samgha*. Early Buddhist religion gained many adherents especially from among those who did not belong to the brahmin caste. Among these converts was the emperor Ashoka (c. 274–232 B.C.) who also united India. While he appeared much earlier in history than Constantine, he served the Buddhist religion in much the same role as Constantine did for Christianity.[2]

Buddhism began as, and remains very much, a monastic religion, with large monasteries functioning as institutions of higher learning where monks studied the words of the *sūtras* and debated over their meaning – in this respect much like the situation in medieval Christianity. With an increase in monastic and lay following, Buddhism also became more divided. Eventually, it engendered two branches, the Theravādar, the 'school of the elders' (sometimes pejoratively called Hīnayāna or Smaller Vehicle), and the Mahāyāna or the Greater Vehicle. The major difference between the two had to do with whether enlightenment or salvation is universally accessible. The Theravāda school teaches that salvation is difficult to attain, and impossible outside the monastic life; the Mahāyāna school teaches that all can become enlightened. The former school is still dominant in Southeast Asia: in Sri Lanka, Burma, Laos and Cambodia where the Buddhist religion remains visible through the monastic presence; the latter school spread to China, Korea, Vietnam and Japan.[3]

The celibate, monastic discipline in Buddhism offers a good parallel with Christian monasticism. Interestingly, the devout layman in early Buddhism was usually inducted into the monastic order before death, as a token of assurance of his future well-being, much as a lay Catholic member of a 'third order' used to be buried in monastic garb.[4]

The Anglo-American philosopher Alfred North Whitehead has

said that Christianity has been 'a religion seeking a metaphysic', in contrast to Buddhism which is 'a metaphysic generating a religion'.[5] For Westerners, Buddhism was initially very difficult to comprehend and scholars were not certain whether to call it a religion, since the place of God, so central to Western beliefs, has always been ambiguous, especially in Theravāda Buddhist sects. And yet, Buddhism engendered many scriptures and rituals, as well as important monastic orders – all of which Westerners would call religious. Only with increasing openness, especially in the twentieth century, has the West learnt to accept Buddhism with more appreciation. In this respect, the German theologian Paul Tillich has contributed his own understanding of religion as 'the state of being grasped by an ultimate concern, a concern . . . which itself contains the answer to the question of the meaning of our life'.[6] With this, a religion need not always profess personal theism. It only has to be concerned with life's ultimate meaning.

To understand Buddhist doctrine, one has to get accustomed to many terms. With the advent of Mahāyāna Buddhism, the difference in meaning almost disappears between the Buddha-figure as an enlightened being and the role of the Bodhisattva who is ready for *nirvāna* but forgoes it and returns to *Samsāra* to save others. A Westerner could appreciate the importance of such issues when it is understood that Buddhism is essentially a religion of salvation, with doctrinal disputes focused on the accessibility of such salvation, which is also explained as *nirvāna*, Buddhahood, or enlightenment.

As saviour figures, the Bodhisattvas have exercised enormous appeal in Mahāyāna Buddhism, and have been compared to the Christ figure as suffering saviour. The essential difference between the two is the essentially *historical* character of Jesus Christ. While certain Bodhisattva figures are believed to have become historically incarnate, they do not derive their religious importance from being in any sense historical.[7]

2   The Introduction of Buddhism

Possibly a contemporary of Confucius, Gautama, the *historical* Buddha, is reported to have died either in 544 B.C. – or, as most modern scholars would have it, about sixty years later. The presence of both in the same century gives some substance to Jaspers' hypothesis regarding the 'axial ages' in human civilisation. But given the geographical distance that separated the two countries, Buddhism was introduced into China only some time before the first century

A.D., roughly five to six hundred years after the deaths of the two men.

By that time (1st century A.D. or earlier), this religion of Indian origin had already undergone several centuries of development both in theory and practice. It acted as a harbinger of civilisation in many areas, introducing knowledge of Indian languages and scripts, especially Sanskrit and eventually a technical vocabulary in Chinese for translation purposes, as well as inspiring art, literature and philosophy. But China was already home to a vigorous civilisation with an ancient canon – the Confucian classics – and time-hallowed traditions. The meeting of the Buddhist religion and Chinese culture was a momentous one, marking an encounter between the Indian world view and the Chinese. In many ways, the pre-Buddhist Chinese ways of seeing things was much closer to the Western ways than to the Indian. We are referring to the three-tiered universe (Heaven, Earth, and the Yellow Springs or 'Hades') and a single lifespan. With Buddhism, the universe and human existence would be seen in much more complicated fashions. The encounter became the occasion for conflicts and controversies, which were resolved only when Buddhism adjusted itself to the Chinese environment, taking account of Confucian moral values, such as filial piety, while making use of Taoist ideas and terminology for its own survival and advancement.[8]

Buddhism introduced the presupposition of rebirth or transmigration, and the practice of monastic life, into a society where ancestors were venerated and descendants desired. But Chinese realism and pragmatism also influenced Buddhism, affirming this life and this world, including the values of family, longevity and posterity. The big historical question Buddhism has introduced into China remains: has it been the 'Buddhist conquest of China', or the 'Chinese conquest of Buddhism'?[9] And a related historical question is: would the course of Christianity have been different, had it allowed more cultural adaptation, and to what extent could it have been possible, given *its* dogmatic presuppositions?

The Buddhist encounter with Chinese culture also has its parallel in the meeting of Jewish Christianity and Hellenistic culture. Where Greek culture contributed to the speculative legacy of the interpretation of Judeo-Christian doctrines, Chinese culture rendered simpler, and more pragmatic, the highly speculative and analytical doctrines of early Buddhism, while harmonising the doctrinal inconsistencies that have crept in through factionalism in India. Besides, Buddhism witnessed the development of two different branches in its religious history, much as Christianity became known under two forms, the Greek and the Latin.

Conflicts and Confluences
Buddhism's arrival in China is associated with the interpretation of dreams. According to the story, a Chinese emperor, Ming-ti (r. 57–75 A.D.) saw in a dream a golden giant entering his palace. On asking courtiers for an interpretation, he was told that the giant represented Gautama, the wise man from the west. Immediately the emperor sent a delegation to India to inquire after this wise man. Buddhist monks from India were also invited to China to preach their religion to the Chinese.

Even with this imperial welcome, its introduction was met with resistance. From the Confucian side, there was incredulity that any wisdom might come from outside the country, and without having been mentioned in the Chinese classical texts. There was also revulsion that Buddhist monks did injury to their bodies (received from parents) by shaving their heads, and that they even abandoned family and society by embracing celibacy and asceticism, therefore going against the demands of the ancestral cult and of filial piety. And there was unease that the Indian belief in transmigration was incompatible with the same Chinese veneration for ancestors as well as the custom of eating meat. On the Taoist side, there were also misgivings born of rivalry and competition. The counter-claim was made that the Buddha was no other than Lao-tzu, who had gone west and preached to the barbarians! There was also disappointment that Buddhism (an other-worldly religion) had no great contribution to make to the information on elixirs of immortality.[10] Indeed, the earliest Buddhists most welcome in China turned out to be those with magical, including healing, powers, that is, 'wonder-workers'.

But Taoist philosophy was much more compatible with Buddhist teachings, with metaphysical propensities and a language of negation. Due to their own preference for solitude, Taoists were able to appreciate Buddhist asceticism and monasticism. Eventually, Taoist ideas and expressions were used in the translation of Buddhist scriptures into Chinese, resulting in a blending of Indian and Chinese thought. And Buddhism prospered in China, especially under the patronage of various rulers. Its rich and elaborate imagery and concepts fascinated many Chinese minds, who strongly preferred the Mahāyāna teachings of universal salvation. Perhaps this had to do with the character of Chinese society, which was less stratified and more open than that of India. Perhaps it had also to do with another preference that developed within Confucianism, for human perfectibility and the universal accessibility of the goal of sagehood.

3   The Translation of Buddhist Scriptures

The translation of Buddhist literature from Pali and Sanskrit hastened the process of acculturation of Buddhism in China. This may sound simple, but it was not, on account of the enormous vastness of the corpus of books called Buddhist scriptures, the differences between the Indian languages and Chinese, and the fact that the translation effort itself took over a thousand years. All in all, such an effort defies comparison with the translation of any other body of religious texts, whether in Christianity or in any other religion.

One difference between the Indian and the Chinese civilisations is that the change from the oral tradition to the written one was slower to take effect in the case of India. It therefore took longer for Buddhist scriptures to be put into writing than it took the Confucian classics or the Christian New Testament. Sometime during the two centuries between the death of the historical Buddha and the birth of the first great Buddhist emperor, Ashoka (3rd century B.C.), some sort of Buddhist canon in the form of *oral* tradition had appeared. After that came the 'Three Baskets' of palm leaves, on which the oral tradition was recorded. This name '*Tripitaka*' refers to the tripartite Theravāda scriptural canon preserved in Pali, including the Sermons or *Sūtra* (in Pali, *Sutta*) *pitaka*, Further Discourses or *Abhidharma* (in Pali, *Abhidamma*), and Monastic Discipline or *Vinaya*.[11]

When Buddhism first came into China, the people there knew nothing of its previous history. The Chinese were ignorant of the fact that Buddhism had already splintered into sects in India and Central Asia, and that the scriptures that had been written down were to a large extent sectarian writings attributing various teachings to the historical Buddha long after his death. Instead, they imagined that the scriptures were the Buddha's *ipsissima verba*, recorded by disciples around the time of his death and stored in caves and libraries before they were discovered and taken to China. The facts, actually, were quite different, especially where Mahāyāna is concerned. There was no fixed corpus, no original *Tripitaka* (such as Theravāda's) that was gradually being translated. The ensuing difficulties experienced by converts led to the creation of a *Chinese* Buddhism. It was a response in part to the problems of hermeneutics and textual interpretation. These problems far exceeded Christianity's, where a much smaller corpus of texts is claimed as sacred.

The Selection of Scriptures

We shall start with the translation process, dwelling upon the choice made of texts for translation and the quality of the work, as well as who did the translating. Actually, many of the translations are all that remain of texts that have become lost in their original languages, whether Pali or Sanskrit. Indeed, with its 3,053 entries, but including many commentaries as well as so-called original scriptures, the Japanese *Taishō* edition of the Chinese 'Tripitaka' (1922–33) has become essential for the study of the Buddhist religion.[12]

In the beginning, the Chinese had little choice to exercise about what to translate and what not, as they knew too little. The matter was left to the discretion of foreign monks. As the translations were subsequently read, there was little doubt as to which books were preferred. So choice can be discerned in repeated translations of more popular texts, a fact that would mark the character of Chinese Buddhism. The *Vimalakirti sūtra* was translated nine times, the *Surangama sūtra* nine times, the *Lotus sūtra* three times. The *Small Perfection of Wisdom*, introduced earlier, had been translated nine times. The number of times depends also on how early the scripture was first introduced, and the versions varied in length. By the end of the T'ang dynasty (A.D. 906), the formation of the Chinese Buddhist canon was practically completed.

What did the Chinese find so attractive about these scriptures? This question holds the key to understanding *Chinese* Buddhism. Frequently, this was decided on the basis of the content of the scriptures already known through earlier and shorter versions. The Chinese found certain Mahāyāna doctrines more appealing, especially that of the Bodhisattva as a compassionate saviour who refrains from entering *nirvāna* in order to help more people. A related doctrine is that of the universal accessibility of Buddhahood, a prominent theme in the *Lotus sūtra*. There is also the ideal of the lay Buddhist in the *Vimalakirti sūtra*. Chinese Buddhists developed such ideas further, to include in the 'pale of salvation' all sentient beings, even stubborn unbelievers, expressing this metaphorically to embrace also the entire universe. The language is somewhat reminiscent of the Pauline epistles, especially Colossians 1:15, about Jesus Christ reconciling all things in heaven and on earth.

However, let us remember that the word 'canon' does not have the same normative sense it has with the Hebrew or Christian

Scriptures, or even with the Theravāda (Pali) Scriptures. There was, for example, never a serious effort to define scriptural authority. The Chinese Mahāyāna canon still keeps something of the tripartite structure of Theravāda's Pali canon. But this has become artificial on account of the great influx of new 'discourses' or *sūtras* composed much later, claiming to be the words of the historical Buddha, and translated as such into Chinese. I am using the word 'canon' because the collective work did have some normative value, since it was believed to contain the religious founder's teachings, and includes as well monastic rules and discipline. But the specific normative value of many entries, including commentaries, is open to question. Besides, the Chinese themselves added new works to the corpus, including one work given the status of a *'sūtra'* without being ascribed to the historical Buddha – the *Platform Sutra of the Sixth Patriarch*, a Ch'an work.

Why did the state support translations, and promote the spreading of their words? Pious sovereigns did this for merit and devotion, or to please the believing multitudes. Besides, patronage was one way of controlling the religion. The Buddhist canon was useful to the state, serving as a 'constitution' for the *samgha*, and the state exercised its prerogatives by making the final decision about which translations were fit for inclusion in the canon. Such decisions were made on the advice of the experts. But it was the state's *imprimatur* that made a collection of books the 'Buddhist canon'. The Buddhist religion was never able to become another power, a challenge to the state, as did the Christian religion in medieval Europe. And the state used the canon as a sanction; it could and did punish those members of the *samgha* for moral or ritual transgressions against the prescriptions and proscriptions of the scriptures.

Early Translators
Scant information is available regarding the authors of the Confucian classics, and even less regarding the authors of the Taoist scriptures, or the original composition of the Buddhist scriptures – outside of the fact that the Buddha himself did *not* write them. By comparison there is ample information about the process of translation that built up the Chinese Buddhist canon, and about those men who translated the scriptures into Chinese. We know the names of over two hundred translators, not to mention their assistants – since, in most cases, the translators cannot be said to have personally done the work word for word, but worked with teams of collaborators.[13]

The earliest texts were copied by hand, sometimes from dictation, but printing was used from very early on to help with wide dissemination. As new books were written, and always *attributed* to the Buddha himself, they were taken to China for translation, practically before the ink was dry. Thus to the Chinese, it must have seemed a miracle that so many texts should claim to give the Buddha's own words. We might even speak here of some kind of '*sūtra* industry' in India, seeking to satisfy the demand in China for Buddhist scriptures for translation!

Foreign monks who knew little Chinese had successors like Dharmaraksa (A.D. 232–309), born in Tun-huang (Dunhuang), who translated over a hundred Mahāyāna texts. He dictated, often from memory, for his Chinese copyists. His important contribution was the *Lotus sūtra*, called in Sanskrit the *Saddharmapundarika* (A.D. 286), a text of paramount importance for the development of Mahāyāna. But the work of translation was spurred on as well by a succession of Chinese monks travelling west on pilgrimage. This was a quest unparalleled in religious history, certainly unknown in the history of Christianity, even when we consider that Jerome, the translator of the Latin Vulgate, pursued scriptural studies and worked on his translations in fourth-century Palestine.

The first of these actually to reach India was Fa-hsien, who went in search of an original monastic code in A.D. 399. Till then, it appears that the *Vinaya* had been passed down only by oral transmission.[14] By the time of Fa-hsien's return to China, and unknown to him, the entire *Vinaya* had already been translated by someone else. That more than one person was dedicated to finding and translating it shows the strength of Chinese Buddhism.

Two Great Translators: Kumārajīva and Hsüan-tsang

The monumental task of translating scriptures required the support of the state and its enormous resources. It also called for a certain kind of genius, and one such was the famous Kumārajīva (A.D. 344 – c. 413), a native of Kucha in Central Asia. This region is historically important for religious encounters, including that of Buddhism with Christianity, with Manichaeism, and with Islam.[15] Kumārajīva's fame as a scriptural scholar reached the northern Chinese court (the country was then politically divided), and the ruler literally plotted wars to 'kidnap' him. Eventually, he was brought to Ch'ang-an by another ruler in 402, honoured with the title of 'National Preceptor', and surrounded by a thousand monks and lay people including some of the best scholars in the country. His task was to retranslate the most influential of Mahāyāna scriptures, and produce definitive editions with authoritative interpretation. Until his death in 413, Kumārajīva and his collaborators poured forth a steady stream of translations. Their output included the *Amitābha sūtra*, basic text of the Pure Land school in China, the massive *Treatise on the Great Perfection of Wisdom*, and the two important Mahāyāna scriptures, the *Lotus sūtra* and the *Vimalakirti sūtra*.

Until that time, translators of Buddhist scriptures had sought mainly to make use of words and concepts coming from Taoist texts to make the Buddhist scriptures more comprehensible as well as more acceptable. This was the method called *ko-yi* (matching of meanings). But it did not always permit the accurate communication of the content of the original texts, and sometimes even distorted them. Readers noticed the difference with Kumārajīva's translations.[16]

However, Kumārajīva appeared not to have been able to read or write Chinese. After all, he was already forty-six years old when he arrived in Ch'ang-an. His greatness lay in his immense learning and understanding, and the leadership he exercised in the translation of the scriptures, a task he accomplished with the assistance of his teams of assistants. But his reputation as a genius was such that the Chinese ruler in the north thought it a waste for him not to have progeny, and offered him concubines. Kumārajīva acquiesced to the royal wishes, for which he has been severely criticised by the Buddhist monks. But we know of no child prodigies from him.

The T'ang dynasty (618–906) also witnessed a flowering of translation activity. The most famous person in this era was a Chinese. Hsüan-tsang, pilgrim and translator himself, brought back to the country hundreds of *sūtras*. He remained after that for twenty years in the capital, Ch'ang-an (today's Xi'an). A man of peerless energy and determination, Hsüan-tsang took care to translate entire works, rather than being content with partial translations. With him, the corpus of Mahāyāna scriptures was made available, as well as its most important treatises and commentaries. In the twenty years before he died, he completed the translation of seventy-five works.[17]

Hsüan-tsang left China for India without official permission, but returned to a royal welcome, and had to decline offers of high office. His adventures as a traveller and a pilgrim (he was nearly killed on his way from China to India by some cannibals, who only spared him at the last minute for fear of reprisals from a higher power) inspired eventually the famous novel, *Journey to the West*.[18] In this piece of fiction he is given as companions a monkey, representing quick wit and loyalty, and a pig, representing sensuality. Indeed, the monkey becomes the hero in the novel, whereas the monk seems quite helpless in difficulty, resorting only to prayer and meditation.

To return to the subject of translations: the Buddhist texts were coming at an uninterrupted rate, leaving no leisure for reflection. But once people realised the complexity of the doctrines, other problems presented themselves. What should one do when contradictory teachings were all ascribed to the Buddha himself? How to sort out, to coordinate, to systematise the new strands of Buddhist doctrine became the burning question.

4   The Great Philosophical Schools: A Hermeneutical Adventure

In early Christianity, the dissemination of the New Testament was followed by doctrinal controversies and ecumenical councils that sought to draw lines between orthodox and heretical doctrines. In the case of Buddhism in China, diverse schools of opinion also developed, but they sought mainly to reconcile a difficult range of often contradictory teachings attributed to the Buddha. While sectarian rivalries were not absent, the goal of harmonisation was never overlooked. This alone would be anathema to many a jealous defender of the Christian faith in the West. In our own days, with the growth of the ecumenical spirit, dialogues between Christians of different persuasions have witnessed a genuine desire to find common ground, a desire extended also to dialogues between Christians and Buddhists. Still, an important difference exists. For Buddhism, truth means religious truth, which includes myths as well as divergent doctrinal formulations. And these are secondary to salvation, as the means are secondary to the end. For Christianity, history is essential to an understanding of salvation, and an emphasis on revelation within history tends to force an uncompromising attitude toward specific points of doctrine as factual assertions.[19]

The Buddhist schools that developed in China included both Theravāda and Mahāyāna schools. But the Theravāda soon disappeared, whereas the Mahāyāna prospered and grew. Of its schools, two (San-lun and Fa-hsiang) were basically Indian imports, reducing everything either to Emptiness or to Consciousness. Their doctrines influenced the subsequent development of other schools of thought, including the response to Buddhism that is called Neo-Confucianism.

Emptiness: The Middle Doctrine in China

On examination, Buddhist philosophy usually postulates higher and lower levels of truth, much as does Gnosticism, but with many more nuances. The San-lun (Three Treatises) and Fa-hsiang (Yogācāra) schools both have to do with the Indian Mahāyāna philosophy known as the Middle Doctrine. This was developed by the great philosopher Nāgārjuna (c. 100–200), who taught the doctrine of Emptiness: that everything in the phenomenal world is ultimately unreal. By a process of paradoxical logic, he also claims that this Emptiness is itself unreal, although it may be experienced in meditation with directness and certainty. He summed up his discovery in an eightfold negation:

> Nothing comes into being,
> Nor does anything disappear.
> Nothing is eternal,
> Nor has anything an end.
> Nothing is identical,
> Or differentiated,
> Nothing moves hither,
> Nor moves anything thither.[20]

The great translator Kumārajīva himself introduced this teaching into China, with the translation of two treatises by Nāgārjuna, and a third by his disciple Deva, which became the foundation of the San-lun or Three Treatises school. This philosophy had an able exponent in Kumārajīva's disciple Seng Chao (A.D. 374–414).[21]

The Fa-hsiang (Dharma Character) school is also derived from Nā gārjuna's Middle Doctrine. It teaches a philosophy of pure idealism, somewhat like that of Bishop George Berkeley and David Hume. The universe exists only in the mind of the perceiver, being but a fabrication of consciousness. Impressions are called 'seeds' which lead to acts or thoughts.

> A seed produces a manifestation,
> A manifestation perfumes a seed.
> The three elements (seed, manifestation, and perfume) turn
>   on and on,
> The cause and effect occur at the same time.[22]

According to Yogācāra, mountains and rivers are all manifestations of the pure and tainted ideas in our mind's 'storehouse consciousness'. Through yoga and spiritual cultivation, one could purify this storehouse consciousness, exhausting it until it becomes identical to ultimate reality or (*Tathatā*), which corresponds to Emptiness.

Importantly, Buddhist philosophical schools should not be regarded only as representing abstract or even abstruse opinions. They project ideas with soteriological implications, ideas that were born of meditation and mystical experience. They often make use of a language of negation, which serves as expression of their effort to go beyond the realm of discursive thought. Theirs may be termed a *theologia negativa*, a theology that refuses to pin identifications and definitions down. It is a theology born of experience that offers resistance to critical thought. Interestingly, Buddhists often find the Christian belief in revelation uncritical, whereas Westerners are wont to call paradoxical logic abstruse.

The imported Buddhist schools survived until the ninth century, and then quickly declined under the persecutions. Some of their ideas influenced other schools of thought. (In our modern period, especially in 1920s and 1930s, there has been a revival of interest in the Fa-hsiang school among a group that included the monk-reformer T'ai-hsü and the philosopher Hsiung Shih-li.)[23] The other great Mahāyāna schools that developed in China may be regarded as the responses of the new converts to the great diversity of doctrine they discovered in the scriptural corpus. Here I am speaking of the great schools of T'ien-t'ai and Hua-yen (Avatamsaka) Buddhism.

Reconciling Contradictions: The Lotus School (T'ien-t'ai)

The T'ien-t'ai (Tiantai) school, named after its place of origin on a mountain in Chekiang, in south-east China, had a great systematic thinker in Chih-k'ai or Chih-yi (538–97), who enjoyed imperial patronage as well. A self-proclaimed practitioner of meditation rather than a philosopher, he left behind a truly architectonic synthesis to reconcile and harmonise all Buddhist teachings. According to him, doctrinal divergence within Buddhism and its many scriptures comes from the Buddha's having taught different things at different times, as well as addressing multiple audiences at the same time. So he distinguishes between periods in the Buddha's life of preaching, methods of teaching the *sūtras* or scriptures, and different modes of doctrine. We shall concentrate on the periodisation.

Chih-yi explains that after the enlightenment experience, the Buddha remained in an ecstatic state, and preached first the *Avatamsaka sūtra*, which teaches that the universe is but the revelation of the absolute spirit. But few could understand him during those three weeks. So the Buddha decided to accommodate his teachings to the listeners, and spent the next twelve years teaching Theravāda doctrines of the Four Noble Truths, the Eightfold Noble Path, and dependent co-arising. In this way, he gathered together huge crowds who were converted. After that, he moved to another period of eight years, teaching the simple Mahāyāna truths, especially of the Bodhisattva, who forgoes his own *nirvāna* to save others. Then came twenty-two years of the fourth period, when he discussed metaphysical problems like those taught in the *Prajñāparamitā-sūtras*. The fifth or last period of eight years was spent on the reconciliation of apparent contradictions, in accordance with the *Lotus sūtra*.

T'ien-t'ai Buddhism represents a genuinely ecumenical attempt to establish a great eclectic school recognising all forms of Buddhism, giving a place to all the scriptures by regarding them as the product of a gradual process of the Buddha's revelations. Its successes underscore the Chinese preference for harmony. But there are limitations to its successes, as Chinese Buddhism continued to engender different schools or sects. Generally speaking, however, sectarian differences were less severe than in Christianity. Religious wars were not fought over doctrines, although the jealousy of another religion (Taoism) occasioned persecution by the state.

T'ien-t'ai's emphasis was on the *Lotus sūtra* and its teaching of the universal accessibility of enlightenment and Buddhahood.[24] It was introduced into Japan and established its base on Mount Hiei near Kyoto. There it evolved under Shintō influences, and eventually incorporated practices from Tantric Buddhism as well. Tendai Buddhism remains a vital force in today's Japan.

All in One: The Flower Garland School (Hua-yen)

The Hua-yen school is best represented by Fa-tsang (643–712), who had worked as a translator with Hsüan-tsang, and served as preceptor to four emperors. It relies particularly on the *Avatamsaka* or Flower Garland *sūtra*. This school explained reality under the two aspects of *li*, the noumenal, and *shih/shi*, the phenomenal – much as Immanuel Kant used in his philosophy. These concepts would exercise a profound influence on the later Neo-Confucian metaphysics of *li* and *ch'i/qi*. Its chief representative is the monk Fa-tsang.

Fa-tsang enjoyed the favour of Empress Wu (r. 684–705), who frequently listened to his sermons. Once he had a statue of a golden Buddha placed in the middle of a palace room, with mirrors surrounding it on all sides, above and below as well. A burning torch was placed next to the statue. He then explained that the Buddha is present in all of its images and reflections just as *li* is present in the *shih*.

> In each and every reflection of any mirror you will find all the reflections of all the other mirrors, together with the specific Buddha image in each.[25]

'One is in all and all is in one' – a statement of harmony and interpenetration. This was the way in which the Hua-yen teaching would be remembered.

5   The Buddhist Conquest of China?

As philosophical reflection followed scriptural study, we find a harmonisation of alien teachings with the native, especially with Taoism. Like Buddhists, Taoists had always taught the two levels of truth. Like Buddhists, Taoists pursued mystical insight and expressed their discoveries in a language of negation. But while Taoist philosophy served as an intermediary for Buddhist ideas, Taoist priests were less than happy with the growth of Buddhist influence. Time and again, they urged the ruler to suppress the foreign religion. Yet Taoism itself was profoundly influenced by Buddhist thought and eventually transformed by this influence. Were we to look superficially at today's China, we might conclude that Buddhism is a thing of the past. Should we, however, seek to probe more deeply into the study of Chinese thought and culture, we would have to say that Buddhism has profoundly transformed the Chinese modes of thought and expression, of religious belief and ritual practice.

Buddhist monks who have studied under the T'ien-t'ai and the Hua-yen lineages are still found today, even if Chinese Buddhism as a religion no longer benefits from a multiplicity of schools or sects. In the next chapter, we shall speak of the Pure Land school and the Ch'an school. These will be treated more as sects or denominations, because they remain living forms of Chinese Buddhism. In Japan, however, Tendai and Kegon (i.e., Hua-yen) still survive as living forms of Buddhism. But that is another story.

8

Mysticism and Devotion: Buddhism Becomes Chinese

1 Buddhism: Rise and Decline

Is there a law of rise and decline, followed by revival, that governs the history of Chinese Buddhism? Here we encounter the historical fact of persecutions against Buddhism before the Communist era. That of A.D. 845 effected the decline of most Buddhist schools described in the last chapter. According to the census of 845, there used to be a quarter of a million monks and nuns, 4,600 temples and over 40,000 lesser shrines in China. The wealth and power of the *Samgha* invited envy and provoked persecution. The severity of the persecution meant that most of these temples were destroyed, and most of the monks and nuns were forced to return to lay life.

The questions may be asked: 'What has happened to Buddhism since the ninth century? How is it now faring in the new, Marxist society?' In short, what is the Buddhist legacy in China, and what importance does it still have? The answers to these questions, I believe, will underscore the *limitations* of the 'Buddhist conquest of China' to demonstrate that the religion was never totally accepted, even before the ravages of the Communist revolution. On the other hand, there is no denying that Buddhism also made a tremendous impact on Chinese culture, which has never been the same again.

2 The Growth of Buddhist Sects

Hua-yen and T'ien-t'ai were philosophical schools with importance in themselves and as preparation for the Ch'an school. Hua-yen philosophy presents a noumenal world of *li* and a phenomenal world of *shih/shi*, which interpenetrate each other, with all phenomena manifesting the one, unchanging noumenon. This established a totally integrated system, in which everything leads to the Buddha in the centre, as Fa-tsang demonstrated in his hall of mirrors. T'ien-t'ai philosophy harmonised the many differences found in the diverse scriptures by formulating a classification of the *sūtras* and their doctrines, while claiming that the *Lotus sūtra* represents the culmination of the Buddha's final teaching. This was one more testimony to the Chinese propensity for the harmony of opposites. And indeed, this harmony of opposites will be reflected once more in the success of Ch'an and Pure Land and their eventual merging in China.

On the one hand, the growth of Chinese Buddhism required the translation and interpretation of the Buddhist canon. On the other hand, the very intellectual emphasis of scriptural study became an obstacle to spiritual experience and mystical fulfilment. At issue, indeed, were the central Mahāyāna questions of salvation: is it really accessible to all? Must one first know all the scriptures? Is there not a more direct approach, we may say, a shortcut?

The two sects, Ch'an and Pure Land, might be called the 'short-cuts' to salvation. Interestingly, both are expressions of belief in universal salvation, and both subordinated scriptural study to other pursuits. But Ch'an Buddhism believes that enlightenment (or salvation) is produced by 'self-power' (in Japanese, *jiriki*), while Pure Land Buddhism believes that it may only be attained by faith in 'other-power' (in Japanese, *tariki*). There is some parallel here to the tension between justification by faith or by 'works', so well known in the history of Christianity. Artistically, however, the parallel does not hold. Ch'an meditation halls often show a preference for simplicity, with little religious ornamentation, and reflect a history of iconoclasm. Pure Land temples, on the other hand, manifest a baroque-like exuberance with a multiplicity of Buddha- and Bodhisattva-figures, together with representations of numerous saints or 'Lohans' – usually historical figures who have fought the good fight and now find themselves in paradise.

Meditation and Mystical Enlightenment: Ch'an Buddhism

The word *Ch'an* is the Chinese transliteration of the Sanskrit *dhyāna*, meaning 'meditation'. Also known by the Japanese pronunciation of 'Zen', it refers basically to the religious discipline aimed at calming the mind and permitting the person to penetrate into his or her own inner consciousness. As meditation exercises, *dhyāna* had been developed in India over the ages, but as a Buddhist school, *Ch'an* is a Chinese development.

In common with other Mahāyāna systems, *Ch'an* teaches that ultimate reality – *śūnya* (emptiness), sometimes called Buddha-nature – is inexpressible in words or concepts, and apprehended only by direct intuition, outside of conscious thought. Such direct intuition requires discipline and training, but is also characterised by freedom and spontaneity. This has led *Ch'an* to become somewhat of an iconoclastic movement, relativising such other practices as studying or reciting the Buddhist *sūtras*, worshipping the Buddha images, and performing rituals, which are regarded as being of no avail to the goal of spiritual enlightenment (in Chinese, *wu*; in Japanese, *satori*).

Ch'an Buddhism claims a direct legacy from the historical Buddha, who allegedly made a wordless transmission to his disciple Mahākāśyapa simply by holding a flower while smiling. In China, its first patriarch was the semi-legendary Bodhidharma, who entered the country in the early sixth century, and spent nine years meditating in front of a wall.

From its distaste for book-learning Ch'an became known as a special tradition 'outside the scriptures', that is, not dependent on 'words or letters', but 'pointing directly' at the human mind or heart, to enable its followers to 'see into' their 'own natures'. Such a tradition is only transmitted 'from mind to mind', that is, without the intervention of rational argumentation. It advocates the 'absence of thoughts' to free the mind from external influences. Here it is useful to recall a competition in verse between the young monk Hui-neng (638–713) and the older and more learned Shen-hsiu. The latter emphasises the need for careful preparation for the enlightenment-experience in the following words:

> The body is the *bodhi* tree,
> The mind is a bright mirror.
> At all times diligently clean it,
> Keep it free from dust.

To which Hui-neng's response is:

> *Bodhi* is originally no tree,
> Nor has the bright mirror any frame.
> Buddha-nature is always clear and pure,
> Where is there any dust?[1]

This came like a thunderbolt. The metaphysical rebuttal was complete, and the poem has been interpreted as a counterplea for *sudden* enlightenment – an assertion that this goal can be achieved at any time, in any situation. It denies the separation of subject and object, mind and body. And it invokes the mirror image only to supersede that too.

The difference between these two monks supposedly character-ises the difference between the northern and the southern schools. After Hui-neng, Ch'an Buddhism continued to divide into many sub-sects or branches, depending on the varying emphasis on meth-ods and techniques. What was involved were also different beliefs regarding whether the goal of spiritual enlightenment is a sudden experience, or one that is achieved after a gradual process of cultiva-tion. The southern school is especially associated with the allegedly illiterate Hui-neng, who focused on the abrupt character of the enlightenment experience. This is reflected in the 'breakthrough' achieved in our stream of consciousness, much as *Nirvāna* is a breakthrough achieved in the cycle of rebirths called *Samsāra*.

The story of Hui-neng in the *Platform sūtra* also stresses the importance of ordinary life, even of finding enlightenment outside meditation. A logical development for the Mahāyāna movement which acknowledges the presence of the absolute in the relative, of *Nirvāna* in *Samsāra*, it had the result of affirming the value of this life and this world.[2] Chinese Ch'an, especially as represented by Hui-neng's school, became known for freedom of expression and respect of the natural – what we may also call Taoist characteristics. These attitudes contributed to a creative genius in discussions of spirituality and mysticism as well as in art and culture.

The problem is, should Ch'an be considered as Buddhist, if it does not give a prominent place to scriptures, images and even the Buddha himself? The Ch'an masters would, of course, reply in the affirmative. According to them, the religion is defined not by its scriptures but by the realisation of the experience of enlightenment, and this can be best done by looking inside one's own nature. Ch'an represents an effort to return to the sources of Buddhist inspiration – and hence to certain features of Theravāda Buddhism, especially that of 'saving oneself by one's own efforts'. It involves as well a Taoist effort of discovering one's own original nature, that would also influence Neo-Confucianism. Such Taoist affinity, as well as Ch'an's practical bent, has led to its being called a Chinese religion.

Ch'an Buddhism has been introduced to the West through the

efforts of the Japanese Buddhist Daisetz Suzuki and others, and is better known under its Japanese name of Zen. So far, we have not hesitated to use the term 'mystical' to denote the Zen experience of spiritual enlightenment. But there are those who might not be comfortable with its usage. Buddhists and Christians alike have been for long accustomed to see mystical experience in terms of union with a personal God, who is not present as such in Zen. Suzuki himself acknowledges this, while finding common experiential ground between Zen practitioners and Christian mystics like Eckhart, Suso and others.[3] Our own understanding of the term 'mysticism' is, however, much broader, focusing on the spiritual experience itself as a transformation of human consciousness.

Western interest in Zen has been twofold: in itself and for the sake of emulation. Here, Catholic missionaries and theologians, coming from a long contemplative tradition, have sought to learn from Zen insights as well as techniques. Many have written on the subject of a common ground of religious wisdom between the two traditions.[4] At the same time, the Zen experience (like Taoist meditations before it) has also attracted the attention of experts in depth psychology.[5]

The Sects of Ch'an Buddhism
With its focus on practical matters of spirituality, Ch'an Buddhism developed subsects with rival teachings on enlightenment and how this might be acquired.[6] For example, Tsao-tung (in Japanese, Sōtō) emphasised silent meditation as a means toward enlightenment. This does not mean inactivity or passivity. Rather, silence is considered to be the primal stillness of the ultimate ground of the enlightened mind, which is naturally radiant and 'shining'. On the other hand, Lin-chi (in Japanese, Rinzai) aims at sudden enlightenment through the use of shouting, beating, and riddles called *kung-an/gongan* (in Japanese, *koan*) to provoke an experience of enlightenment, for which it is claimed that no slow preparation is necessary or possible. By posing an insoluble problem to reason and the intellect, the *kung-an* is supposed to lead to the dissolution of the boundary between the conscious and the unconscious in the human psyche, and bring about a sudden experience, described metaphorically like the blossoming of a lotus, or like the sun emerging from behind the clouds.

The difference between the two subsects is much more in nuances of emphasis than in practice. But the nuances were important enough, having to do with maintaining a balance between the 'gradualist' preference for spiritual cultivation (hence 'works') and the 'subtilist' focus on mystical enlightenment (bordering on faith alone). And a steady exchange of Chinese and Japanese monks, from the middle of the twelfth century on, brought to Japan these two Zen Buddhist subsects, which are still active there today.

The vigorous growth of Ch'an Buddhism in eleventh and twelfth century China is reflected in the written word. It produced numerous recorded dialogues giving the words of wisdom of its various masters. And while Ch'an Buddhists placed less importance on studying the *sūtras*, they sought to prove themselves the legitimate heirs of the historical Buddha, producing numerous works outlining the transmission of Ch'an insights through allegedly correct lineages. Such proliferation of texts was in direct contradiction to original Ch'an principles of not establishing written directives, and some have seen in this the beginning of the decline of the true Ch'an spirit.

Devotional Religion: Pure Land Buddhism and the Kuan-yin Cult
Pure Land Buddhism is named after *Sukhavati*, a Sanskrit word representing an ideal Buddhist paradise this side of *Nirvāna*. This form of Buddhism presents the strongest parallel in doctrine and practice to Western theism – be this Christian, Jewish, or Muslim. Its paradise is believed to be presided over by the Buddha Amitābha (in Chinese, Omitofo; in Japanese, Amida), a much earlier (and thus mythical) figure than the historical Buddha. He is assisted by the Bodhisattva (in Chinese, *p'u-sa*) Avalokiteśvara (in Chinese, Kuan-yin; in Japanese, Kannon). It is based especially on the *Pure Land sūtra*, which has two versions. The longer one emphasises the equal importance of faith and devotion to the Buddha as well as good works. The shorter one says that faith alone is enough – faith in the infinite compassion of the Buddha, shown in prayerful and meditative repetition of the name, O-mi-to-fo.[7] This refers to the practice called *nien-fo/nianfo* (in Japanese, *nembutsu*), by which the faithful invoke, with faith, the name of Amitābha. Such recitation is usually done while fingering beads. And the assistance of the Buddha is especially promised for the hour of death. Thus Pure Land Buddhism shows strong and multiple resemblances to Christianity, with a God-figure (Omitofo), a mediator (Kuan-yin), a doctrine of faith and grace and a prayerful devotion that resembles the rosary.

As a Chinese religion, Pure Land Buddhism has especially appealed to the masses seeking not only ultimate salvation but also a power that responds to their ordinary needs. In this respect, the P'u-sa Kuan-yin attracts the most devotion. Originally a male figure, it eventually became transformed into a female in religious iconography probably through Tibetan influences (10th century A.D.). Clad in white, this 'goddess of mercy' became rather early a symbol of the 'giver of children' to whom women pray for issue. It offers a curious contrast to the otherworldly thrust of Indian Buddhism, and shows how *Chinese* the religion has become in a totally different cultural environment. It is also the Buddhist parallel to the Christian cult of Mary, the mother of Jesus.

Pure Land Buddhism, especially in its Japanese form, has impressed the Christian theologian Karl Barth with its parallels to Christianity. He has even called it 'Japanese Protestantism'.[8] At issue is the concept of faith or the 'will to believe' as a pure gift from the Buddha: 'Once this faith is aroused, salvation is assured.'[9]

Fusion of Mysticism and Devotion: Two Sects Combined

With its emphasis on faith in Omitofo, a God-figure and a dispenser of grace and salvation, Pure Land differs immensely from Ch'an and its more pantheistic tendencies. However, in spite of obvious differences, the Chinese tendency toward the harmonisation of opposites led to a gradual syncretism of Ch'an with Pure Land, of meditation and the study of scriptures, by which devout Buddhists combined the Ch'an practice of meditation with the Pure Land practice of calling on the name of the Buddha. Such joint practice considered invocation as another form of meditation, involving visualisation of Omitofo, and combining self-reliance with reliance on other power. It might be compared with the Byzantine practice of combining yoga with the invocation of the name of Jesus in that school of mysticism called Hesychasm. The introduction of yoga into this 'Jesus Prayer' could have happened through Hindu (or Buddhist?) influence.[10] In the Buddhist case, the argument was that since *nien-fo* could terminate discursive thought, it could lead as well to enlightenment, a Ch'an goal. By such means, Paradise became interiorised, just as Buddha-nature itself had become interiorised in Ch'an, in T'ien-t'ai or Hua-yen Buddhism.[11]

Popular Buddhism and the Mi-lo Cult

We are now speaking about a process of syncretisation within Buddhism, as well as between Buddhism and Taoism, or between all the Three Religions of China, until we have a popular religion embracing various strands from all three traditions. Here a well-known Chinese development is the metamorphosis of the Maitreya cult.

Maitreya, the Buddha of the Future, is a well-known figure in the Buddhist *sūtras* and may represent also Messianic influences from beyond India, perhaps Persia. Because of such connotations, it has been the focus of certain political rebellions even in China itself, including that which eventually led to the founding of the Ming dynasty (1368). But the image of Maitreya also underwent a transformation somewhat akin to that of Avalokitesvara or Kuan-yin. I refer here to the earlier large and heroic figure before the seventh century A.D., which reappeared in the fifteenth century and afterwards, in the shape and appearance of a wrinkled, laughing monk, with an exposed pot-belly, carrying a hemp-bag, and in a reclining posture, with small children climbing on top of him and surrounding him. This image is extremely popular, not only in a devotional cult in the whole of East Asia, but also as an artistic decoration in the world at large, and often presides over monastic dining halls and even ordinary restaurants.

In this guise, we see once more the embodiment of Chinese values within a Buddhist image. This Maitreya figure, called Mi-lo, affirms the importance of worldly happiness and prosperity and performs the same function as the goddess figure Kuan-yin, since it is alleged to have the power of giving children to those who pray to it. And this desire for posterity, so much a part of the Chinese ancestral religion, stands in diametrical opposition to the Buddhist call for renunciation of all desire. Moreover, with his happy expression and carrying a bag on his shoulder, Mi-lo reminds one of the Western Santa Claus, a religious figure with Christian origins who has come also to represent worldly prosperity. Indeed, the metamorphosis of both Kuan-yin from Avalokitesvara and Mi-lo from Maitreya is a good indication of the Chinese appropriation of the Buddhist religion. If Buddhism survived in China, it did so by serving Chinese goals, including Confucian family values, thus confirming a basically Chinese affirmation of the importance of this life and this world.

3 Tantric Buddhism: The Mongolian-Tibetan Religion

Although not strictly a *Chinese* religion, Mongol-Tibetan Tantric Buddhism is becoming more widespread in the world, through the propagation by Tibetan monks or Lamas in exile.[12] It has also attracted a small number of Chinese adherents in Hong Kong, Taiwan, and among the diaspora. It deserves to be better known, all the more as it represents a *living* form of Buddhism and not just a philosophical school of the past.

When we speak of Tantric Buddhism, we are referring to the Sanskrit *tantra*, which means spreading knowledge, and also an esoteric literature. The Tantras are the texts on which the sect is based, which include new and different teachings, much borrowed from Hindu myths and symbols, which originated in North India in the late seventh and early eighth centuries. These include a pantheon of many gods, often presented in the *mandalas* or symbolic circles or diagrams of deities in their cosmic connections, the practice of magic, either in invoking the gods or to increase prosperity, or to attack one's enemies, often done with the help of *mantras* or mystic syllables and *mudras* or gestures. The best-known *mantra*, recited by everyone and printed on banners and prayer wheels, is *Om mani padme hum*, 'O the Jewel in the Lotus'.

To the extent that Tantric Buddhism practises esoteric rituals requiring religious initiation, one may call it a kind of 'mystery religion'. But the German scholar Kurt Rudolph has called this exercise a dangerous one, since Hinduism and other religions also do so, representing a ritualisation of esoteric teachings that can in turn be traced back in part to older foundations.[13]

Tantric Buddhism places importance especially on the *Mahā vairocana sūtra* (The Great Sun *sūtra*), the basis of the 'womb mandala' with its thirteen divisions and four hundred and five deities. In a Tantric mandala, the central figure is Mahāvairocana, or the Great Sun Buddha. He is flanked by the Buddhas of the four directions.[14] It is characteristic of Tantric Buddhism to give to the Buddhas and even the Bodhisattvas (for each Buddha is accompanied by a Bodhisattva) female counterparts, thus increasing the number in the pantheon. These deities have dual aspects, pacific and angry, according to the functions they have to perform, such as to repel evil forces or to assist in beneficial functions. Indeed, the union of wisdom and compassion, considered as key to Mahāyāna enlightenment, is represented by the father–mother image, i.e., the deity locked in embrace with its consort. Initiation is very important to this school, and is done, among other things, by a series of baptisms.

Introduced into China in the eighth century, Tantric Buddhism enjoyed there only a very brief period of prosperity. It was the official religion of the Mongol emperors of the thirteenth century. In Tibet, the religion has existed since the eighth century, and has developed numerous lineages.[15] But the best-known representative is Tsong-kha-pa (1357–1419), a reformer, who started the

Gelugpa, a lineage of celibate monks to which the Dalai Lama also belongs.[16]

The line of Dalai Lamas started in the early fifteenth century as incarnations of the Bodhisattva Avalokiteśvara. It assumed political importance in a country which came to be governed by monks. Succession is decided with the discovery of a child who has the alleged characteristics of the deceased Lama. In the sixteenth century, the Dalai Lamas allied themselves with the Mongols, whom they definitively converted, and the religion has become known as Tibetan-Mongolian Buddhism. It is also referred to as the Left-hand Tantra, on account of the role given to ritual sex, and so differentiated from the Right-hand Tantra, which is still found in today's Japan as Shingon Buddhism. The Manchu rulers of China took strong interest in this religion, and served as patrons. During the Ch'ing or Manchu dynasty, each successor as Dalai Lama was confirmed by the Chinese government. In the early twentieth century, Tibet was caught up in Anglo-Chinese conflicts. After the invasion of Tibet by the Chinese Communist army, the fourteenth Dalai Lama (1935–) fled to India in 1959. He has emerged as a world figure, becoming a spokesman not only for Tibetan Buddhism in particular, but also for Buddhism in general. In 1989 he was awarded the Nobel Peace Prize.

One problem with this Mongolian-Tibetan religion has to do with ritual sex. Little in fact is known about this secret practice, as it is only for the initiated and those advanced in cultivation. Surprisingly, wisdom is identified with the female, and compassion with the male. In spite of the prominent role given to the female in symbol and ritual, we have no evidence of sexual equality or anything near it between monks and nuns, men and women, in the *Samgha*.

4   Buddhism and Society

Historical Buddhism has been mainly a monastic religion, the only exception being Japan, where monastic celibacy has long been abolished. As such, it has emphasised otherworldly values while also encouraging almsgiving and the protection of life. In our own days, the Buddhist religion of all persuasions has been active in promoting the cause of world peace. But it is not possible to deal with the entire range of Buddhist attitudes toward a variety of social problems. We shall single out for discussion two special issues: the position of women and the problem of suicide.

The Position of Women

In the case of women's position within Buddhism, the records allegedly tell us of the Buddha's initial opposition to having nuns at all in the Samgha. When his foster mother pleaded with him to allow an order of nuns, he acknowledged that women 'are competent . . . to attain to the fruit of conversion, to attain to . . . saintship'. Only after the repeated intercession of his disciple Ananda did he finally acquiesce, however, to her request, and then under this condition:

> A nun of even a hundred years' standing shall salute, rise to meet, entreat humbly, and perform all respectful offices for a monk, even if he be but that day ordained. This regulation shall be honored, esteemed, revered, and worshiped, and is not to be transgressed as long as life shall last.[17]

The Buddha's alleged reluctance to be influenced by his foster mother reminds us of Jesus' response to his mother when told that she and his brethren had come to take him away – he then designated as mother and brothers those who do 'the will of my Father' (Mark 3:34–5). In each case, the image is of a male figure who seeks to protect his own mission from the interference of a mother. However, we are unable to ascertain the historicity of these encounters. For example, some scholars regard the Buddhist passage we cited as representing the opinions of later monks rather than those of the Buddha himself.[18]

Moreover, there has been an assumption that a woman cannot achieve salvation without having been first reborn a man. We have an anecdote from the *Lotus sūtra* about the Naga princess, a beautiful, mermaid-like creature complete with all the virtues of a true Bodhisattva. She offered to the Buddha the precious jewel set on her forehead – often interpreted as her own female sexuality, and he accepted it. Turning then to the Buddha's disciples, she said:

> 'I offered the precious gem to the Buddha and he accepted it. Was that not very quick?'
> They replied: 'Yes, very quick indeed.'
> She responded: 'Well then, you will now see me achieve Buddhahood even more quickly.'
> Then the multitude saw the Naga Princess in an instant of time turn into a man and have all the distinguishing marks of a Buddha.[19]

The position of women in the world's religions is generally low, as it is in Buddhism. In the case of Christianity, religious orders of women rank after those of men in the Catholic church, and priestly ordination is still forbidden to women.[20]

Buddhism and Suicide

A problem that has flared up in modern times is that of suicide within Buddhism. This came to public notice during the 1960s in Vietnam, when the south was governed by an anti-Communist government headed by the Catholic Ngo Dinh Diem.[21] Apparently, the Buddhists found themselves in conflict with the régime, and several were fired on and killed for carrying the Buddhist flag in public during a procession. Then the world witnessed the self-immolation of several monks and nuns, events that made headline news everywhere. The first incident, in May 1963, was that of an elderly monk, Thich Quang Duc, who, accompanied by other monks and nuns, took up a position on a busy street in Saigon, assumed the cross-legged lotus position, and had gasoline poured over him. Then he calmly struck a match and became a human torch. And throughout it all, until he expired, he maintained a calm and meditative exposure, in contrast to the wailing of the people around.

When we search the scriptures, we find that the Buddha had allegedly proscribed suicide in these words:

> Monks, let no one destroy himself, and whosoever would destroy himself, let him be dealt with according to law.[22]

And yet, when we turn to the Mahāyāna tradition, we find the *Lotus sūtra* apparently accepting suicide when it is undertaken for a good cause. This was the case with the Bodhisattva Medicine King, a popular figure in China and beyond, who vowed to offer his own body to heal the sicknesses of human beings. For this, we turn once more to the *Lotus sūtra*:

> . . . he wrapped his body in a garment adorned with divine jewels, anointed himself with fragrant oils, with the force of supernatural penetration took a vow, and then burnt his body. The glow gave light all around to the world-spheres equal in number to the sands of eighty millions of Ganges rivers. Within them the Buddhas all at once praised him.[23]

Historically, there have been a few instances of monks in China who offered themselves physically as demonstration of their piety or in protest to persecutions. Sometimes, they offered a part of themselves, such as cutting off their arms or fingers. It was in fact such instances, together with the veneration of relics, that the Confucian scholar Han Yü (786–824) cited in his criticism of the Buddhist religion.[24]

Buddhism in Today's China

As a religion which has survived the Cultural Revolution, Chinese Buddhism faces peculiar problems. I am referring not merely to the fear of renewed persecution, but to certain changes that the religion has sustained. It appears, for example, that many secularised monks are returning to the temples – but as married men. Although novices are presumably trained to remain celibate, one cannot help but wonder what the future form of the Chinese *Samgha* will be like.

And yet, can we say that Buddhist influence is over? Has Chinese Buddhism not also moved to the West, especially to North America? In those areas where an immigrant community is well established, be that in California, New York, or Toronto, we find Buddhist communities, not only from South or Southeast Asia, but also from Japan and China, active, and even assuming a role of leadership in organising communal religious life and in spreading the knowledge of Buddhism beyond the ethnic community. Just as Christianity has evangelised East Asia, so too Buddhism is evangelising North America and Western Europe. Its gains may be numerically small, but these are frequently among the intellectually sophisticated.

The historical transformation of Buddhism in China leaves behind many questions for students of the history of religions. On the one hand, as we have seen, Buddhism adapted itself to Chinese culture to the extent of becoming a Chinese religion, while maintaining its distinct identity in the company of Confucianism and of religious Taoism. On the other hand, it was never completely accepted by the country's political and intellectual élite, suffered severe persecutions, and has been threatened with near-extinction. Has the Buddhist openness to acculturation served the religion well? What would have happened if the religion had been less adaptable?

My own answer is: Buddhism could not have survived in China the way it did, had it not adapted itself culturally to the environment. Acculturation also accounts for its transformation, and its ability to contribute positively to Chinese civilisation. True,

Buddhism had been on a steady road of decline ever since the ninth century, and, with all its efforts of renewal and revival, it has generally been regarded, in the twentieth century, as peripheral to the concerns of Chinese society and even irrelevant to modern life. However, in spite of its decline, its strength may be discerned in its continual ability to resurrect itself after persecutions. We need not overestimate the importance of Buddhism in today's China; but ought we to overlook its resilience?

5   Buddhism in Korea and Japan

The Buddhist legacy is also present in both Korea and Japan – mediated through China, and to this day using Chinese translations of the Buddhist scriptures. In Japan, we find a wealth of diverse Buddhist sects and lineages, whereas in Korea there is much more evidence of syncretism with local shamanistic religion. Also, except for some Japanese influence, the Korean monks have largely remained celibate, where the Japanese now have mostly a married clergy – their practical application of the Mahāyāna insight that *Nirvāna* is to be found in *Samsāra*, that the ultimate is to be found in the relative, and that salvation is to be found here and now.

Three important sects of Japanese Buddhism are not known in China. They include the esoteric Shingon (True Word) sect of Tantric Buddhism, which went from India to China, and was introduced from early-ninth-century China by the Japanese monk Kukai, although it has since disappeared from China; the Jodō Shinshū or True Pure Land sect, started by Shinran in the thirteenth century, with its exclusive faith in and devotion to the Buddha Amida, its principal focus upon the exercise of *nembutsu* and its greater readiness to adapt itself to modern exigencies; and the Nichiren (Sun and Lotus) sect, named after its founder and started somewhat later, also in the thirteenth century, and known for its exclusive exaltation of the *Lotus sūtra* and its association with Japanese nationalism. It was Shinran who broke the tradition of monastic celibacy. Since then, Japan has had a married Buddhist clergy.[25]

Buddhism is uniquely Japanese in Japan, as it became Chinese in China. This is an important dimension of *all* Japanese religions, in spite of discernible Chinese influences. Theoretically, one finds more continuity between China and Japan, in the case of both Confucianism and Buddhism. Practically, however, the blending of the traditions, such as of Shinto and Buddhism, have given Japanese Buddhist sects a new visage, different from their Chinese antecedents. Japan has not witnessed the merging of Zen and Pure Land, although it has known a greater Tantric influence on various Buddhist sects, including Tendai.

In today's Japan, Buddhist sects tend to be associated with the rituals surrounding death and mourning, and the temples have shrines which honour the ashes of the departed. Indeed, Japanese Buddhism is so closely associated with the memory of the dead and the ancestral cult, that the family shrine dedicated to the ancestors, and still occupying a place of honour in homes, is popularly called the *butsudan*, literally, the Buddhist altar. For the same reason, Buddhism is frequently called the religion of the dead, whereas Shinto is labelled the religion of the living, on account of its association with the joys of life.

Has Buddhism any contemporary relevance in Japan, aside from mainly ministering to the memory of the departed? The question has sometimes been asked. Its influence is certainly present, even speculatively, as discerned in the modern Japanese philosophy developed by Nishida Kitarō and his followers, which blended Buddhism with continental European philosophy.[26]

And so, what of the importance of Buddhism today? The West may still be aware of the role of Buddhism in Japan and Korea, with its traditional sects and temples – even if its influence is subtle and ill-defined. In Japan, more than in Korea, there is the richness of sectarian transmissions, although in Korea, perhaps more than in Japan, the monastic discipline has been better preserved. The West knows also of the enduring Buddhist influence in Southeast Asia, especially in Burma and Thailand, but also, to some extent, in the Chinese circles of Taiwan, Hong Kong, and Singapore, where folk religion shows a very eclectic face. But what of mainland China with its Communist society?

6   The Buddhist Legacy in East Asia

As a rule Buddhism was better tolerated and promoted under those governments of non-ethnic Chinese or of mixed ethnic backgrounds. This shows how the religion continued to have a reputation of being an alien cultural influence. Besides, for those conquerors of China from the steppes, Buddhism helped to fill a spiritual vacuum. In the case of Tantric Buddhism, it also offered a sense of special power.

The Buddhist legacy in China represents a religion which has taken on many Chinese moral values while retaining its concern for deliverance from suffering, and its various monastic lineages and communities as centres for the transmission of the teaching or *dharma*. But the legacy includes as well Buddhist contributions to Chinese culture, which has never been the same since. Buddhist philosophy contributed to the development of Neo-Confucian metaphysics and spirituality. Buddhist faith and devotion expressed themselves in the fine arts, and sculpture, such as we see today in the rock-cut 'cave temples' of Yün-kang (Yungang), Lung-men (Longmen) and Tun-huang (Dunhuang). And Buddhism contributed to the architectural landscape as well: the well-known Chinese pagodas are evolved from Indian stupas where relics were kept. And there are various literary motifs and genres, including poetry and folk literature, which bear the imprint of Buddhist influence.

In the 1920s, the monk T'ai-hsü started a reform movement within Buddhism, while prominent lay devotees extended their activities to social work and popular education. These became part of the Buddhist mission in those areas and countries where the monks and believers still have the freedom to pursue these goals. Buddhists in Sri Lanka as well as Japan have been active in voicing their concerns for world peace. The Dalai Lama, in exile from Tibet, has emerged as the best-known spokesman for the Buddhist religion. He has been encouraging good relations with other religions while expressing peaceful political dissent against the Communist government in China. In the aftermath of the 1989 democracy movement in Tian'anmen and elsewhere in China, he was awarded the Nobel Peace Prize, to the world's acclaim.

9

Metaphysics and Spirituality: Neo-Confucianism as Response to Buddhism

1 A New Orthodoxy: Later Confucianism

The German sociologist Max Weber has offered us insights about charisma and its bureaucratisation. In the case of Confucianism, after it became a state ideology in the first century A.D., it was as if truth became institutionalised and something was lost in the process. Later thinkers sought to recover the lost truth by returning to the sources of their original inspiration. Each time, however, they could only do so within their own historical and existential contexts, so that each time, they too produced a new synthesis. The problem was that in its turn, each *new* synthesis became established as state doctrine. Here we are talking about problems that have plagued Confucian society through the ages, as they have also affected Christendom: problems that come in part with success and prosperity. Like any official orthodoxy, Confucianism abhorred dissent, thus stifling creativity and spontaneity. Confucianism has always been the tradition of lay people, which developed without a priesthood and without a church that could effectively stand up to the state. It took the combined popularity of Taoism and Buddhism to arouse a movement of return to the roots of Confucian inspiration, a movement which may be compared historically with that of Christian scholasticism.[1]

2 Compromises with Other Schools: Han Confucianism

The Han period is important in religious history because during that time Confucianism became a state orthodoxy (some would say, the state religion), Taoism became an institutional religion, and Buddhism was introduced into the country. Han China represents an epoch when all under Heaven was unified under one emperor ruling by Heaven's mandate with the help of Confucian orthodoxy. It was a development parallel to early Christendom under Constantine, who had a 'political theology' of one God, one Logos, one Emperor and one World – with philosophical monotheism applied to the monarchical order. No wonder the name Han has been identified with the majority population of China, which has been so marked by the transformations that took place during that dynasty.[2]

Kingship: Real and Ideal

The Han scholar reputed to be the most influential in consolidating Confucian gains was the 'political theologian' Tung Chung-shu (179–104 B.C.), who sought with metaphysical arguments to persuade the ruler to exercise benevolent government. Systematising traditional thought, he established Heaven, Earth and Man as a horizontal triad or trinity, with kingship as the vertical link between them:

> Those who in ancient times invented writing drew three lines and connected them through the middle, calling the character 'king'. The three lines are Heaven, earth and man, and that which passes through the middle joins the principles of all three . . .
> Thus the king is but the executor of Heaven. He regulates its seasons and brings them to completion . . . . [3]

And also:

> The ruler of men uses his love and hate, his joy and anger to change and reform the customs of men, as Heaven employs warm and cool, cold and hot weather to transform the grass and trees . . . . Therefore the great concern of the ruler lies in diligently watching over and guarding his heart, that his loves and hates, his angers and joys may be displayed in accordance with right.[4]

This is an example as well of Tung Chung-shu's expression of the 'unity between Heaven and man', which he describes somewhat mechanically, and with the help of Yin-yang philosophy. Another aspect that emerged in Han thought may be termed 'Messianic'. That was pointed out by those who asserted that Confucius always sought to promote the ideas of the ancients, including the ideas of the ancient Shang dynasty. It has been claimed that the Shang people had looked forward to a Messianic king from their line, expected within five hundred years after the dynasty's fall. Confucius, as a scion of a family that looked back to the Shang progenitors, was in a sense the fulfilment of these hopes.[5] Such Confucian Messianism was native to China, having emerged long before the birth of Christ. A similar phenomenon developed in the Taoist religion around the figure of Lao-tzu. Like Jesus, Messianic fulfilment for Confucius was not to be in the political arena, but in the spiritual sphere. Confucius became very much exalted and nearly deified. Following logically the idea that the sage ought to be king, Han scholars also called him the 'uncrowned king' who ruled the world through his works, namely, the classical texts attributed to him, especially the didactic *Spring-Autumn Annals*. Interestingly, images of Christ as king came into prominence only in the early Byzantine empire, which was contemporaneous with the Han, and where the ruler sought to control the church as well.[6]

Cosmology: Yin-Yang and the Five Agents

Tung Chung-shu and Han Confucians also incorporated ideas from the Yin-Yang and Five Agents schools. These were independent and ancient schools, but their ideas gradually fused with one another and were absorbed into both Taoism and Confucianism. We are here referring to cosmological ideas of two opposing yet complementary forces, *yin* and *yang*, as well as to a system of thinking focused on five primal elements that were also viewed as active cosmic agents always engaged in a process of mutual interaction and change. These five agents are water, fire, wood, metal and earth. Each has power over the other; that is, water is over fire, fire over earth, earth over metal, metal over wood, wood over water. These five agents thus differ from the Greek or Hindu 'Four Elements' of earth, air, fire and water.[7] Not only does the Chinese group include an organic substance, wood, but it appears to exclude the very important and all-pervasive air. Actually, air or *ch'i* had always been regarded as fundamental and indeed, all-pervasive. The Five Agents, however, served another purpose. Together with *yin* and *yang*, they formed a system of correlation which integrated life and the universe.

Han Confucianism was tolerant of exaggerations and superstitions. Together with the reconstructed Five Classics, many apocryphal texts were also accepted; indeed, each classic had at least one apocryphal text associated with it. We hear of Confucius' alleged miraculous birth and many other legends. There were also widespread beliefs in omens and portents, supported by a wide array of prognostication and divination texts. Eventually, scholarly consensus would subordinate the non-rational and non-historical materials to stricter scrutiny. But the Chinese belief in omens and portents continued until our own times. During centuries of history, eclipses of the sun and moon were carefully predicted and studied for their values as portents or omens. Natural disasters, whether floods or droughts, were also regarded as signs from Heaven of displeasure of misrule. The earthquake in Tangshan, North China, that just preceded Mao Zedong's death in 1976, was widely seen as an omen, predicting drastic change.

3   Neo-Confucianism as a Response to Buddhism

As a term, 'Neo-Confucianism' is also a Western coinage. The usual Chinese usage is to refer to the later development of Confucianism as the 'Metaphysical Thought' (*Li-hsüeh*, literally 'the learning of principle'). This was a *new* expression of Confucian thought, based on a smaller corpus of classical texts, reinterpreted in response to Buddhist challenges. In this respect, the Neo-Confucian movement parallels scholastic philosophy in the West, which sought to reinterpret Christian teachings with the assistance of Greek philosophical concepts. Ironically, since the rise of Neo-Confucianism signalled the decline of Buddhism, Buddhist influences on Chinese thought are best discerned afterwards in the structure of Neo-Confucian thinking.

During the Han dynasty and the later T'ang dynasty (when Buddhism became prominent), many commentaries and sub-commentaries were written on the classical texts themselves, which also became the core of the examination curriculum. But all this was largely the work of philologists. The Neo-Confucian philosophers made a different kind of contribution, as they developed their new thinking in response to Taoist and Buddhist influences. These thinkers also turned away from Han philology and superstitions. They looked for the spiritual legacy of Confucianism itself – the 'legacy of the mind and heart' that we may call spirituality. It was a new development, quite different from the direction of Han

Confucianism, which oscillated between the rationalism of Hsün-tzu and the superstitions of signs and omens. It also marked all later Chinese thinking, drawing the wealth of spiritual doctrine into mainstream philosophy. While Western spirituality has its rightful place in ascetical and mystical theology, it remains the domain of the monks rather than the laity, and has never been part and parcel of Western philosophical heritage. In the Chinese context, the spirituality of Confucius and Mencius, and even of Lao-tzu and Chuang-tzu, became strengthened through the Buddhist experience and the Neo-Confucian response to this experience, which was primarily the response of lay teachers and thinkers on a quest for sageliness.

The Neo-Confucian movement also strengthened a new understanding of lineage, so central to Chinese religious as well as philosophical thought. According to Chu Hsi (1130–1200), the true understanding of Confucius' teachings was lost after Mencius, and only rediscovered by his own intellectual predecessors – the eleventh-century thinkers Chou Tun-yi, Chang Tsai and the Ch'eng brothers.[8]

The Four Books as a New Canon

The Five Classics had stimulated philological exegesis, but had not promoted sufficient philosophical and religious commentaries. The Sung dynasty Neo-Confucian philosophers reformulated Confucian philosophy on the basis of a smaller corpus of texts, the *Four Books*. They contained the following texts:

* The *Analects* of Confucius (*Lun-yü*) includes twenty chapters, divided into nearly fifty sections, some of which are very brief. The earliest text with any historical information about Confucius, it goes back to about one century after the Master's death and gives the conversations between Confucius and his disciples. The chapters are not organised systematically, and the dialogues they offer are fragmentary.
* The *Book of Mencius*, a work in seven chapters, each subdivided into two parts, presents the conversations between Mencius and his disciples. Probably compiled after Mencius' death, although perhaps not that much later, it too is not systematically organised. But the passages are longer and the contents livelier, and include many anecdotes.
* The *Great Learning* is a brief chapter taken from the *Book of Rites*. Its concern is less ritual, but rather moral and spiritual cultivation, considered the beginning of good rulership.

- The *Doctrine of the Mean* is a slightly longer text, also taken from the *Book of Rites*. Its spiritual and philosophical content focuses on the inner life of psychic equilibrium and harmony.

In giving these texts pre-eminence, Chu Hsi and the other Neo-Confucian philosophers oriented Confucian scholarship increasingly to metaphysical and spiritual questions, at a time when Buddhism had made great inroads. In fact, their own thinking shows signs of Buddhist and Taoist philosophical influence. The result is a new synthesis, a *Weltanschauung* that builds on the old moralist answers to questions about life and the world, with a clearer metaphysical framework and spiritual profundity. The basic Neo-Confucian quest, while it has its scholastic roots, is definitely oriented to self-transcendence in the achievement of sagehood, rather than to rising on the bureaucratic ladder simply by passing official examinations. The synthesis took shape especially during the Sung (960–1279) and Ming (1368–1661) dynasties.

Chu Hsi on the Absolute: T'ai-chi and Li

Chu Hsi's philosophy represents a conscious synthesis of previous philosophies, combining as it does the 'naturalist' legacy of the Taoists and Buddhists, and the psychist and culturalist legacy of the Confucians themselves, modified also by an undercurrent of Buddhist influences. His theory of human nature draws from both sides. For Chu Hsi, as for the mainstream of Chinese philosophy, the human being and the cosmos are each paradigms, one of the other, so that evil loses its significance in the affirmation of human perfectibility, as expressed through the doctrine of sagehood.

A terse expression of the world regarded as an ontological paradigm is given in the philosophy of the Great Ultimate (*T'ai-chi*), which Chu Hsi took over from Chou Tun-yi. This is a symbolic expression of cosmology which emphasises the interrelatedness of the world and man in macrocosm / microcosm terms; it also hides within itself a secret Taoist formula for alchemy and yoga. And it points possibly to early Chinese beliefs in a supreme deity under symbols of astral bodies.

Chu Hsi interprets the *T'ai-chi* with the help of the concept of *li*, those 'principles' which constitute all things, and which had been given prominence by the Ch'eng brothers, especially Ch'eng Yi. *Li* may be defined as forms or essences, as organising and normative principles, belonging to the realm 'above shapes'. It is prior – although not in a temporal sense – to its co-ordinate, *ch'i*, translated sometimes as 'ether', or 'matter-energy', which belongs to the realm 'within shapes'. All things are constituted of both *li* and *ch'i*, somewhat as with Aristotelian form and matter, with the difference that *li* is passive and *ch'i* is dynamic.

The Great Ultimate is the most perfect *li*, a kind of primal archetype. It is also the *totality* of all the principles (*li*) of the myriad things, as brought together into a single whole. It serves in Chinese philosophy the function of the Form of the Good in Platonism, and that of God in Aristotelianism.

In place of a personal deity, Chu Hsi was speaking about an absolute which he clearly identified with both Heaven and the Lord-on-high. He asserted that it is not correct to speak about 'a man in Heaven' who is lord of the world, but that it is equally wrong to say that 'there is no such Ruler'. He was removing the anthropomorphic overtones of these terms while affirming the presence of a higher power, a metaphysical more than a personal Absolute.

> The Book of Poetry and the Book of History speak as though there is a human being there above, commanding things to come to pass, as in [passages] where they mention the Lord (*Ti*) as being filled with wrath, etc. But even here what they refer to is [the action of] *Li*. There is nothing more eminent under Heaven [i.e., in the universe] than *Li*. Hence it is called Ruler. 'The august Lord-on-high has conferred even upon the inferior people a moral sense.' [The word] 'conferred' conveys the idea of a ruler.[9]

Christian missionaries, especially the Jesuits of the sixteenth and seventeenth centuries, preferred to go back to the ancient Lord-on-high as a personal deity. But Chu Hsi's ideas have their parallels in Nicholas of Cusa, who spoke of the world as having no centre and no circumference, unless God be described as both. They have also an echo in modern philosophy, especially in the process philosophy of A. N. Whitehead, for whom God is more becoming than being, more absolute than personal.

> It is as true to say that God is permanent and the World
>   fluent, as that the World is permanent and God is fluent.
> It is as true to say that in comparison with the World, God
>   is one and the World many, as that the World is one and
>   God many.

It is as true to say that the World is immanent in God, as that
God is immanent in the World.
It is as true to say that God transcends the World, as that
God is immanent in the World.
It is as true to say that God creates the World, as that the
World creates God.[10]

Such ideas, identifying apparently contradictory concepts such
as transcendence and immanence, show the convergence between
Whitehead's thinking and Chinese thought, both Buddhist and
Neo-Confucian. They are also reflected in the work of German
theologian Paul Tillich, for whom God is the ground of being. And
they are echoed by the French paleontologist and mystic Teilhard
de Chardin, who lived many years in China without learning the
Chinese language or philosophy:

God reveals himself everywhere . . . as a 'universal milieu',
only because he is the 'ultimate point' upon which all realities
converge.
However vast the divine milieu may be, it is in reality a
'centre.'
The Creator, and especially the Redeemer, have steeped themselves in all things and penetrated all things.[11]

Chu Hsi was probably the greatest mind, and the most prolific
author among the Neo-Confucian giants. Though he was not
accepted as an orthodox thinker during his own life, his
commentaries on the Four Books were eventually integrated
into the curriculum of the civil service examinations (1313),
making his philosophy the new state orthodoxy for six centuries
to come. The history of Chinese philosophy after Chu Hsi may be
described as a debate between those who, like him, wished to give
more importance to *li*, and others who wished to give more emphasis
to *ch'i*. The protagonists of *li* tended to presuppose a pre-established
pattern of harmony in the universe and in human nature, to be
recaptured and maintained by a proper balance of reason and the
emotions. The protagonists of *ch'i*, on the other hand, were inclined
to minimise the opposition between reason and the emotions. In
other words, the tendency was toward either idealism, in the first
case, or materialism, in the second. It is interesting to note that
Chinese Marxist scholars have consistently sought to discover in
ch'i a materialist ancestry for Chinese Marxism.

Chu Hsi on Human Nature

In the metaphysics of Chu Hsi, the human being represents the summit of the universe, participating in the excellence of the Great Ultimate and possessing the nature which has come to him or her through the interaction of *yin* and *yang* and the Five Agents. Human nature is originally good, or 'sincere' (*ch'eng*). Whence, then, comes evil, that ugly fact of human life and experience?

The explanation is that *li*, though wholly good in itself, loses its perfection with actualisation through *ch'i*, owing to the limitations imposed by the latter. This is true of physical things as well as of human nature, owing to impediments to the 'manifestation' of *li*. Physical endowments vary in human beings: there are differences of 'translucency' or 'opacity'. People who receive the *ch'i* in its purity and transparency are endowed with a natural ease for sageliness; those who receive it in its impurity and coarseness will experience a stronger attraction for evil.[12]

And how, specifically, is the task of self-cultivation to be carried out? Chu Hsi proposes the double effort of maintaining an attitude of reverence (*ching*) toward one's own inner nature and its capacity for goodness, as well as 'the investigation of things and the extension of knowledge'. This double formula includes intellectual pursuit. Here we find a controversial issue, disputed by his contemporary and rival thinker, Lu Chiu-yüan, as well as by Lu's spiritual heir of three centuries later, Wang Yang-ming. They point out a serious problem in making intellectual pursuit the cornerstone of moral striving: that it makes sages necessarily intellectuals. This implies the inaccessibility of sagehood to those deprived of the luxury of intellectual striving. Chu Hsi's critics prefer to emphasise the power of the human mind and heart to choose good (*liang-chih/liangzhi*) and to perfect itself by the practice of virtues; they see intellectual pursuit a useful but not necessary component of cultivation. They prefer the dynamism of moral action, as the expression of the whole personality, oriented to the highest good.

Chu Hsi on Spiritual Cultivation

Acting under Buddhist influence, Chu Hsi gives some importance to the practice of meditation, or 'quiet-sitting'. What is implied here is a *cyclical* movement: the return to one's original nature, the recapture of the springs of one's being, and the enabling of this state of original equilibrium of nature and the emotions to permeate one's daily living. Such a form of meditation differs from

the scripture reading which precedes much of Christian meditation, and the tradition of point-by-point reflection on the gospel
episodes. It differs also from the Buddhist tradition of meditation
by visualisation, in which the person imagines the presence of
Buddhas or Bodhisattvas, but comes closer to the Ch'an (Zen)
ideal of emptying the mind or heart of its concepts and feelings.
Unlike Buddhist meditation, however, Confucian meditation has
as its goal less the attainment of mystical experience (which is not
excluded), and more the enhancement of one's moral nature. Here
we are speaking of *spirituality* as well as moral doctrine. And it is
especially as a spirituality that Neo-Confucianism – both the school
of Chu Hsi and the school of Wang Yang-ming – has deepened the
religious character of the Confucian tradition.

Chu Hsi's double formula of self-cultivation includes moral and
spiritual attentiveness over oneself, that of 'keeping [one's self]
recollected' (*shou-lien/shoulian*) or 'not getting dispersed' – also a
doctrine of spirituality. To quote Canon Jacques Leclerq:

> . . . recollection . . . is the chief disposition required for the inte-
> rior life . . . . It is simply the calm which is born into the soul
> through solitude and silence . . . . Man has need of it to find
> himself as well as to find God.[13]

Even the arguments between two schools of Neo-Confucian thought
reflect the later arguments between schools of Christian spirituality, formulated in terms of the primacy of the intellect of of the
will in the soul's union with God. Within the Catholic Church,
the Dominican order prefers the intellect, and the Franciscans the
will.[14]

4 Neo-Confucianism as Protest Philosophy

Chu Hsi enjoyed a certain reputation during his lifetime, but he
was regarded more as a heretic than as an orthodox thinker, if only
because of the novelty of his thought. His philosophical synthesis
of Neo-Confucianism was not accepted as a genuine expression
of Confucian thought until over a century after his death, when
the Mongol rulers decided to enshrine it in the curriculum of
the civil-service examination system (1313). And once again, we
might debate the merits of such official acceptance, as it risked
turning creative ideas into mere formulas, to be memorised by
examination candidates. It was this process that disgusted some
later, more independent thinkers, including Wang Yang-ming.

Wang Yang-ming's philosophy may be called a protest philosophy, because of his criticisms of Chu Hsi and, even more, of the state orthodoxy that was making use of Chu Hsi. Besides, it played a role somewhat parallel to Martin Luther's Protestant movement with regard to Roman Catholicism. Its much more subjectivist orientation precluded its ever being manipulated by state authorities. Wang Yang-ming speaks of the mind as absolute. But the mystical, subjective mind cannot be so easily controlled, whereas Chu Hsi's emphasis on *li*, located in human nature as well as in the world – including the world of classical texts – lent itself more to such control through the state examination system.

Wang Yang-ming on the Absolute and Human Nature

Where Chu Hsi begins with the world, and speaks of the Great Ultimate as present in both the world and the self, Wang Yang-ming, following the footsteps of Lu Chiu-yüan, prefers to begin with the self, and speaks of ultimate reality in terms of a subjectivity which infuses all objectivity. Such a school of thought has been described as the school of mind (*hsin/xin*), in contrast to Chu Hsi's school of *li*, sometimes translated as principle.[15]

As a philosophical concept, the mind-and-heart (*hsin*) occurs frequently in the *Book of Mencius* and in Buddhist scriptural texts, where it refers to ultimate reality. Neo-Confucian thinkers restored the word to its pristine meaning, as a psychic principle, while retaining the undertones of Buddhist metaphysical connotation. Lu Chiu-yüan, for example, identifies mind with *li*, while also speaking about the 'mind of the sages' as the 'moral mind' or the mind of Tao:

> Sages appeared tens of thousands of generations ago. They shared this mind; they shared this *li*. Sages will appear tens of thousands of generations to come. They will share this mind; they will share this *li*.[16]

As Lu's spiritual heir, Wang Yang-ming continued the process of interiorising this metaphysical principle. For him, the mind explains the meaning of both the world and man, containing levels of profundity of meaning and presence:

> The original substance (*pen-t'i/benti*) of the mind is nothing other than the heavenly principle (*T'ien-li/Tianli*) . . . It is your True Self. This True Self is the master of [your] physical body. With it, one lives; without it, one dies.[17]

Such philosophical terms as 'original substance' and 'heavenly principle', as well as 'true self', are not taken from Confucius or Mencius. They come rather from Buddhist and Taoist vocabulary. In taking over their usage, Wang Yang-ming, like Chu Hsi before him, was reintegrating Buddhist and Taoist insights into the Neo-Confucian tradition. For him, one must take good care of the True Self, always keeping intact its original substance. And then, as one shreds off the superstructures which the 'false self' – the ego – has erected as barricades behind which one has formerly attempted to hide oneself, as one clears away the selfishness which hinders the inner vision, a person will discover this innermost core of his or her own being. This in turn will lead to the realisation of perfect goodness, which is the ultimate revelation of the Absolute in the self. In fact, the concept *jen*, originally an expression of intersubjectivity, became absolutised, gaining cosmic connotations without losing certain qualities of relativity.[18]

Wang Yang-ming emphasises the presence of the Absolute in the subjective and relative, in the human mind. With mystic fervour, he speaks of a process of spiritual cultivation culminating in an experience of enlightenment which is essentially the discovery of the True Self. His language is reminiscent of that of Christian mystics, especially Meister Eckhart, for whom the divine spark in the soul 'is the light of God's reflection, which is always looking back to God'.[19]

Eckhart's distinction between God and the Godhead probably offers the best analogy for an understanding of this kind of subjective Absolute, described in terms of increasing immanence in relation to both the world and man. Such terms as original substance, heavenly principle, *li* and even *jen*, came to refer to the Confucian 'Godhead' as distinct from the Confucian 'God'. The former is reality, hidden at the heart of things, especially in the human heart, where the latter is its manifestation in human consciousness:

> The 'I' is there reduced to utter nought and nothing is left there but God. Yet, even God she [the soul] outshines here as the sun outshines the moon, and with God's all penetrativeness she streams into the eternal Godhead where in an eternal stream God is flowing into God.[20]

5   Neo-Confucianism in Korea and Japan

Confucian thought and culture spread from China, usually through Korea to Japan, and retains its importance today as a diffused moral philosophy. Unlike Korea, Japan never adopted civil-service examinations, although Confucianism has traditionally been associated with the task of education. The Tokugawa period (1600–1868) especially encouraged the development of Confucianism and Neo-Confucianism at the expense of Buddhism as well as Christianity. Where the Chinese and the Koreans were scholar-officials, the Japanese Confucians were scholar-samurai, fighting men who always wore swords and lived in readiness for an honourable death, according to the code of ethics called the Bushidō ('way of warriors'). This shows a principal difference between Confucianism in Japan, and the same tradition in China and Korea. Of the five relationships, the Chinese have emphasised the parent–child relationship, thereby celebrating filial piety, where the Japanese *samurai* have focused more on the ruler–minister relationship, with the commitment of absolute loyalty from generation to generation. In this light, we can better understand the Japanese 'emperor-cult', and its tendency to divinise the emperor – a cult that was never found in China.

Of the two countries, Confucian influence appears stronger and more visible in Korea than in Japan. Historically, Confucianism in Korea, like its counterpart in China, has been associated with education, and with a civil-service examination. Once introduced, the philosophy of Chu Hsi became supreme in Yi dynasty Korea, producing such Korean thinkers of the *Songni hak* (Learning of Human Nature and Principle) as Yi T'oegye (1501–70) and Yi Yulgok (1536–84), whose discussions centred on the relationship between human nature and the emotions. Confucian influence is especially discerned in the Korean emphasis on filial piety, shown also in ritual mourning for the dead – a reason why Koreans have traditionally preferred to wear white (the colour of mourning in East Asia), since they were always mourning for some member of the large, extended family.

6 Neo-Confucianism in Modern Times

During most of the last thousand years, Neo-Confucianism has been the official philosophy for China. But the Jesuit missionaries, including especially Matteo Ricci, preferred classical Confucianism to the later development. They opposed the metaphysical dimensions of Neo-Confucian philosophy, which bore a pantheistic imprint of Buddhist influence. Actually, it has become impossible to separate Neo-Confucianism from earlier Confucianism, so that an onslaught on one meant the same on the other. In the late nineteenth century,

Chinese intellectuals began a soul-searching questioning of the cultural heritage, particularly Confucianism. It was regarded by many of them as a weight and a burden – an intellectual shackle on the mind, preventing the country from modernisation. Its strongest critic was probably the early-twentieth-century writer Lu Hsün, whose short stories attacked the 'cannibalistic' ritual religion that stifled human freedom and individual initiative in the name of passive, conformist virtues. These critiques satirised the dehumanising elements in a fossilised tradition until then inextricably bound up with the social-political establishment. They were also expressive of the newly awakened nationalism, desirous of asserting independence against the coming of the Western Powers and Japan. It was in the midst of these anti-traditionalist, anti-Confucian voices of the May Fourth Movement (1919) that the Chinese Communist Party was born (1921). What began as a search for intellectual freedom entailed finally a repudiation of the monopoly of tradition, with the Communist takeover of the mainland (1949).

Mainland scholars have sought as well to point out for the sake of attack the *religious* character of the Neo-Confucian movement, including Chu Hsi's teachings on meditation and spiritual cultivation and Wang Yang-ming's penchant for mysticism. However, Liu Shaoqi, former head of state in Communist China, had lauded both Confucian and Neo-Confucian ideas in his address, *How to Be a Good Communist*:

> The Chinese scholars of the Confucian school had a number of methods for the cultivation of their body and mind. Every religion has various methods and forms of cultivation of its own. The 'investigation of things, the extension of knowledge, sincerity of thought, the rectification of the heart, the cultivation of the person, the regulation of the family, the ordering well of the state and the making tranquil of the whole kingdom' as set forth in the Great Learning also means the same. All this shows that in achieving one's progress one must make serious and energetic efforts to carry on self-cultivation and study.[21]

During the Cultural Revolution (1966–76), the Anti-Confucius movement entered a new phase, with diatribes in 1973–74 linking the fallen Defence chief Lin Piao with Confucius. This was the most vehement attack ever mounted. Long before that, Liu Shaoqi had become 'enemy number one' to Chairman Mao. His writings were banned, and the Confucian and Neo-Confucian ideas he had praised also came under heavy attack.

While Marxist scholars were vigorously criticising the entire traditional legacy, a group of philosophers and scholars in Taiwan and Hong Kong expressed their concern for the survival of Chinese culture, which they identified especially with Neo-Confucianism. I refer here to the plea for a return to Neo-Confucian sources, in 'A Manifesto for the Reappraisal of Sinology and Reconstruction of Chinese Culture', made public by a group of Chinese philosophers in Taipei in 1958. This statement speaks of the harmony of the 'way of Heaven' (*t'ien-tao/tiandao*) and the 'way of man' (*jen-tao/rendao*) as the central legacy of Confucianism. It also challenges Western Sinologists to give greater attention to Confucian spirituality as the core of Chinese culture, which it claims was not properly under-stood by the missionaries of the sixteenth and seventeenth centuries. In saying this, these scholars interestingly concurred with mainland scholars in the judgement that Neo-Confucianism in particular possesses an undeniably spiritual and religious character.[22]

The Question of Women's Place

In reassessing the relevance of Confucianism and of Neo-Confucianism, one must not overlook certain obvious problems. In the Confucian social order, human relationships tended to become hierarchically fixed and rigid – with the superior partners, the fathers, husbands, rulers, exercising more right and privilege, and the inferior partners performing more duty and submission. Speaking historically, this was the combined product of Confucian philosophy and the influence of the Legalist theory of power and Yin-Yang philosophy with its arbitrary correlation of cosmic forces and human relationships.

The patriarchal family system was consolidated with the assis-tance of Confucian ideology. And women were increasingly rel-egated to a subordinate role. The obligation of providing a male heir became woman's sacred duty, to assure the continuation of the ancestral cult. It also offered an excuse to the husband to take on secondary wives, in cases when the principal wife was childless or had only a daughter. In other words, the more Confucian the society became, the less freedom the women enjoyed. Impregnated with Yin-Yang ideas, the Appendices to the *Book of Changes* represent the male–female relationship in terms of the superiority of Heaven over inferior earth. And the ritual texts sum up the woman's place in society – which means family – in the 'Three Obediences': she is to obey her father while at home, obey her husband when married, and obey her son if widowed.[23]

Women usually enjoyed more freedom during those periods when the country was disunited, under alien rule, or under the influence of non-Confucian teachings. By Sung times, with the restoration of an ethnic Chinese dynasty as well as more 'civilised' moral principles, women became largely confined to the home. Although no law forbade a widow to remarry, those women who lost their spouses were encouraged to remain unmarried – especially by the school of Ch'eng Yi and Chu Hsi. Female chastity, or loyalty to one husband, was made parallel to political loyalty, or the man's commitment to one dynastic government. Society's double standards for men and women increased in importance, until women from good families had to bind their feet from infancy to assure their chances of making a good match. The custom in itself probably arose in the emperor's harems, and had nothing initially to do with Confucian teachings. But the custom imposed enormous suffering, and the assumption made women the mere playthings of men. Only with modern times, under Western missionary influence and especially with the May Fourth Movement (1911) which espoused Western ideas of science and democracy and attacked the old Confucian order for its stifling of individual freedom, did women begin to experience their liberation from some of society's harshest rules.

7 Neo-Confucian Rationalism as Preparation for Modernisation

For a long time, modernisation in East Asia has been exclusively attributed to Western influences, such as those of science and democracy, industry and high technology. But recent decades witnessed the coming of age not only of modern Japan as an economic giant, but also the rapid growth of the Pacific Rim countries. These countries and regions have never formally repudiated their cultural heritage. In Japan, the economy is capitalist and the government is a liberal democracy. There, traditional symbols (including the Emperor system and religious beliefs associated with Buddhism and folk religion), as well as an ancestral cult and Confucian ethical values (especially the 'work ethic'), continue to dominate the life of the people, including that of many of their intellectual leaders. During the immediate post-war period, Japanese scholarship reflected a popular mood of uneasiness over the military defeat. An eminent Japanese scholar, Maruyama Masao, criticised traditional Japanese culture and thought, including Neo-Confucianism, as obstacles to modernisation.[24]

Since then, Japanese scholars have argued about the causal factors leading to the modernisation of their country. Although the stimulus from the West has been essential, their argument has favoured a 'traditionalist' interpretation focusing upon the forces already present in Tokugawa Japan. Among these forces, the most prominent is Neo-Confucian rationalism, that dominant school of thought in the cultural circle which includes China and Korea as well. It is a well-known fact that the earliest Japanese 'modernisers' were usually from the *samurai* class, which had a Confucian classical and literary education, could afford a Western scientific and technological training, and were motivated by a desire to 'enrich the country and strengthen the armed forces', a slogan directly attributable to the utilitarian branch of Confucianism.[25] Such a desire fostered nationalism, and in its Japanese manifestation, nationalism *was* the moving force behind the country's phenomenal economic success. The same slogan and this same desire inspired the Chinese and Koreans as well – whether Marxist or anti-Marxist – in their modernising efforts. Increasingly, Western business circles are now aware of the need of better understanding the Confucian ethos behind trade and industry in East Asia. This points to the importance of finding the traditional in the modern, of a process of cultural and possibly religious integration as well as continual transfomation which has been going on in contemporary East Asia.[26]

10

Ethnic Survival: Islam and Other Middle Eastern Religions

1 Foreign Religions in China

We now move from Buddhism to the other religions of foreign origin. Like Buddhism, these reached China from the west; unlike Buddhism, they originated in or beyond Iran. These include the lesser-known ones like Zoroastrianism and Manichaeism, both arriving from Persia (as did Nestorian Christianity), as well as the better-known Islam. While the other religions from Persia are hardly alive any more in today's China, Islam remains strong, with its adherents numbering in the millions. Were we to discount Confucianism and Taoism as religions, Islam might even be competing for first place with Buddhism in today's China. For while it is difficult to know exactly how many Buddhists there are in China (outside of Mongols and Tibetans, known to be Buddhists), it is somewhat easier to count Chinese Muslims, many of whom belong to visible ethnic populations concentrated in certain regions of the country.

Buddhism and Christianity are missionary religions both in China and elsewhere. It is interesting that Islam, usually considered a missionary religion, should have become the non-proselytising religion of an ethnic minority in China. Likewise Zoroastrianism, an established imperial religion in Persia before Islam, became that of an ethnic minority in China. It is harder to classify Manichaeism, also a religion from Persia, but very much of a syncretising religion, with ideas infiltrating Taoism and Buddhism, and itself eventually losing its own identity and being considered a Buddhist sect.

2   Persian Religions in China: Zoroastrianism and Manichaeism

Several religions came to China from Persia. Besides Zoroastrianism and Manichaeism, we have also mentioned Nestorian Christianity. For people who are not specialists in comparative religion, these can be difficult to distinguish one from another. The Chinese have often confused the three groups, as they have also the Muslims and the Jews. We shall start with Zoroastrianism, sometimes known in Chinese as *Po-ssu chiao* (Bosujiao, 'the Persian religion') and sometimes as *Pai-huo chiao* (Baihuojiao, 'the religion of Fire-worshippers'). After all, it is believed that it arrived in China before the others.

Prior to the emergence of Islam in the seventh century, trade through Iran and Central Asia had linked the Mediterranean with China, along what historians refer to as the 'Silk Road', named after China's principal westward export. Trade in commodities may have been accompanied by some cultural exchange, but not on the whole by large-scale permanent settlement of populations. Things changed with the advent of Islam. It appears that the Arab Muslim pressure on Persia caused the migration of peoples belonging to different religions like Zoroastrianism, Manichaeism, and Nestorian Christianity. A large number of Persians settled in T'ang China, spreading to Ch'ang-an, Loyang, Kaifeng, Yangchow, Taiyuan and elsewhere.

The 'Fire-worshippers'
Zoroastrianism is named after the ancient Persian prophet Zoroaster, who lived some time before the sixth century B.C. This religion has a priesthood, a belief in Ahura Mazda, the great good God, represented by light and by fire, an elaborate ritual system, and a high ethical code. Its followers are sometimes called Majūs (Arabic for Magians, from *magus*, 'priest'), or Mazdeans ('followers of Mazda'). The established religion of Sasanian Persia before the country was overtaken by Muslim Arabs, Zoroastrianism still survives through a very small minority in today's Iran and also through a somewhat larger group that had migrated to western India and survives in Bombay and nearby as the Parsees, i.e., 'Persians'. In China, it is known as the religion of 'fire-worshippers'. Historically, fire temples are known to have existed in T'ang China, especially at Ch'ang-an, the capital.

Zoroastrian migration to China followed upon the Arab conquest of Sasanian Persia (637–42). The last Sasanian emperor, Yazdegird

III, had appealed for help to the T'ang court. As he did not get the support he wanted, he took refuge among the Turkic tribes in Central Asia but was betrayed by them. The Chinese extended protection to his son Peroz, who came with other refugees, and these were permitted to build their temples and practise their religion. Peroz himself was recognised as king of Persia and named a general of the imperial guard. He died at Ch'ang-an and left behind a son, Narseh, who succeeded to his royal title and attempted to regain Persia with Chinese troops, but in vain. These Sasanian refugees stayed in China for at least two hundred years, and were usually left in peace until the great persecution of 845, directed at all foreign religions but especially Buddhism.[1]

There existed, and still exist in many places like Ch'ang-an, Loyang and Kaifeng, sites of former temples dedicated to the God of Heaven. Early speculation was that these could have been former synagogues; but the Australian Sinologist Donald Leslie thinks they were Zoroastrian temples. This is surprising, as it would make the number of Zoroastrians in China much larger, and the period of their activities much longer.[2]

In the nineteenth and early twentieth centuries, following the maritime trade of the British, Zoroastrians from India, namely, the Parsees, came to the coastal big cities in China as traders. They had a community in Shanghai until the Second World War, and they still number over a hundred in Hong Kong, where they have a community hall and a cemetery. There are also Parsee graves in Macau, though no community survives there.

The Religion of Light (Manichaeism)
Manichaean experiences in China are a long and fascinating story. Mani was born under Persian rule in Mesopotamia (today's Iraq). Heavily influenced by Gnostic ideas prevalent among Syrian Christians, he lived and worked in the first half of the third century in Persian Mesopotamia, and wrote in Babylonian Aramaic. As a religious leader, he advocated a syncretistic world religion with elements borrowed from Christianity, Zoroastrianism and Buddhism. Manichaean faith is based on a dualism of good and evil with the aim of liberating the light within from its captivity by matter. The religion accepted followers on two levels: the celibate priests or 'elect' lived in retirement from the world, and were waited upon by their 'hearers' for their daily needs. Mani himself was put to death in A.D. 274, a victim of Zoroastrian jealousy. The religion he founded had some influence in fourth-century North Africa and

numbered St. Augustine of Hippo as a follower for some time. Although the sources speak of the religion (*Mo-mo-ni*) as having been introduced only in 694, this could have happened much earlier. In 732 it was mentioned in an imperial T'ang edict as teaching an erroneous doctrine and pretending to be a school of Buddhism. However, since it was a religion of the 'Western barbarians' (*Hsi-hu*), it was not to be outlawed provided that its practice was confined to 'the barbarians', that is, if it remained an ethnic religion. Such Chinese treatment was kind compared to the Roman persecution both of Christians and of Manichaeans in the early fourth century.[3]

As time went on, Manichaeism had conflicts with Buddhism but appeared to have been better accepted by the Taoists. In an eighth-century version of the *Lao-tzu hua-hu ching* (Lao-tzu's transformation as a barbarian), an anti-Buddhist polemic, Lao-tzu is alleged to have reincarnated himself as a prince in Assuristan (i.e., Iraq), only to become a monk called Mo-mo-ni.[4] In the early eighth century, the Turkic Uighurs of Central Asia converted to Manichaeism. This was a non-Chinese group that had traditionally allied itself with the Chinese, and that supported the T'ang dynasty during the An-lu-shan rebellion in the mid-eighth century. As Uighurs settled in China, they built Manichaean temples as well. Such were constructed in the late eighth century in Nanking and Yang-chou, at Chinchou (Hupei) and also as south as Shao-hsing (Chekiang).[5]

The turning point for Manichaean fortunes came in 840, when the Uighurs were defeated by the Kirghiz, a people living today on both sides of the northern borders of Sinkiang, straddling China and the erstwhile Soviet Union. In the anti-foreign and anti-Buddhist wave starting in 843, Manichaean properties were confiscated, their temples and books were burnt, and over seventy nuns were killed in Ch'ang-an. The religion never fully recovered, although it survived underground, supporting peasant rebellions at different times and places, including possibly the anti-Mongol struggles of the fourteenth-century founder of the Ming dynasty.[6]

Today, the world's only remaining Manichaean shrine still stands outside of Quanzhou, in coastal China, with its bas-relief image of Mani displayed as the 'Buddha of Light'. Possibly, the name of Mani is close enough to that of Sakya*muni*, the Buddha, to have people confuse the two figures. But the image is very different from any known Buddha image. The head is surrounded by a great halo of light, while two long plaits of hair descend from the head and shoulders. The figure also wears a white garment. A stone inscription there indicates that the image was erected in

1340 by a disciple. This unique shrine may be seen today by outside visitors brave enough to find and take a bus from Quanzhou (Fukien) via an unpaved road to a hill some distance from the city.[7]

The T'ang poet Po Chü-yi allegedly composed a letter on behalf of the Chinese emperor in response to the Uighur court and its request for the protection of their co-religionists. Supposedly, he also left behind a poem about the religion itself:

> I have calmly examined the accounts of Su-lin.[8]
> The doctrine of Mo-ni is truly amazing.
>> The Two Principles display their dignified silence,
>> The Five Buddhas follow the light.
>> The Sun and the Moon render their homage.
>> Heaven and earth acknowledge their origin.
> In matters of self-discipline and purification,
> They are as renowned as the Buddhists.[9]

The problem with Mani's religion had always been its readiness to borrow from others, making it appear more Jewish or Christian in the Near East, and more Buddhist in the Far East. Mani himself accepted Jesus as the prophet of the Jews, Zoroaster as the prophet of the Persians, and the Buddha as the prophet of the Indians. He said:

> My Church is superior in this . . . to all previous churches, for these previous churches were chosen in particular countries and in particular cities. My Church, mine shall spread in all cities and my Gospel shall touch every country.[10]

Manichaeism is an exception among the Persian religions introduced into China because its representatives did active proselytising. It was a religion of an ethnic group that attempted to extend beyond that group. It is thus interesting that Manichaeism should have survived better than Zoroastrianism or Nestorianism, with which it seemed to have had interaction in China. Presumably, this happened because the Manichaeans adapted themselves better to local culture and also made local converts, even if in the end they risked losing their own identity.

3   Jews, Past and Present

The survival of a people with remembrance of their Hebrew origins in contemporary China is a real saga, even if, strictly speaking, these may no longer be considered either ethnically Jewish, on account of the many mixed marriages during the centuries, or religiously Jewish, as they no longer practise Jewish rituals.

It is not known when Jews first arrived in China. References from Arab sources going back to the ninth and tenth centuries speak of Jews in China. But the Chinese Jews themselves like to speculate on their ancient arrival, perhaps in the Han dynasty. During the European Middle Ages, the trade between Europe and both India and China was largely controlled by Muslim Arabs or Persians, who used mainly a sea route across the Persian Gulf and established trading communities along the way. It appeared that Jews were also active in such trade, and that they too used the sea route as well as the land routes opened especially by the Mongols. An Arab record also reports the incident of Canton in 879, when the rebel Huang Ch'ao captured that city and put many inhabitants to the sword. Among the victims were '120,000 Moslems, Jews, Christians, and Magians, who lived in this city and became merchants in it'.[11]

We cannot determine how many of these victims belonged to each of the different religions. But it is quite possible that Jews were present in many coastal cities, living perhaps in quarters close to the Muslims, as they have traditionally done, as they still do today in inland Kaifeng (Honan). But the Arab records would place Jews in the China of the T'ang dynasty, around the same time as Manichaeans, Zoroastrians and Nestorians also entered the country. Jews are known to have lived in Hangchow, Kaifeng, Peking, and elsewhere under Mongol rule (1280–1368), and their presence has also been corroborated by Marco Polo's account.

And there remain people today in Kaifeng who still remember their Jewish ancestry, traced back at least to the twelfth century. Interestingly, this group is not referred to in the early reports, and yet they have left behind their own records in stone and other inscriptions in Chinese, dated back to 1489, 1512, 1663 and 1679; scrolls of the Law, and an almost complete set of prayers in Hebrew; a Chinese–Hebrew Memorial Book of the Dead, closed about 1670. And, of course, there exist reports by Jesuit and other missionaries from the seventeenth to the twentieth centuries.

The stone inscriptions claim that the group arrived at Kaifeng, then capital of the Sung dynasty, probably before 1127. They carried with them 'western cloth' (perhaps cotton from India) although there is no account of their route, whether by sea via India, or by land via Persia. Donald Leslie concludes from his examination of their scrolls and prayerbooks that they might have originally come from the Yemen. He calls them Rabbanites, whose prayers and ceremonies followed Talmudic prescriptions.[12]

An interesting encounter took place in 1605, when the Jesuit missionary Matteo Ricci was living in Peking. He had a visit from a man called Ai T'ien, from Kaifeng, who had heard of the presence there of non-Muslim foreigners worshipping the true God. Ricci first mistook the visitor for a Christian, but later realised he was a Jew. And, of course, the Jewish visitor had also mistaken the Jesuit to be Jewish. Anyway, the visitor informed the missionary that there were then about ten or twelve clans of Jews living in Kaifeng, and that they had recently restored their synagogue at a cost of ten thousand crowns. He knew as well of Jews in Hangchow, with their own synagogue. But while he could recognise the Hebrew language, he was unable to read the Bible. At that time, the Jews of Kaifeng were circumcised, observed the Sabbath as well as other feasts like the Passover, the Feast of Tabernacles, and the Day of Atonement, and married within their own community. They wore blue headgear in contrast to the Muslims' white.

The visitor was most impressed with Ricci. So when the Jews of Kaifeng lost the chief of the synagogue in 1608, they even suggested that Ricci take up that job – on condition that he give up pork. So apparently, the community was already feeling the results of isolation, even if there were other Jewish communities in China. The decline of the Jewish communities could have been due to intermarriage with ethnic Chinese, and perhaps to conversions to Islam, as the Muslims had always been more numerous, and the Chinese tended to confuse the two groups.

Jesuit missionaries kept up contact with the Jews. Fathers Gozani, Domenge, and Gaubil all visited them in Kaifeng, in the years 1704 and 1721–23. The community was still flourishing, with a beautiful synagogue, and the group was known by the local Chinese as practising a religion that 'extracts the sinews' – which also gave rise to the street name in their quarter in Kaifeng.[13]

After that time, the community went into decline. The last rabbi died around 1800. Contact with the outside world was only re-established in 1850, when two Chinese Protestants were sent from Shanghai to visit the community. They found the synagogue in a state of decay, and the community impoverished and ignorant of Hebrew. The struggling community even sold the surviving scrolls and prayers to the visitors. When the Anglican bishop, William Charles White from Canada, took over protection of the synagogue site and the two extant stones in 1912–13, the Jews were no longer distinguishable by race, culture or religion.

Since Communist China opened up the country in 1977, more outsiders have been able to visit Kaifeng, and many scholars and journalists, especially from Canada, contacted the Jews there. In 1981, I went there in a small group of three and was received by a member of the Chao clan, the nephew of the man who had assisted Bishop White in his amassing of information. Our conversation took place in his house, which is built on the old synagogue grounds. Other families of Jewish origin also live nearby. According to him, there are about two hundred families who still remember their Jewish ancestry. While these people now eat pork, they still refrain from raising pigs.

We should mention the new wave of Jews who entered China in modern times, following those treaties that opened Chinese ports to foreigners. In the mid-nineteenth century both Oriental (or Sephardic) and Ashkenazic Jews arrived in Chinese cities from places like Russia and Great Britain. After the Communist revolution in Russia (1917–20), many more Jews went to China from that country, settling first in Harbin, Manchuria, and later moving to Tientsin and Shanghai. Even during the Sino-Japanese War of 1937–45, 19,000 Jews fleeing persecution in Europe arrived in China to live under Japanese occupation. Many of these would later move on to the United States or Israel.

4 Islam in China

We move now to a discussion of Islam in China. As a world religion, Islam is often identified with the Arab Middle East and North Africa, or with the Turks and Iranians of the Middle East. But most of its adherents are east of Iran, among the non-Arabic-speaking peoples of South and Southeast Asia. Today's Indonesia is the country with the largest Muslim population.

On account of its historical links with the Middle East and with Judaism, Islam has been called, together with Christianity, an Abrahamic religion. And Muslims today still regard themselves as spiritual or even ethnic descendants of Abraham through his son Isma'il (Ishmael). Moreover, on account of the towering stature within Islam of the Prophet Muhammad, God's messenger, Islam also considers itself very much a prophetical religion.

Etymologically, Islam means 'surrender to God', and the Muslim is one who so surrenders. As a historical phenomenon, the religion had its origins in the caravan and oasis towns of early-seventh-century Arabia. After twelve years of struggle in Mecca, Muhammad and his followers migrated to Medina in 622, the year that marks the beginning of the lunar Islamic calendar.

Muslims are usually known as either Sunnis (etymologically, 'followers of custom') or Shi'is (literally, 'partisans'). Their differences have more to do with politics than with theology. The Sunnis claim that rulers must come from the Prophet's tribe – as has often been the case – but not necessarily from his clan or family. The Shi'is, on the other hand, claim that Muhammad's son-in-law 'Ali and his lineal descendants were the legitimate heirs to the Prophet as religious as well as political leaders of the community. Shi'is celebrate in a kind of passion play the historical tragedy of the death of the Prophet's grandson Husayn. Some Shi'is hold that Muhammad ibn Hasan al-'Askari, the twelfth in their recognised line of hereditary leaders or Imams, did not die but went into hiding and will one day return as the Mahdi, a Messiah figure who will restore righteousness and legitimacy. While there are more Sunnis than Shi'is in most of the Islamic world, the Muslims in Iran are mostly Shi'is, and there are a large group of Shi'is in today's Iraq and substantial minorities in Lebanon and India.

The Muslims' religious obligations have been summed up in the 'Five Pillars' of Islam. These include the profession of faith in the one God and in Muhammad as God's Messenger, the recitation of prayers five times a day facing Mecca, the fast of Ramadan, almsgiving, and a pilgrimage to Mecca if possible. Among an omnivorous nation like the Chinese, they were conspicuous, especially for their abstention from pork.

Origins

Missionary zeal is usually strong within the lifetimes of great religious leaders. Both the Franciscan and the Jesuit missionaries went to China either during their founders' lifetimes or immediately afterwards. The religion of Islam also arrived in China within a few decades of the Prophet's death, although knowledge about it was scant until about the seventeenth century.

Actually, the legend concerning Islam's beginning in China would put it some time before the Prophet's decisive move from Mecca to Medina. This has to do with the story concerning Sa'ad Waqqas, who Chinese Muslims say was Muhammad's maternal uncle and the builder of the first mosque in Canton, South China, in the late sixth or early seventh century. The Huai-sheng Mosque still stands, as does the adjacent minaret, as well as a sepulchre claiming to go back to 629, holding his remains within a cemetery of Chinese Muslims. The sepulchre and the minaret appear to be quite old, but there is no way they could have been associated with Muhammad's uncle, even if the present structures were fourteenth-century reconstructions on an earlier site. Presumably, Sa'ad Waqqas was an important namesake. In any case, the first Muslims to reach Canton and Ch'üan-chou (Quanzhou) probably came by sea before the end of the eighth century.[14]

Islam's overland entry into China via Central Asia is sometimes dated to 651, when an envoy from the Caliph 'Uthman arrived at the T'ang capital of Ch'ang-an, and was received with high honours by the Emperor Kao-tsung, the son of the ruler who had received the Nestorians. This event took place because the emperor had received pleas from the Sasanian rulers, and wanted to have information about their Arab opponents as well. Otherwise, we find no mention of Arab traders or Muslims in China before the mid-eighth century, and certainly no mention of any mosques, even though Zoroastrian fire temples and Nestorian churches were built in the seventh century. While the Nestorians and Zoroastrians were Persians, the earliest Muslims were Arabs, and later arrivals were Central Asian converts, sometimes Persians.

But the actual entry of Muslims into China was probably in the mid-eighth century, perhaps during the An Lu-shan rebellion in the north-west. The rebellion was defeated with the help of Arab and Uighur mercenary troops, presumably Arab Muslims and Uighur Manichaeans. Thousands of these were permitted to settle down within the country. Some thirty or more years later, other Arab troops assisted the Chinese in the south-west against Tibet, and some of these settled in today's Yunnan province.

Muslims in China: The Prophet's Religion
An early-ninth-century Arab traveller, Ibn Wahhab, has left behind a record of his own travels, including his visit to the Chinese court. He claimed to be of the family of the Prophet Muhammad, and was asked many questions about the Arab conquest of the Persian kingdom. Then the question turned to religion:

> He ordered the interpreter to ask me if I knew my Master and my Lord, and if I had seen him. I made answer, 'How should I have seen him who is with God? . . . . Then he called for a great box and opening it took out another contained therein which he set

before him, and said to the interpreter: 'Show him his Master and his Lord.' And I saw in the box the images of the prophets . . . I saw the image of Mohammed riding on a camel and his companions about him on their camels, with shoes of the Arabesque made on their feet and leathern girdles about their loins.[15]

It appears that these were painted scrolls. And the collection included Noah in the Ark, Moses with his rod and the Children of Israel, and Jesus sitting on an ass.

Also during the T'ang dynasty, Arab traders were frequently in Canton, the centre of a sea-borne trade with the Persian Gulf. The Muslim community there was governed by an elected Qadi, and followed Qur'anic law. Ch'üan-chou (Quanzhou) had also its Muslim community, with a cemetery there and tombstones that are well-preserved until today. Recent scholarship in the twentieth century has dated a tombstone with Arabic inscriptions in Quanzhou to the years 1009–10, the year in which the big mosque was built there. The large structure of a medieval mosque still stands in today's city. Its walls are intact, but it has no roof. Some claim this mosque was the earliest.[16]

During the T'ang dynasty, Persians settled in China as refugees from Arab Muslim conquerors. Arab traders, however, came and went, usually staying outside the city walls during their sojourns. Under the Mongols in the thirteenth and fourteenth centuries, more Muslims entered China, from Central Asia and beyond, enjoying imperial protection, and often serving as officers and bureaucrats. They supervised the bureau of astronomy and collected taxes from the Mongols' Chinese subjects. They introduced Arab science, including astronomical instruments and battling catapults, and helped in the calculation of the calendar. It was roughly that time when Muslims became known in Chinese as *Hui-hui* (literally: return) – we are not sure why. Perhaps the name had to do with their custom of turning to face Mecca when they prayed; or perhaps it sounded like 'Uighur', since Uighurs had converted to Islam.[17]

Distinguished Muslims in China included the thirteenth-century bureaucrat named Ahmad, finance minister to the Mongol emperor Khubilai. In 1267 the Persian astronomer Jamal al-Din built an observatory in today's Peking, while Muslim engineers made weapons to help Mongol troops. Persian physicians also introduced new drugs and new hospitals. A Central Asian Muslim, Sayyid Ajall Shams, governed Yunnan province for the Mongols, also in the thirteenth century, and encouraged irrigation projects. His troops settled there, many as ancestors of today's Muslim population. The imperial palace in Peking, which still stands today, was built by a Muslim architect. Muslims were often permitted a certain degree of self-rule. Ch'üan-chou (or Quanzhou) was known to Marco Polo by its Arabic name, Zaitun. Under Mongol rule, the Muslim community there had its own leader, its own judge, and bustling religious and secular activities.[18]

Muslims spread into all parts of China, and were distinguished by their food and by other customs, including circumcision, marriage and funeral rites. They shunned usury, divination and geomancy, and built mosques and schools where Arabic was taught and instructions in the Qur'an given. The founder of the Ming dynasty (r. 1368–98), who turned against the Manichaeans, favoured the Muslims. So did a successor, Wu-tsung (r. 1506–21) of playboy fame, who was surrounded by Muslim advisers and eunuchs, and welcomed Muslim envoys to his court. The early-fifteenth-century eunuch, Cheng Ho, who led naval expeditions to southeast Asia, and even reached Hormuz on the Persian Gulf, was of Muslim origin. A Ming thinker, the iconoclastic Li Chih (1527–1602), came also from a Muslim family, although he later turned to Neo-Confucianism and Buddhism.[19]

As the Muslim population increased and as Muslims became more and more Chinese through intermarriage and cultural adaptation, conflicts also took place between them and the majority population.[20] Muslim grievances were frequently due to official maltreatment, such as during the late eighteenth and the entire nineteenth century, when Muslims in both Northwest and Southwest China rebelled many times, and were severely crushed. This happened also under Communist rule, especially during the Cultural Revolution, when Muslims were sometimes forced to eat pork. By nature militant, many Muslim groups have often been restive under Communism. One account tells of the flight of the Kazakhs out of China as a tragic episode with few survivors. In the early 1960s, it is said, 100,000 Uighurs, Kirghiz and Tajiks crossed the border into the Soviet Union. In 1989 and afterwards, including 1991 when the Communist Party was banned in the Soviet Union, there have been sporadic reports of Muslim unrest in Sinkiang. Presumably, the situation remains explosive, since many groups, including Kazakhs, Uzbeks and Kirghiz, continue to inhabit both sides of the border between China and the erstwhile Soviet Union, and trouble on one side can easily spill over.

Muslim vicissitudes under Communist rule parallel those of the other religious groups. In 1953 a Chinese Islamic Association was formed with purposes similar to those of the Buddhist, Taoist and Christian Associations, namely, to collaborate with the government in monitoring their believers. In 1956 an Islamic Institute founded in Beijing (Peking) had 130 students. Muslims also suffered greatly during the Cultural Revolution.[21]

How Many Chinese Muslims Are There?

We are not sure of the exact number of Chinese Muslims. The Communist government's published number of fifteen to eighteen million in the 1980s is considered too low by many believers. Chinese Muslims themselves sometimes estimate their number to be close to one hundred million in the 1980s, although they have no way of substantiating this figure. In any case, even if we cannot be certain of the number of Chinese Muslims (that presumably is a state secret), China is most probably one of the world's most populous Muslim countries.[22]

Muslims make up a minority in Taiwan as well. The figure given in 1992 is around fifty thousand. The mosque in Taipei is a beautiful structure, and overshadows the nearby Catholic cathedral. It was built with the help of Middle Eastern funding. There are four other mosques on the island.

The Challenge of Acculturation

Chinese Muslims are generally Sunnis. They have had to live among a larger population whose dominant ideology used to be Confucianism, and they have sought to acculturate themselves accordingly. The earliest extant Chinese Muslim writings come from the seventeenth century. Their authors include Wang Tai-yü and Liu Chih. Each wrote apologetic treatises that sought to emphasise common ground between Islam and Confucianism. Wang's *Cheng-chiao chen-ch'üan* (True explanations of the orthodox Religion) used Confucian language and methods of argumentation to explain Islamic tenets. He emphasised the moral character of social relationships and added these to the Muslims' obligations of almsgiving and pilgrimage to Mecca. He also pointed out Confucius' reference to terms like Heaven and Lord-on-high, while highlighting Islamic beliefs in God and in divine intervention. Li's *T'ien-fang hsing-li* (The philosophy of nature and principle from Arabia) has a title with Neo-Confucian resonances. And indeed, in this work as well as others, he sought an accommodation of his Sufi interests with Neo-Confucian philosophy.[23]

Sufism represents the mystical side of Islam. Sufi teachings had reached China already in the seventeenth century. Ma Ming-hsing was a Chinese Sufi of the eighteenth century, whose supporters danced and chanted and went into trances in public in their efforts to achieve union with God. Many Muslims and non-Muslims alike were threatened by his pleas to return to the original inspirations of a purer Islam without compromises with other teachings. In the late eighteenth century, Ma and others sought to carve out a Muslim state along China's borders. Their revolt started in Kansu (1781), and was crushed by the Manchu Ch'ing troops.[24] As a consequence, many Chinese Muslims crossed over into Russia, where their descendants may still be found.

True, Chinese Muslims did little to propagate their faith actively. While they acquired converts through intermarriage and adoption, their general isolation resulted in their decreasing knowledge of Arabic and of the Qur'an. Besides, the religion did not encourage the translation of its scriptural text, and while Chinese translations exist, few Muslim families own such a work. Under Communist rule, observance of Islamic rules and customs became even harder. Chinese Muslims are known to keep their fast at Ramadan, to have visited Mecca in delegations from 1955 to 1966, and after the interruptions during the Cultural Revolution (during which time all public religious activities ceased), the pilgrimage was reportedly resumed in the 1980s. Although prayer in public outside of mosques is seldom witnessed among Muslims in China, they appear generally to have remained loyal to their religion. But there have also been many losses. Ambition to climb up the Chinese civil-service ladder has been one reason for some losses. This was actually what the Jew Ai had confided to Matteo Ricci in Peking, when he compared the Jewish situation with that of the Muslims.[25]

Chinese mosques sometimes have a special room reserved for women worshippers. Chinese Muslim women do not cover themselves with a veil, as do many Arab, Persian, and Indian women. Even small scarves are seldom worn, except in the mosques.[26]

5   Islam's Success as an Ethnic Religion

By nature, Islam is a proselytising religion, but it entered China as the religion of certain ethnic groups. So too, did the earliest Christian group in China, the Nestorians, who had a Syriac liturgy. Even the Catholic Franciscan missionaries of the thirteenth century, who worked in Mongol China, appeared to have proselytised relatively little, ministering mainly to those Europeans who were already Christian. Thus Islam survived in China as a religion identified with ethnic minorities, without making many inroads into the population of the Chinese *Han* majority, who remained Confucian, Taoist and Buddhist. But the *later* Christian missionaries, both Catholic and Protestant, were of a different order. They resembled more the Buddhist missionaries of an earlier age who came from South and Central Asia.

I consider this an important point, distinguishing the Christian missionaries from the Muslim *settlers*. Whereas Muslim and Christian Nestorian visitors and settlers went into China usually as migratory peoples from neighbouring countries, the later missionaries went principally, and often exclusively, for the purpose of converting the natives. This is one reason why Christianity met much stronger opposition than did Islam or Judaism, the followers of which sought merely to *survive* in the midst of an alien culture. The Jews appeared to have been always a small group, incapable of exerting a large influence. Culturally and ethnically, they have become assimilated into the majority population, and many are ignorant about the religion of their Semitic ancestors. The Muslims were and remain numerically strong. While their size is relatively small when compared to the country's total population of one billion, it exceeds greatly the number of Chinese Christians. The Muslims of mixed origins who live in the large cities and in areas populated mostly by the majority group or Han Chinese have become culturally assimilated without always abandoning their faith. Others, who inhabit Chinese Central Asia, belong to various groups, usually of Turkic origin, for whom religion is an important hallmark of communal identity.

Why did the Muslims refrain from the proselytising effort? We may adduce certain reasons for this behaviour. Their relatively small number is only one of these. A better explanation is the cultural cohesion of the host country itself. If Islam had won over many steppe peoples of Central Asia, these converts appeared to have lacked a high culture of their own at the moment of conversion. Besides, where Islam is concerned, conversion frequently follows war and conquest, involving sometimes the strangulation of an earlier religious tradition, such as happened with the Arab conquest of Persia. In the course of China's long cultural history the country has been overcome time and again by various 'steppe peoples', such as Mongols and Manchus, from outside her frontiers. Indeed, many of them came in time to accept the high culture of China, with her three religions of Confucianism, Taoism and Buddhism. But none of the conquering peoples were Muslim to begin with. Chinese history therefore does not feature an era of Islamic dominance to compare, for example, with Catholic Spain's or Hindu India's.

11

Cultural Assimilation: The Dilemma of Christianity

1 Europe and Asia: Mutual Stereotypes

For a very long time in history, Europe and Asia knew little of each other, even though sharing the same Eurasian land mass. This was all the truer of Western Europe and East Asia, as the distance between the two is greater. A common view in Christian Europe of non-Christian Asia was as a continent of pagans and idolaters. Alternatively, some Europeans thought of the Orient as a land of wise men, of learned philosophers and astrologers – in part a legacy of the story of the Magi in Matthew's gospel, chapter 2. A third and in-between tendency was to look upon some Orientals, for example, the Chinese, as quasi-Christians, or at least as including among them a Christian community. This involved the legend of the priest-king, Prester John, sometimes thought to be in Ethiopia, sometimes thought to be as far away as in China. He must have been considered an immortal, or at least the founder of a long-lasting dynasty, since he was invoked during the course of many centuries. Perhaps there had been rumours from other sources as well regarding a distant Christian kingdom. After all, Marco Polo made mention of Nestorian princes he had met in the Far East. And the quest for such a Christian kingdom served as a moving force to bring the earliest adventurers or 'missionaries' to China, in search of a Christian Cathay.[1]

On their side, the Chinese were just as ignorant of Europe and its religion. Seeing their own country as centre of the world, they regarded the western regions as the origin and home of the Buddhist religion. Records say that the Chinese knew about Rome, or rather about the Eastern Roman empire, which they called Ta-Ch'in (after their own early empire), and later, in the seventh century, Fu Lin. There were official contacts, including Byzantine embassies or missions in the seventh, eighth, and even eleventh centuries, as late as 1081.[2] In those early days, Europe's interests were in Chinese silk, and moth eggs were smuggled out by about 553. But whatever knowledge or information that existed about the early Byzantine empire faded away, with the series of misfortunes that empire suffered, from the Crusades in the eleventh century, and eventually with the fall of Constantinople to the Turks in 1453. Even after Portuguese traders and travellers had settled in Macau on the coast of southern China in the sixteenth century, the Chinese continued to regard them as believers in a 'Buddhist sect'.

2 Christianity Comes to China

Such early mutual ignorance is in itself instructive. Each of the two great civilisations of western Europe and eastern Asia understood the other in terms of its own self-knowledge. There appeared no strong reason on either side to deepen such mutual acquaintance as did exist. And so the situation remained until the Jesuit missionaries came to China in the sixteenth and seventeenth centuries. Western intellectual curiosity, religious zeal and expansionism finally led to the European discovery of China and its native philosophical and religious traditions.[3] But the Jesuits were not the first Europeans to discover China. Long before the Society of Jesus was founded, other Christian missionaries had preceded them. Speaking historically, in the course of some thirteen centuries, Western Christianity had sought to penetrate China at least four times, only to be driven out each time.

The First Wave: Nestorians in China

The first Christians to come to China were the Nestorians in the seventh and ninth centuries. These were followers of the bishop Nestorius, at one time Patriarch of Constantinople (428), who was declared a heretic in 431 by the Council of Ephesus for not accepting Mary as *Theotokos* (Greek for 'God-bearer') and preferring the term *Christotokos* ('Christ-bearer'). This was basically a political and theological triumph of the Alexandrian school of Cyril over the rival Antioch school, from which Nestorius had come. Deposed, he was exiled to Egypt. Although Nestorius never started a sect or a church, the 'Assyrian' or Ancient Church of the East, which refused to accept Ephesus on the grounds that the emphasis of Christ's unity with God jeopardised the integrity of his human nature, has been identified with his name. Today, this church still forms the easternmost branch of the Syriac Church of Antioch, and many live in northern Iraq. The so-called St. Thomas Christians of India (of the Malabar rite) are basically of Nestorian background. And indeed, Nestorian Christianity is the only kind that so early pushed eastward, to India, Indochina, Tibet, Java, Central Asia, and China itself.

Where China is concerned, records are still extant. The *Book of Jesus the Messiah* probably dates from 637. Historical remains include a stone tablet unearthed in the early seventeenth century, recounting the arrival in T'ang China of the monk Alopen, probably from Persia. This is the so-called Nestorian Monument of 781, which still stands in a museum in Xi'an (Sian) in the province of Shensi. As so many rubbings have been made from the stone, the Monument is now encased in glass, the only one so protected among many other stone monuments collected in the 'Forest of Monuments' that fill the museum. Its discovery in 1625 occurred during the sojourn of the Italian Jesuit Matteo Ricci in China. The Jesuit missionaries were overjoyed at this indication of the ancient presence of Christianity in a country that venerates antiquity. More recently, ancient Nestorian texts were also discovered in the so-called Buddhist caves of Dunhuang.[4]

The Monument itself is ten feet high, three and a quarter feet wide, and nearly one foot thick. It commemorates the arrival in China of a Nestorian mission that was received in 635 by Emperor T'ai-tsung. The inscription includes a description in Chinese of the mission's arrival and settlement in China, with a list of names of over seventy monks, all apparently aliens, in both Syriac and Chinese. This mission took place at the time the Scottish-Irish monk Aidan brought Celtic Christianity to England, and when some German tribes were yet pagans. Once given a foothold in China, the Nestorians were able to have their texts translated, and monasteries built in both Ch'ang-an and Loyang. An edict of toleration of Christianity was also issued.

Interestingly, Syriac, the liturgical language of the Nestorian church, helped to engender several Asian writing systems. As a group, the Turkic-speaking Uighurs, who converted from Buddhism to Manichaeism in 762 (although a minority turned Nestorian), adapted the Syriac script for their own use. Their script, in turn, was adapted by the Mongols in the thirteenth century, and later replaced by a partly Tibetan-influenced script based on the Uighur alphabet (1310). In its turn, the Mongol script became the basis for the Manchu, a southern Tungu language. Interestingly, Uighur, Mongolian, and Manchu were all rotated ninety degrees and written in the vertical manner of Chinese. Although today's Uighurs in China tend to use either the Arabic script also used by the Ottoman Turks, or else the Latin alphabet, the Syriac-inspired forms of Mongolian and Manchurian can be seen, in conjunction with Chinese, on the palace gates of the former Imperial Palace in Peking, the capital of the Mongols and the Manchus as well as of Ming China.[5]

The Nestorian church had its own liturgy and symbols. Instead of the humiliating crucifix, they preferred the 'Cross of Victory' which, in China, sometimes emerged from the lotus, a Buddhist symbol. For this kind of acculturation, and for collaboration with Buddhists in the mid-eighth century on textual translations, it has sometimes been criticised by other Christians.[6] Nestorianism enjoyed a brief prosperity in China, as their name, *Ching-chiao/Jingjiao* ('the Brilliant Religion') indicates. The persecutions of A.D. 843–45 were mainly directed against Buddhists, but affected all alien religions in China. A decline set in on that account, although Nestorians were found in China much later. In the thirteenth century Marco Polo said that the trade routes from Baghdad to Peking were lined with Nestorian chapels, and that in 1265 there were twenty-five Asiatic provinces under the church's ecclesiastical administration, with seventy bishoprics. Many were still there much later. Since so many Nestorians were on the periphery of China, it was always possible for new ones to enter the country from outside. The final decline of the Nestorian church took place in the fourteenth century in the wake of the Islamisation of Mongols and Turks, and the severe persecution of Tamerlane in 1380. Today, Nestorians are mostly found in Iraq and South India. Nestorian Christians were found in China as recently as 1933, among the Erküt tribe of Ordos Mongols. But this remains an isolated instance.

The Second Wave: The Franciscan Friars

The Order of Friars Minor, the official name of the Catholic religious order of itinerant preachers from which come the Franciscan Friars, was founded by St. Francis of Assisi (1181/2–1226) of legendary fame. He was the rich young man who turned his back on his family to give himself to the service of God and the poor. He was the knight troubadour of Lady Poverty. He was also the friend of birds and animals. And he was the intrepid adventurer, the missionary who sought to convert the Saracens without recourse to the sword.

In the thirteenth century, the Franciscan friars were fearless travellers and missionaries at Mongol courts, both in Karakorum, Central Asia and later beyond. It was a time when the papacy was hoping to win the Mongols over as allies against the Muslim Turks. These missionaries eventually came to Mongol China, and still found Nestorians there, although these were no longer actively missionary. The Franciscans gave China its first Catholic archbishop, John of Montecorvino (1307), who came over the arduous land route between Europe and China, and resided in the city of Cambaluc (Peking). Supposedly, he baptised six thousand people before his death in 1328. Most of the early converts to Catholic Christianity appear to have been Nestorians of Turkic origin, especially subjects of an Öngöt prince called King George, whose capital lay between Inner and Outer Mongolia. Others included choir boys from poor families whom he bought and instructed. The Christian mission was extended also to Zaytun in the south, or present-day Quanzhou, where tombstones with Latin inscriptions can still be found. In the Middle Ages, it was a veritable cosmopolis, where Arab travellers and traders rubbed shoulders with Europeans.

But the Franciscan interlude proved even more short-lived than the Nestorian, and neither group appear to have paid much attention to Chinese religions. Before the Franciscans arrived in Cambalac, however, Marco Polo, with his father and uncle, had already spent seventeen years (1275–92) in Mongol China. He would stir Europe with accounts of his experiences, and he also described the Chinese as pagans.

The Third Wave: Jesuit Missions in China
Many circumstances contributed to the ebbing of missionary interest after the middle of the fourteenth century. Among these we may mention problems like the Black Death in Europe, and problems in China, like the replacement of Mongols by a new native dynasty, the Ming (1368), a word meaning 'light'. Interestingly, the name of the dynasty might have something to do not only with the Buddhists, as has always been claimed, but also with Manichaeans and their 'Buddha of Light'. But the new dynasty preferred ethnic religions and ideologies to foreign ones. And, until the coming of the Jesuits, Christians in China had made little visible impact on the country's culture. Besides, each new wave of Catholic missionaries seemed to have gone to China in ignorance of those who had been earlier.

The Jesuits went to China at the time of the high Renaissance in Europe, when the Counter-Reformation had also energised the Catholic Church. Mobilising their best resources of culture in its service, the Society of Jesus (founded in 1540 by the Spaniard, Ignatius of Loyola) was eager to spread its wings to Asia – to both India and China. They were aided by the interest of Portuguese travellers and traders, who were already in Japan in 1543. Francis Xavier followed, preaching (without really knowing the native languages) in India and Japan. At that time, Japan was ruled by a number of feudal lords, called *daimyos*, who often fought among themselves. Some were eager to make foreign allies and profit from foreign trade. And the general populace found Christianity appealing, with Xavier, for example, at first using the term *Dainichi* (the Great Sun God) for God. (He later switched to *Deus*.) By 1606, the number of Japanese Christians was about 750,000. Indeed, the sixteenth century has been called the 'Christian Century' in that country, even if severe persecutions brought the religion almost to extinction three decades later.

Francis Xavier died on a small island near Macau within sight of the mainland without having set foot on China. His successors in the Society of Jesus had better luck. Matteo Ricci, the best-known China missionary, was educated under distinguished teachers in Europe and also studied for four years in India before reaching China. He arrived there in 1583 in the company of Michele Ruggieri. They first wore Buddhist monastic garb, with shaven heads, but found that the Chinese had little respect for a religion already in decline or its monastic representatives. So the Jesuit missionaries decided to switch their alliance to Confucianism, let their hair grow, and changed to the robes of the Confucian scholar. It marked the general attitude of the Jesuit mission in China, which opted for acculturation in that foreign country. Indeed, Ricci and others used all the resources of Western learning and science to convert the Chinese. They won over some significant converts from among the Confucian élite, including especially the famous three – Hsü Kuang-ch'i (Paul), who had held the office of Grand Secretary (like that of prime minister), Li Chih-tsao (Leo), who became Ricci's collaborator in several publications on religion and science, and Yang T'ing-yün (Michael). At the time of Ricci's death in 1610, Chinese Catholics numbered about 2,500.[7]

The Jesuits also introduced European mathematics, calendrical reform and the telescope, although they refrained from speaking about the heliocentric theory on account of Rome's condemnation of Galileo. Jesuit successes continued, and even multiplied, under

the Manchu Ch'ing dynasty (1644–1912). The German astronomer Adam Schall von Bell reached high office under the Shun-
chih emperor. Another Jesuit, the Flemish Ferdinand Verbiest, was
entrusted by the K'ang-hsi emperor with the supervision of the
calendar. In 1670, the number of Catholic Christians in China
reached 273,780.

However, a storm was gathering on account of the different
opinions of Ricci's successor as mission chief, Nicola Longobardi,
who strongly opposed the policy of acculturation. Jesuit involve-
ment in court intrigues also cost them dearly. The Jesuit mission in China was eventually brought down by the controversies over the Rites as well as over differences about translating
Christian terms. We are now referring to a conflict that began
among missionary circles and spread into European philosophical
circles: the so-called Rites Controversy, regarding the permissibility
of 'Chinese Rites' to Christians, and the so-called Terms Controversy, regarding the manner of rendering into Chinese words like
'God'.

A Special Topic: The Rites and Terms Controversies
It is interesting to consider the 'Rites' and 'Terms' controversies
in the context of the frequent suggestion that traditional China
knew no religion as such. The question arose among missionary
circles regarding how they should deal with 'Chinese rites'. Should
Christian converts be permitted to continue the practice of the
ancestral cult, so central to the entire family and clan system, as
well as the veneration of Confucius, in those temples dedicated to
his name which were attached to every school in the country? As
Christianity had been accustomed to regarding itself as the only
true religion, the positioning of missionaries on one or the other
side of the question was quite revealing and even ironic. Those who
were more tolerant of 'Chinese rites' were missionaries favouring
greater cultural adaptation, who also declared these rites to be
non-religious. Others, who opposed such acculturation, regarded
the rites as not only religious, but part and parcel of a pagan and
superstitious society. Interestingly, the Jesuits, who were working
with the educated élite, tended to be more tolerant and accepting,
while the other missionaries, whether Franciscans or Dominicans,
working usually with peasants, tended to oppose the rites as pagan
superstitions.

In the Terms controversy, the Jesuits and other missionaries
grappled with the problem of translating, much as did the early

Buddhists. In the Buddhist case, certain Sanskrit terms were trans-literated into Chinese, words like *nirvāna* and *samsāra*, while oth-ers were given equivalent Chinese terms, often taken from Taoist usages. In the Christian case, many were happy to make use of classical terms like *T'ien* (Heaven) for God. But others resisted for theological reasons, regarding it as having pantheistic over-tones. Some insisted on a new coinage, such as 'Lord of Heaven' (*T'ien-chu/Tianzhu*). For a time, even this could not satisfy the more fundamentalist-minded, who preferred *Deusu* (Latin: Deus), as God was called in Japan. Indeed, to assure theological purity, the three persons of the Trinity had been transliterated in Japanese as Deusu Patere, Deusu Hiiryo, and Deusu Supiritsu Santo, while key concepts were rendered as *persona* (person), *susutanshija* (substance), *garasa* (grace), and *diidesu* (faith). The problem that went undetected for some time was that *Deusu* sounded like *dai-uso*, Japanese for *big lie*.[8]

Under the leadership of Matteo Ricci, the Jesuit missionaries, with the support of a few others, approved for their converts the veneration of ancestors and of Confucius. But opposition to this move caused the spread of the so-called Rites Controversy as well as the Terms Controversy from China to Europe. The acculturation moves were reported to the Pope in Rome, Clement XI, who sent as envoy to China the Patriarch of Antioch, Maillard de Tournon, to sort out the question. Incidentally, Tournon was a conservative who was also to condemn the 'Malabar rites' of India, which the Jesuit Robert de Nobili had accepted. The Jesuits in China promptly sought help from the Chinese Emperor, K'ang-hsi, who gave his official confirmation – that Confucius was not worshipped as God, but venerated as a model teacher; that ancestral veneration was regarded as a memorial service rather than as a worship of the spirit; and that the ancestral tablet offered a focus for filial attention and devotion, and no more; and that Heaven and Lord-on-high were identifiable, not with the physical Heaven, but the Lord of Heaven and Earth and all things. But this was regarded by the other side as political intervention in religious questions. As Tournon preferred to rely on a member of the Mission Étrangère de Paris, Charles Maigrot, Vicar Apostolic of Fukien, who had meagre knowledge of the Chinese language, the emperor was less than impressed, and indeed, quite insulted that Rome should deign to regard itself as an authority on things Chinese.

The controversy lasted for a long time; it was considered by eight popes, and involved leading universities in Europe. Rome vacillated in the beginning, depending on who had its ear. In the end, Rome was to support those who opposed the rites, whose judgement was: that the ancient Chinese were idolaters and the modern Chinese, atheists; that the Confucian classics themselves, and even the Jesuit works published in Chinese, taught doctrines contrary to the Christian faith; that ancestral rites were illicit because they were offered to spirits of ancestors and so involved idolatry and superstition; that Confucius himself was a public idolater and a private atheist, and should not be honoured by Christians as a saint. In a decree of 1704, reinforced by a bull of 1715, Pope Clement XI banned the rites. And, in 1742, Pope Benedict XIV decided 'definitively' in favour of those who opposed acculturation. His decree, *Ex quo singulari*, condemned the Chinese rites and imposed an oath on all Catholic missionaries in China to oppose the rites. Two years later, the Malabar rites were also definitively proscribed.[9]

Here, it may be useful to quote a European scholar who has shown enormous loyalty to the popes of history:

> The prohibition of the rites was a decision of incalculable consequences. Things were forbidden to the Chinese Christians which, in their estimation, were demanded by decency and good manners, and on the basis of an interpretation that was at variance with that given by Emperor Kanghi and the Chinese scholars.[10]

Whose interpretation of Chinese rites should we consider correct? This is not an easy question to answer, even today. The fact was that the more learned Jesuits were in contact with the educated Chinese gentry, whose understanding of the rites was much more rational. Other missionaries, working with people on the grass-roots level, found their prospective converts much more superstitious in their attitudes toward the ancestral cult and other rites.

As a result of the papal decision, Chinese converts could no longer attend Confucian schools, and their religion became known as the Religion of the Lord of Heaven (*T'ien-chu chiao/Tianzhu jiao*), to be distinguished from the later Protestant Christianity, usually called *Chi-tu chiao/Jidu jiao* (the Religion of Christ) or *Ye-su-chiao/Yesujiao* (the Religion of Jesus). Basically, it meant that one had to choose between 'being Chinese' and 'being Catholic'. In 1724, an imperial edict also banned Christianity from the country. Soon afterwards, the temporary suppression of the Society of Jesus by Rome (1773) effectively closed an important chapter in the history of the Catholic Church.

In their desire to win friends and influence people, Jesuit missionaries dispensed information about China and the rites question to intellectuals and philosophers in Europe. Thus, in the seventeenth and eighteenth centuries, the strife that began among missionary circles had spread into European philosophical circles. European philosophers were less concerned about the practical missionary dilemma, but likewise divided about whether Chinese civilisation was compatible with Christianity. G. W. Leibniz considered the Chinese as religious and theistic, but derived his judgement partly from reading the treatise of the Jesuit missionary N. Longobardi, who tended to favour the other side. Christian Wolff, Leibniz' good friend, praised the Chinese for their 'natural morality', one grounded in strictly philosophical concepts, with no reference to religion and no belief in God.[11]

Almost two centuries after *Ex quo singulari*, during the Second World War, Pope Pius XII in 1939 reversed the decision of 1742, authorising Christians to take part in ceremonies honouring Confucius and to observe the ancestral rites. By then, however, the veneration of Confucius had been largely discontinued, since the country had put in a modern school system to replace the traditional Confucian-oriented 'temple-related' institutions. Besides, the Chinese were at war with Japan, and hardly had the time to spare for ancestral rites.[12]

The Fourth Wave: Protestant Missions in Modern Times
With the imperial ban on Christianity, the religion virtually went underground in China, and remained so until another wave of evangelisation reached the shore. This time, Protestant missionaries became more prominent, although Catholic missionaries returned, enforcing the papal decision on the rites and terms. It happened in the nineteenth century, when Manchu China was finding itself increasingly incapable of defending the country against the stronger military might of the imperialist Western powers. And this new wave of evangelisation was supported by the gunboat diplomacy which so characterised Western dealings with the non-Western world of the time.

The first Protestant missionaries in China were the Dutch in Formosa, today's Taiwan, in the mid-seventeenth century. But their sojourn there was very short. The later missionaries were especially from Scotland. They were of pietistic or evangelical persuasion, and little interested in Chinese culture. They made few converts, but contributed to the translation of the Bible. An early pioneer in this area was the Presbyterian Robert Morrison, who landed in China in 1807.[13] Among the few Protestants interested in the problem of acculturation, James Legge, translator of the Chinese classics into English (1861–72), stood out. He reawakened the Terms controversy with his rendition of 'Lord-on-high' (*Shang-ti*) as 'God' in English, and his proposal that the reverse should be adopted in Christian translations of the Bible into Chinese. Eventually this did occur, so that Chinese Protestants today call on God as Lord-on-high while Catholics continue to invoke the Lord of Heaven.

A word may be added here about theological emphasis. Matteo Ricci and other Jesuits who favoured acculturation, had also been inclined to approve of the Confucian doctrine of human perfectibility with its implicit teaching of original human goodness. On account of the reverses they suffered in the rites and terms controversy, the situation changed rather drastically. The later Protestant missionaries were mainly of pietist persuasions, and emphasised divine grace and human depravity. We might characterise this as a hallmark of Christian evangelisation in general, which stood in opposition to mainstream Confucianism, and made the Christian religion less acceptable to educated Chinese.[14]

A Special Episode: The T'ai-p'ing Rebellion
An episode that lasted several decades was a Chinese rebellion with Christian overtones: that of the T'ai-p'ing or 'Heavenly Kingdom'. Its leader was the southerner Hung Hsiu-ch'üan, who had failed the state examinations, but learnt about Christianity from some tracts derived from Morrison's translation of the Bible. He and his Christian-influenced friends soon gathered a group of 10,000 people disaffected with the Manchu régime, called the 'Worshippers of God'. These turned against the imperial government in late 1850. The following year, Hung proclaimed himself Heavenly King, the younger brother, he claimed, of Jesus Christ, God's first-born. Military successes took the rebels to Nanking (Nanjing) in 1853. For a time, they were on the winning side, as the imperial forces continued to lose ground. But their iconoclastic attitudes toward traditional Chinese religions, including Confucianism, brought them the enmity of the educated gentry, who rallied to the dynastic cause and eventually, with the help of foreign (Western) military support, defeated the rebellion and repossessed Nanking in 1864.

It appears that diplomats and traders felt more comfortable dealing with the known establishment than with an unknown quantity. Yet the T'ai-p'ing rebels were undeniably Christian-influenced. They had planned to replace the Confucian classics with the Christian Bible in their examination system. But the question arises: 'Had the T'ai-p'ing rebellion been successful, could China have been converted to Christianity?' My own answer is: probably not.

The rebels' Christianity was what the twentieth century would call Protestant fundamentalism, with prohibitions against smoking, drinking and illicit sex, although some of the leaders exempted themselves from the general rule. With their foreign beliefs, they had a revolutionary vision for the country. But both the vision and their attempts to implement it were naïve. Interestingly, the Communist régime in mainland China has tended to look favourably at this historical interlude, seeing the T'ai-p'ing rebels as (kind of) predecessors to their own adventure. Their palace in Nanking is now a museum, and their printed propaganda of religious as well as political agenda may still be read.

Protestant missionaries would continue their activities with the help of treaty rights wrested from a government suffering many reverses. In the late nineteenth century, more enlightened missionaries like Timothy Richard renewed an effort of acculturation, and sought as well to make the missions self-supporting and self-managing. In 1900, however, Chinese Christianity suffered from the so-called Boxer Rebellion, which was a xenophobic anti-foreign effort manipulated by the Manchu empress dowager. This in turn led to a multinational Western invasion of China and the further weakening of the dynasty. Christians would be among those revolutionaries who sought to topple Manchu rule, and the greatest of these was Sun Yat-sen, leader of the Chinese Republican revolution (1911). Missionaries founded schools and universities, as well as hospitals, all over republican China in the early twentieth century. Their influence helped to modernise the country, spreading literacy and promoting more equality between the sexes.

But the modern effort of evangelising China proved once more to be only a wave. While it made various contributions to the country's modernisation, it also aroused criticism and opposition, both among the educated and among those belonging to the grass roots. At issue was the foreign character of the Christian religion, seen also as an ally of the Western powers. Besides, Chinese intellectuals (like Ch'en Tu-hsiu, the founder of the Communist Party) were searching for a political ideology to revive nationalist interests, and found

Christianity wanting in this respect. And the Communist takeover in 1949 effectively put an end to this period.[15]

3 Christianity under Communism

Chinese Communists are militant atheists, intent on controlling religion, and suspicious of religious believers. Their first move was to cut the ties between Chinese Christianity and the outside world. For the institutional churches, collaboration with the government has meant accepting the 'Three Self' principles (self-administration, self-finance, self-propaganda). Many mainline Protestant denominations accepted these principles rather quickly in the Three Self Movement (1951), although some more evangelical groups resisted. Catholics were harder hit, as they regarded the Roman pontiff as the head of their church. Those who collaborated with the government formed the Patriotic Association, sometimes called the 'Patriotic Church' which is not in communion with Rome.

With the devastating Cultural Revolution (1966–76), all religious organisations and activities went under, until it seemed as though China had no more religion. Red flags were placed over Christian churches in place of crosses, objects of veneration were removed from the premises and Bibles were burned. For the population at large, a new pseudo-liturgy was enforced as people paid respect to their Mao portraits in a quasi-religious manner. The political leader had become a living god, and the Little Red Book of his quotations a scripture.

However, when a new political leaf was turned, outsiders learned that worship had never ceased, as, for example, among Christians who had gone underground and held home services in cities and villages. Such activity remains proscribed by the régime, especially after the military crackdown on the Tian'anmen demonstrations of 1989. In 1982, the official figure put Catholics and Protestants at three million each. In 1992, unofficial figures put the total number of Christians in China at about thirty million, which would indicate a phenomenal growth under Communist rule. Officially, Protestants no longer have denominational cleavages. They now have many seminaries, including a prestigious Union Seminary in Nanking, and there are also many Catholic seminaries in operation, of which the best known is in Sheshan, outside Shanghai.[16] Since the Tian'anmen crackdown in 1989, the régime has imprisoned a number of 'underground' Catholic bishops and priests. The Chinese Church Research Center in Hongkong reports on the growth of underground Christian sects in China, many of which are evangelical Protestants preaching an apocalyptic Christianity seasoned with traditional Chinese beliefs in spirits and ghosts, and carry out faith-healing activities. Indeed, the interest in religion has even grown since the 1989 crackdown on the democracy movement, causing anxiety to the government, which is seeking to stem the tide of conversions not only to Christianity, but to all religions.[17]

4 Christianity in Korea and Japan

Christianity was also introduced into Korea and Japan. Korea has frequently been perceived as a country of conservative inclinations; yet the number of Christians has steadily risen, till in 1992 it was about twenty-five per cent of the total population. Even the growth in Taiwan and Hong Kong, and elsewhere among Chinese communities in Southeast Asia, cannot match this phenomenal upsurge. In Japan, on the other hand, except for the so-called Christian century (1550–1650), with mass conversions followed by severe persecutions, Christian missionaries have met with occasional curiosity and general indifference. The present proportion of Christians there is less than half of one per cent.[18]

Why such a difference regarding acceptance of Christianity in Korea and Japan? Some association may be made with the differences between shamanism as it is known in Korea, which favours a kind of monotheism, and Japanese Shinto, with its eight million gods. Possibly, the stronger Confucian influence in Korea has also been favourable to the development of Christianity, whereas the stronger Buddhist influence in Japan is more of a deterrent. And then, differences in national character can also be alleged between the Koreans and the Japanese.

The differences between Korea and Japan also leave us guessing regarding the future of Christianity in China: should there be no more official prohibitions or limitations? A better indication may be found in the relative openness of the Chinese population in Taiwan and Hong Kong as well as Singapore: their response has been more positive than the Japanese, and less enthusiastic than the Koreans.

Besides, the question may also be asked: what *differences* has Christianity, as a universal religion, made to Japan and Korea? In the case of the Second World War, the Japanese Christian churches, with some exceptions, rallied to the support of the government, perhaps all the more in their desire to prove their own patriotism, whereas the strongest opposition group, in spite of their numerical and political weakness, was the socialists.

The minority status of Christians in the various East Asian countries brings with it a concomitant feeling of insecurity. It is not known whether the post-war Japanese Christians have overcome this feeling. This appears less the case in Korea, where Christians are also prominent in the dissident movement. But this remains very true of the Christians in China today, who are sorely aware of the accusation levelled against them as being collaborators with 'cultural imperialists'. Judging from the recent upsurge in the number of conversions, however, the consciousness of cultural imperialism appears to be subsiding.

5 Christianity: A Foreign Religion in China

We may perceive a certain resemblance between the introduction of Buddhism and that of Christianity into China. In spite of their very basic doctrinal differences, each made immense proselytising efforts. The Buddhist missionaries came from nearer lands, and frequently, though not always, as invited teachers. Indeed, many Buddhist missionaries were invited to China because of the initial curiosity of the Chinese regarding the Indian religion. The Christian missionaries, however, invited themselves. They proselytised less to satisfy the curiosity of their hosts, and more to follow their own religious imperatives. Entering China in an age of Christian triumphalism, they were intent upon the task of saving souls that many believed to be otherwise destined for eternal damnation.[19]

It has been said that Christianity could learn from the Buddhist example of acculturation. This might be so, but the acculturation of Buddhism took many centuries, and risked the loss of the religion's identity. Moreover, sixteenth- and seventeenth-century China was not sixth- or seventh-century Gaul, which turned Christian in mass conversions, or even sixth-, seventh- or eighth-century Central Asia, which fell first for Buddhism, and later for Islam. As an ancient civilisation, China, like India, was difficult to penetrate. After sweeping across North Africa and westward into Persia, Islam could rule northern India but was unable to win over the majority of its Hindu population. As successors to the Mughals, the British Raj could bind India together with railroads and educate the upper classes in English, but had only a minuscule effect in extending the Christian religion in the subcontinent.

Communism remains the reigning ideology in mainland China

today, even after its recent fall in the erstwhile Soviet Union and its many republics. But, as we observe in the case of formerly Communist Eastern Europe, the demise of the ruling ideology was followed by a revival of the indigenous religion, that is, Christianity, alongside the introduction of capitalist market principles and modern values that are secular. In the Chinese case, my prediction about the future is that, with freedom of religion, Christianity should prosper, as should the native religious traditions. However, the acceptance of Christianity will be especially by those sectors of the population today that desire greater Westernisation. And as the country becomes more Westernised, secular values may very well supersede religious values.

Am I therefore predicting a grim future for religion in general in China? Not exactly. I shall elaborate the matter further toward the end of this book.

Part Three
The Legacy of Syncretism

12

The Vitality
of Syncretism: Popular
Religion

---

1   What is Popular Religion?

In this book, syncretism amounts to a nebulous affair between indigenous traditions and foreign intrusions, with progeny that are not always easy to identify. Chinese Buddhism is obviously a product of syncretism. Taoism shows the imprint of heavy Buddhist influence, yet it remains somehow native. Neo-Confucian philosophy would not have appeared in the form it did were it not for Buddhist stimulus, even if it defined itself in opposition to both Buddhism and Taoism. Syncretism, I would maintain, that is historical interaction and mixture, has been at work in all the world's religions. It has moulded Christianity just as it has moulded Buddhism. However, to the extent that Chinese religions are themselves 'religions of harmony', they have permitted more latitude to the workings of syncretism than have the more exclusivist Western religions, including Christianity and Islam. For this reason, an earlier popular religion has largely been suppressed in Christianised lands.

Popular religion has a history, although its past is less studied than that of the more institutionalised and 'established' traditions. It also has a present, which is an important proof of its continued survival and vitality. And this vitality is also an index that it has a future. Chinese popular religion includes beliefs and practices that are still part of Chinese life among ethnic Chinese communities everywhere. This means Taiwan, Hong Kong, Singapore, Southeast Asia and beyond. This also means mainland China, to the extent that the official tolerance for religious manifestations has permitted the re-emergence of such expressions that have been derogated as 'superstitions'.

Popular religion crosses the lines of demarcation between Confucianism, Taoism and Buddhism. There is no single sacred text or set of documents that can speak for it. Instead, its basic ideas and values coincide with those that pervade the culture as a whole, with particular relevance to human concerns for personal and communal survival in a sometimes harsh world. The belief is shared, between popular religion and the mainstream Confucianism and Taoism, that somehow the spirits have power over this life and yet require sustenance from those who are alive. Thus, offerings and promises are made to the superior powers for help in return, and offerings may be withheld if help is not forthcoming. In their own turn, the 'ghosts' may harass the living by blackmail, and so demand propitiation.[1]

Traditionally, popular beliefs and practices are organised along *yin* and *yang* lines. The realm of *yang* refers to relations with the deities, while the realm of *yin* refers to relations with the dead – that is, those who have not been deified. After all, many, perhaps most, of the spirits or deities (*shen*) in popular religion are human beings rewarded with deification for their virtuous lives on earth. Usually, their spirit status has been verified by the manifestation of miraculous powers.

We see here a parallel to Christian sainthood, especially as this is recognised in institutional Catholicism. In Chinese popular religion, the process is less cumbersome, without a required number of certified miracles on the part of the being to be deified. Frequently, the deification occurs by popular consensus, although historically this was usually confirmed by imperial authority, thus revealing a continued 'Cesaro-papist' character of kingship. Besides, a majority of those deified come from among ordinary, lay people, rather than from among the monastic orders of Buddhism or Taoism. Sometimes, the deified were influential persons on earth, often former bureaucrats or officials in the secular realm. In any case, deification in these circumstances parallel the 'canonisation' of saints, and the gods have limited, often carefully defined powers.

2   The Legacy of the Past

Much of religious ritual and practice on the popular level reminds us of the religion of antiquity, even if forms have changed and religious concerns appear now more peripheral to social priorities. Divination is still practised; shamanism is also important, although the sacrificial offerings are only made now of fruits and cooked foods. And the ecstatic union between human beings and the gods or spirits, so much a part of ancient religion, has contributed to the philosophical ideal of harmony between the human and the divine (or the 'natural'), that became part and parcel of Confucian and Taoist humanism.

This does not mean that popular religion should be traced directly from ancient religion itself. The legacy is never direct or immediate, and the transmission is difficult to identify. There are, besides, many elements that can be historically verified as having come down from various periods – such as through the development of Buddhism or Taoism.[2]

Spirit Mediums in Popular Religion

The quotation below comes from one of the invocations used to call for a spirit in a Chinese spirit-medium cult in Singapore, that city-state on the Equator where the majority population is ethnic Chinese:

> He who shakes the Heavens comes from the west riding on a tiger and a dragon, bearing a holy seal . . . . Your voice like thunder makes the *shen* (spirits) and devils tremble . . . . You can save a myriad of people. Now we invite you . . . to come before this altar. With your sword you can kill evil spirits . . . . Wake, wake, and save us.[3]

In Singapore the male spirit-mediums are called *tang-ki* (or *dang-ki*) (Hokkien dialect, literally, 'divining youth'), not necessarily because they are young, but rather because they are not expected to live long. Such a person is subject to involuntary possession by one or more spirits, and serves as a medium for those who desire to seek out the will of the spirits as regards them. The trances vary with the importance of the occasion. The following is a description of what occurred in a spirit-medium temple:

> First there is a gentle quivering of the limbs, which rapidly becomes stronger. Soon, the *dang-ki's* whole body sways and his head begins to swing round in circles. This may go on for two or more minutes, becoming faster and faster all the time. [His hair, which is usually left very long, flies in all directions, and his neck appears to be at impossible angles . . . . As the drums rise to a crescendo, he staggers to his feet . . . . He slobbers at the mouth

and rolls his head . . . . He prances around on his toes, stagger-
ing from side to side and muttering strange sounds . . . . It is
now that he cuts his tongue with his sword, or . . . sticks spikes
through his cheeks, hits himself with a prick-ball, or climbs a
sword-ladder.[4]

Feats of self-mortification are followed by sessions in personal
consultations. These involved the presentation by worshippers of
charm papers and amulets, or the stamping of clothing and household ornaments with blood marks, or the interpretation of 'speaking
in tongues'. Eventually, the *dang-ki* makes some final gesticulations.
He leaps into the air, is caught apparently unconscious in the arms of
an assistant, and must be revived by having charm water splashed
into his face.

The *dang-ki* and what they represent do violence also to those
among us accustomed to the comfortable idea that the Chinese
are always moderate and reasonable. Among other things, these
divining youths flout Confucian customs by deliberately causing
self-injury in public performances. This can only be understood in
terms of their being instruments of higher powers, cut off from
the world of ordinary mortals.[5] They rather call to mind those
Christian saints and miracle-workers who performed extreme acts
of asceticism.

There are more private or semi-private seances, often involving
communications with the recently deceased, and usually through
female mediums. Ecstatic or trance behaviour takes place here too,
as the medium prays for assistance to seek out a specific soul.[6]

Divination and Geomancy
Divination is a widespread practice in popular religion. We made
passing reference to it in describing the *tang-ki* as 'divining youth'.
There are also more mechanical ways of divining. A common act
in Taiwan is the use of 'divination blocks' – two pieces of wood,
rounded on one side and flat on the other, cut into the shape of a
crescent moon, mirror images each of the other. When dropped on
the floor, the combinations of positions indicate responses from the
deity. Sometimes, these are used in conjunction with joss-sticks. For
even more elaborate questions, people may use divination verses in
temples. First they take out a numbered slip from a vase, to which
corresponds a verse of four lines, usually rather cryptic words
with added explanations. Such usage is widely found, also among
overseas Chinese. It is now being revived in mainland China.

This brings us to the subject of 'spirit writing' (*fu-chi/fuji*), a ritual which has been traced back to the Sung dynasty. Today, these revelations contain a diverse lot, ranging from housekeeping procedures and liturgical instructions through moralistic verses and commentary on the classics, to rarer but elaborate mythological explorations of Heaven and Hell.[7]

A popular divinatory practice that has received widespread attention is geomancy (*feng-shui*, literally, 'wind and water'). An ancient practice, it was earlier applied especially to the selection of burial sites. Today, the *feng-shui* specialist is also consulted in the selection of sites for the living and all their activities, in the construction of office-towers, banks and hotels in Hong Kong, Taiwan and beyond. He works with the geomancer's or astrological compass, an instrument with a magnetic compass at the centre of a disc inscribed with concentric circles and the symbols of *yin* and *yang* and the eight trigrams. *Yin* is called 'white tiger' referring to the west, and *yang* 'azure dragon' referring to the east.

The azure dragon must always be to the left, the white tiger to the right of any place supposed to contain a luck-bringing site . . . . In other words, in the angle formed by dragon and tiger, in the very point where the two (magnetic) currents . . . cross each other, there may the luck-bring site . . . be found.[8]

The various forms of Chinese divination are arousing increasing interest in the West, where astrology remains the most popular pseudo-science. While the New Testament approves of dreams as a means of predicting the future (as in the case of the angel instructing Joseph regarding the child Jesus), the Acts of the Apostles forbids sorcery. On balance, we may say that the central place given to divination in popular Chinese religion marks its distinctive difference from institutional Christianity.

3   Gods, Ancestors and Ghosts

The vitality of popular religion is reflected by the abundance and prosperity of temples and shrines in a region like Taiwan. After all, what are temples and shrines if not the supposed earthly palaces of the deities and spirits? Frequently, the Chinese temple is the only architectural structure in a town or village that still follows the traditional style of roofs with curved eaves. It is built along a north-south axis, with the deity facing south like a ruler or emperor in his palace. The entrance way is usually a triple gate. Large temples rest in walled compounds with many courtyards surrounded by long halls with individual rooms and centering on a main structure housing the image of the deities. Temples are very visible structures when they are well maintained, since the Chinese prefer strong colours like green roof tiles and red pillars even for their holy places. Statues of deities, especially of Buddha-figures, are often gilded. Indeed, there are so many temples, even in Communist China today, that one wonders how the Chinese could ever have been described as an irreligious people. Shrines are miniature temples, the dwellings of more humble deities like the local earth god.

Administratively, Chinese temples are usually independent of one another, maintained by the local communities. These may or may not have the services of a resident priest. But there are priests or other religious functionaries, like spirit mediums, who visit there and render services there, especially on big occasions. Usually, temples are open to the public, who crowd in during festival times, such as on the birthdays of the gods. And, just as in Europe, these feasts are occasions as well for celebrations, processions, and even dramatic performances.[9]

The Domestic Deities

The gods of popular religion often overlap with those of traditional religion, including Taoism and even Buddhism. 'Lord Heaven' and 'Jade Emperor', for example, are the popular names for the supreme deity, names obviously taken over from ancient religion or Confucianism, and from Taoism. But he is regarded as too high, too remote, for most people, who only dare to approach him through other intercessory powers. Fortunately, the pantheon also embraces many others, some of whom have special influence in certain regions. In rural Taiwan, it has been observed that traditional families burn three sticks of incense mornings and evenings.[10]

The stove god (or the kitchen god) goes back to time immemorial, perhaps the eighth century B.C., and his cult used to be found all over China. Indeed, its survival to our own times is testimony to the continuity of Chinese religion. The stove god's presence is actually more like that of a policeman sent from on high to watch over the behaviour of the family and its members, on each of whom he makes a report at the end of the year, submitted to Lord Heaven or the Jade

Emperor, i.e., the supreme deity. This offers as well an example of the bureaucratisation of religion, since the world beyond is a mirror image of traditional society, with an emperor above, ruling over officials who in turn rule over the commoners.

Another deity with a widespread cult is the *t'u-ti kung/tudigong*, literally, an 'earth god'. Tablets marked with his name are found in many places, urban and rural, even in overseas communities. His role is to protect the living from dangerous, wandering ghosts, while keeping a watch over the behaviour of those he protects. He too, reports on them to a higher authority, usually the city god. There are those who ask his permission to build a new house or demolish an old one. Often the family's ancestral altar has the stove god in the lower left-hand corner and the earth god on the lower right-hand corner. The city god, on the other hand, governs all the spirits in a major administrative district.[11]

In the mid- and late 1980s, with the mini-revival of religious life in Communist China, many households pasted images of 'door gods' outside. These are renewed at New Year, much as wreaths are hung on doors at Christmas in the West. These deities are martial figures protecting the household. Historically, they go back to three generals in the service of the second T'ang emperor, guarding his quarters to assure a peaceful night to an insomniac ruler pursued by dreadful spirits. Usually, two of them decorate the front door, and a third guards the back door. Frequently, the inside of the external door is decorated with yet another portrait: that of the god of wealth, either as a civil official or as a martial figure – that of the famous Kuan Yü, also called Kuan Kung, a hero of the Three Kingdoms period (3rd century A.D.)[12]

Three popular images in the home make up the trio known as *Fu Lu Shou*, literally, happiness, high emolument (i.e., success) and longevity. Happiness (Fu) is the tallest figure, with a long, dark beard who stands majestically in the middle, with a boy in front. High Emolument is on his right, also holding an infant. Longevity is on his left, a somewhat shrivelled old man with a long, white beard, holding a peach in one hand. The trio are also stars in the Great Dipper, with Longevity sometimes identified with the Pole Star. All represent historical figures as well, and their portraits decorate the house especially at New Year. But veneration of these (as with the Taoist Immortals) is more folkloric than religious, as their presence often serves artistic purposes more than devotion.[13] Recently, it has been reported that portraits of the deceased Mao Zedong have become icons in many peasant homes during the Chinese New Year festival, presumably to protect the households from floods and disasters. Taxi-drivers in the southern city of Canton (Guangzhou) also carry small Mao portraits as a protection through the increasingly dangerous traffic.[14] We see here, then, a possible deification process in popular consciousness. For many people, a powerful figure like Mao should continue to exercise power after death. Moreover, he *was* already worshipped as a god during his lifetime. The worshippers happen also to be people far removed from the actual reins of power as well as from real acquaintance of Mao as a human being.

A Higher Bureaucracy

The city god is represented as a higher bureaucrat in the robes of a scholar-official. Presumably, he lords over the local earth gods. He is traditionally named by the imperial government from among deceased notables. The city god of Shanghai, for example, was a high scholar-official called Ch'in Yü-po, who was honoured by the founder of the Ming dynasty.[15]

The various deities have the custom of inspecting the regions they govern. Thus there are processions in which the statue of the city god is carried around the city's borders and the local earth god does the same thing for his neighbourhood. They are usually preceded by noisy bands and by firecrackers. By that same token, the gods' powers are not infinite, but carefully defined.[16]

'Holy Mother in Heaven'

A deity of special importance in Taiwan and Fukien is the female Ma-tsu, the Hokkien dialect's expression for 'grandma'. Allegedly, the historical figure was born on an island off the Fukien coast and died young. She is credited with having saved her father and brother when their fishermen's boat collapsed, and commands much loyalty among the fisherfolk.

Ma-tsu's title of 'Holy Mother in Heaven' makes of her a near parallel to the Virgin Mary. This comes not only from a title given from below, that is, from the folk who venerate her, but also from above, since she was named by the emperor (1683) as 'Consort of Heaven'. This is an interesting instance of how earthly emperors considered themselves to have authority over spirits of the deceased, even giving a virgin consort to Lord Heaven himself! Indeed, Chinese deities are made such by emperors. As deities, they are highly anthropomorphic, and reflect the society which offers them worship. Ironically, that society today still represents their deities in the traditional mould as bureaucrats in a celestial empire where power is delegated from above.

Ancestors and Other Ghosts

The domestic altar is a place where ancestral spirits are remembered. It is usually a large table holding ancestral tablets, whether of wood or on paper, venerating the deceased ancestors, male and female. Today, photographs are sometimes placed there, when tablets are absent. Incense is offered, usually every morning, by the woman of the house. On the same table, one may sometimes find a statue of Kuan-yin, and another of the deified Kuan Kung. Most commonly, food offerings are made on special occasions, such as on death anniversaries with communal meals to follow, either at home or in a restaurant. From the ancestors, one asks for blessings and fears punishments. Occasionally, offerings are made of imitation paper money, even paper houses with appropriate furnishings and servants, as well as clothing. These are usually burnt in outdoor rituals.[17]

One class of spirits in Chinese popular religion resembles the Hindu and Buddhist *preta* or 'hungry ghosts' from which they are derived. In Hindu or Buddhist religion, they suffer deprivation as punishment for avariciousness in life. In Chinese popular beliefs, these frustrated and sometimes angry ghosts often require solace and appeasement. They are rather spirits who have no living relative to care for them, and may turn vicious to get attention and offerings. They may be victims of violence, spirits of unmarried women and children who died before they completed a natural life span, and who are not included in the normal domestic cult, or just abandoned spirits.[18] The common fear of these ghosts resembles in large measure the fear in the West of ghosts and spirits, as manifest still in customs surrounding Halloween.

4 Popular Religion and the Great Traditions

A criticism levelled against popular religion is its utilitarian thrust, its preoccupation with *quid pro quo*. While I do not deny this fact, I emphasise that this is true of popular religious devotion everywhere, including in popular Christianity, where most prayers are implorations. Besides, popular religion does not exclude thanksgiving or propitiation, and serves as an efficient vehicle of moral education.

The Moral Influence of Confucianism

The Confucian impact is especially through moral instructions of filial piety, loyalty to country and emperor, fairness in work and trade, concern and compassion for fellow human beings. Filial piety is usually extended to the observance of the ancestral cult, and veneration of ancestors is also a means for procuring more descendants. Confucianism has also influenced both Taoism and Buddhism, making it filially pious, for example, for those monks who entered the monastery to fulfil a parent's vow. Both directly and through these other traditions, it influences popular religiosity, supporting the widespread belief in moral retribution.

Confucian influence has been exercised especially through the family. Family expectations have generally urged the children to work or study hard, and to behave according to the rules of propriety. This has been supported as well by the state, with its own emphasis on political loyalty and civil obedience. Popular sects are also known to call themselves Confucian. In Taiwan, we have the 'Confucian-lineage spirit-religion' (*Ju-tsung shen-chiao/ruzong shenjiao*) which was introduced from the mainland. It is a salvation religion with shamanic features, honouring, among other figures, the Taoist Jade Emperor and the divinised Kuan Kung. Its scriptures are regarded as revealed from on high, sometimes through a form of 'spirit writing' with a heavenly bird as medium.[19]

The Religious Consolations of Buddhism

Several Buddha and Bodhisattva figures are prominent in the popular cult. These include the historical Buddha himself, and Omitofo (Amitābha), the Buddha of the Pure Land, the future Buddha Mi-lo (Maitreya), sometimes called the Laughing Buddha, as well as the famous female figure, the *p'u-sa* Kuan-yin. The order of popularity does not follow the order of priority within Buddhism. Kuan-yin, the female Bodhisattva, ranks ahead of Mi-lo, of Omitofo, and of the historical Buddha in popular devotion.[20] Among the healing figures, there is the Healing Buddha, called Yao-shih.

Buddhism has exercised political influence over people discontented with the government. Popular or sectarian forms of Buddhism have historically given rise to rebellions. The one that led to the founding of the Ming dynasty was inspired by the millenarian cult to Mi-lo as the Buddha of the Future. Historically, this was especially associated with the White Lotus society of the mid-twelfth century, which began as an association of clergy and laymen, devoted to attaining rebirth in the Pure Land,

and committed to vegetarianism, abstinence from wine and killing. In the late fourteenth century, followers of such a group, together apparently with Manichaeans and others, turned against the Mongol government in rebellion. They fought under the aegis of a Prince of Light (*ming-wang*), identified with Mi-lo or the Buddha of the Future. The title was given to their early leaders, the father and son of the surname Han. But the movement was taken over by the man who eventually founded the Ming dynasty.[21]

Taoist Saints: The Eight Immortals
An interesting group of Taoist 'saints' which has influenced folklore and art are the Eight Immortals, all allegedly historical individuals who collectively signify happiness. Interestingly, these include men and women of different ages and stations in life, representing a 'democratic' instinct in Chinese religion in general and its universal soteriological concern in particular. The appeal (again like that of Christian saints) is therefore to a variety of people. Among them are the crippled Li holding an iron crutch and the patron of pharmacists; the imperial relative Tsao, a military commander and the patron of actors; the seemingly androgynous Lan, formerly a street singer and now patron of florists; the fairy maid Ho, daughter of a store-keeper; Chung Li-ch'üan, a stout man holding a peach in one hand and a feather fan in the other; Old Man Chang carrying a fish drum; the famous Lü Tung-pin, carrying a sabre and a fly-whisk; and his disciple, the lad Han, carrying a basket of flowers and a jade flute, a patron of musicians.[22]

5 Is Taoism also Popular Religion?

Popular religion honours Taoist deities or 'saints', and is often practised with the help of Taoist priests on festivals such as the lunar New Year. They serve the interests of the faithful by the performance of a variety of rituals, and also as exorcists against the unwanted harmful ghosts. In these capacities, the Taoist clergy is regarded as having qualifications superior to the other mediums and shamans who have had no rigorous training and can claim no prestigious lineage. But Taoist religion is not the whole of popular religion. After all, the latter includes also many Buddhist beliefs and practices, some of which (but not all) had been incorporated into the Taoist system. Neither should the Taoist religion be identified with the ancestral cult, which can also be traced to the earliest times, but which, while being an ancient tradition, shares bonds with both Confucianism and Taoism.[23]

The lines of distinction between Taoism and popular religion may continue to blur. In the future, there may be only one Chinese religion – a highly syncretised form of popular religion, incorporating elements not only from Taoism, Buddhism and Confucianism, but also from Christianity. It will cater especially to the grass-roots population, although it will not leave untouched the better educated, the mostly secularised élite.

Buddho–Taoist Mythology: Chinese Hells

Whereas Taoism is more concerned with life on earth, Buddhism is more concerned with life after death. It comes as no surprise that popular beliefs in rewards and punishments that come after life bear Buddhist influences. Also, the well-known Chinese hells are derived from Buddhist beliefs even if they have also become part and parcel of Taoism, with Taoist priests hanging scrolls depicting the hell scenes during funeral services.[24]

Although the figure may vary, Chinese hells are usually said to be ten in number. They are sometimes said to be situated under a high mountain in Szechuan, in south-west China. Each is ruled by a king serving as judge, surrounded by ministers and attendants who implement his decisions. In these hells, justice is impartially meted out and punishments are usually described as corporal, doled out with the assistance of torture instruments. Supposedly, the soul of the deceased goes through the series of hells until it is ready for rebirth. Thus Chinese hells are not final, and bear more resemblance to the Catholic purgatory. Like Catholic beliefs, offerings and prayers for the dead can mitigate punishments.

Morality and Retribution: The T'ai-shang kan-ying p'ien

The *T'ai-shang kan-ying p'ien* has been translated as *The Treatise of the Great Exalted One on Response and Retribution* by the Japanese scholar Daisetz Suzuki – and, we may add: as Revealed by the Supreme [Lord Lao], i.e., the divinised Lao-tzu. It appears to have emerged from Taoist circles that venerate the *T'ai-p'ing ching* (Classic of Great Peace), and belongs to the Taoist Canon. Through its popularisation of traditional religious ethics, it has exercised widespread influence over the centuries.[25]

The basic belief of this text is in a superior power who watches over the behaviour of all, to reward good and punish evil by controlling the people's life-span. Accordingly, human beings are responsible for their own good or bad fortune, as each deed, good or bad, will have its retribution, which comes with the judgement of the superior power, the *shen* in charge of the life-span.

But how does the superior power attain detailed knowledge of people's behaviour? And how is such record kept? The text speaks of gods that reside in the human body, especially of astral deities, in particular that identified to the Polar Star, who also resides in the human head and keeps a record of good and bad deeds. There are also others, such as those residing in the abdomen, who control the human life-span. And, external to the human body, there is the stove god, always keeping silent watch over the household.

6   The Vitality of Syncretism: Popular Religion Today

The Three-in-One Religion

An interesting example of syncretism from the historic past comes from the sixteenth-century thinker Lin Chao-en (1517–98), who also became a religious leader, the founder of the 'Three-in-One' religion. After a personal quest that directed him to both Taoism and Buddhism, Lin returned to Confucianism only to merge the three teachings into a new sect which he taught to enthusiastic followers. His focus was basically a spirituality centred on the cultivation of the mind – the mind common to Confucius, Lao-tzu, and the Buddha. This is done with the assistance of inner alchemy or a meditation coordinating both body and mind and directing the self to a higher consciousness. His goal was both spiritual restoration and physical healing. His religion attracted followers from all three traditions, who were urged to make vows to Heaven, clearly committing themselves to the fulfilment of the teachings of their own tradition, while guarding them from the excesses of that tradition. It was also an effort to personalise the relationship of human beings to Heaven. Indeed, it was a courageous move in a country where only the emperor as Son of Heaven had the prerogative of worshipping Heaven, where ordinary citizens only dared address themselves to the minor deities of the city, the locality, or the household. Lin's teachings were banned as a heresy by the late Ming government, which burnt his books and temples.[26]

In spite of severe proscriptions, Lin's religion is still alive as a continuing tradition. Apparently, it spread widely on the southern coast and also to Taiwan, where it survived the Japanese occupation. It is still popularly known as the Three-in-One religion. According to a book published in 1988, there are seven temples in Taiwan where incense is offered to Confucius, Lao-tzu, the Buddha, as well as the religion's founder.[27] We are told also of a new sect, duly registered in 1982, that publicly venerates five figures, including Jesus Christ and Muhammad as well as Confucius, Lao-tzu and the Buddha. It is dedicated to the promulgation of all their virtues, i.e., loyalty and reciprocity, compassion, the natural, universal love, and the pure and true.[28]

The 'Pervading Unity' Sect: I-kuan tao

The I-kuan tao (Yiguandao) demonstrates how popular religion represents the ultimate expression of syncretism. Literally, the term refers to the 'Unifying Tao', and it is sometimes translated simply as 'Unity Sect'. This is an ethical society devoted to the salvation of its members and of all humankind. It claims to embrace Taoist, Buddhist and Confucian teachings as well as the cult of the Eternal Mother, of which more will be said later. It has a very large following. Believers engage in chanting ritual and meditation, participate in scriptural studies, including those of morality books, do T'ai-chi or *ch'i-kung* exercises and abstain from meat.

As the sect was banned for a long time, little is known for certain. It claims to go back to time immemorial through a kind of apostolic succession. But some scholars think that it was founded in North China in the nineteenth century. In any case, it has maintained a tradition going back to the sixteenth century, in late Ming times, when religious syncretism between Confucianism, Taoism and Buddhism was strongly advocated. As an underground religion, it first survived the Japanese occupation of much of China, and then thrived in Taiwan after the war. Membership was through secret initiation at the sect's temples. After many persecutions, the sect emerged above ground and gained legal status in the mid-1980s.

The syncretistic character of the Unity sect is also reflected in its texts. These include 'spirit writing' tracts or scriptural texts borrowed from Confucianism, Taoism and Buddhism as well as from other small sects, dealing with doctrine, ritual, and the important issue of lineage or apostolic succession. Part of its claim is parallel to that of the Neo-Confucian thinkers: that the proper transmission of ancient doctrine, coming down from time immemorial, through both Confucius and Lao-tzu, ceased with the death of Mencius. But it then maintains that this Tao blended with Buddhism in the West (i.e., India), and proceeded through Ch'an in China, to the Sixth Patriarch, Hui-neng. After him it was once again lost, to be recovered by the 'common people' who received his teachings and managed to continue the transmission.[29]

7 The Role of the Female in Popular Religion

The role of the female appears more dominant in popular religious manifestations. We have spoken of the universal importance of the Buddhist 'goddess of mercy' Kuan-yin, and of the particular devotion of fisherfolk to their virgin 'grandmother' Ma-tsu. There is also the mother-goddess Wu-sheng Lao-mu, the 'Eternal Mother', sometimes called Golden Mother – a creator as well as saviour figure. The Eternal Mother reflects the Taoist penchant for venerating an uncreated Tao, later personified as a deity. She had connections with the secret Buddhist group, the White Lotus society. She was also worshipped by a popular sect founded by Lo Ch'ing (d. 1527). Her cult is central to many sects in Taiwan, including the Confucian spirit-religion as well as the I-kuan tao, and the related Hsien-t'ien tao (*Xiantian dao*, literally, 'the Way that is Prior to Heaven') found in Singapore. They rank her higher than the Jade Emperor, or the Maitreya Buddha.[30]

According to this belief, she first created the world, and then engendered human beings, who are her children. Their misbehaviour and contention, however, has brought her grief. With great compassion, she continues to send messages to them through inspired leaders and revealed books, calling on them to recover their true natures and return home. To quote from an I-kuan tao text:

> [Mother], thinking of her children with great pain and limitless sorrow, from the cool native land of utmost bliss has sent all the immortals and Buddhas to save the imperial [children] . . . . She sighs that they are lost . . . and in pity has descended in person to save the world, sending down from on high books written in [her] blood in many thousands of words.[31]

There is an echo here of known Christian teachings, including the parable of the vineyard (Matt. 21:33–40) and Hebrews 1:2. The Eternal Mother is even honoured with the title *Shang-ti* (Lord-on-high or Emperor-on-high). As a female figure, she is interestingly not just a mediator (as with Kuan-yin or Ma-tsu), but the supreme deity. Ironically, she offers conservative moral teachings, including female submission to male dominance in the family.[32]

8 Conclusion

More than any of the other traditions, popular religion represents the survival of the native traditions as well as the fruitful union of the native and the foreign. That is because popular religion has less need to defend its own orthodoxy. It is less self-conscious, we may say. For by 'popular religion' we are referring to religious beliefs and rituals on an unsophisticated level together with their implied beliefs and theories which have never been entirely assimilated into the doctrinal systems of institutional Confucianism, Taoism or Buddhism. In other words, popular religion represents an amorphous mass of accumulated tradition from the past as well as the surviving – sometimes thriving – beliefs and practices of the present. In fact – and except for its shamanic aspects – popular religion (like Pure Land Buddhism and religious Taoism) bears structural similarities to the Christian religion, especially the Roman Catholic faith as this is practised in such places as Latin America or the Philippines.[33] As we reflect upon the past and look at the present, we may well come to the conclusion that popular religion will also be the religion of the future.[34]

13

The Future of Chinese Religions

1 The Question

We pose here the question of what future religion has in China. But an answer to this question cannot be offered until other questions are resolved. These include questions about the legacy of the past as well as about the present situation. And these questions are all the more important as the situation in today's China so contradicts the postulate we have given about harmony and harmonisation. First: to what extent has Chinese culture actually succeeded in harmonising ideas and ideals, beliefs and customs, that have been widely divergent? Second: why has China as a country espoused the radical dialectic of Communism (including class struggle and militant atheism) in the twentieth century, when the historical culture has usually shown a preference for moderation, and for the harmony of opposites? And then: given yesterday's history and today's reality, what will tomorrow be like? Is there a future for religion – and for what *kind* of religion?

2 The Success of Harmony

We have spoken of *three* Chinese religions: Confucianism, the 'moral' and 'ritual' religion, Taoism, the 'theistic' or even 'polytheistic' and 'alchemical' religion, and Buddhism, the 'devotional' and 'mystical' religion. And we have briefly discussed the situation of popular religion as a manifestation of the vitality of syncretism.

However, are there really three principal religions in China? Here we need to keep in mind the entire heritage of Chinese culture, from which the religions cannot be separated. This inseparability between religion and culture has led many to the conclusion that the Chinese have no religiosity of their own. But it also explains

221

why much common ground can be found among the religions of China. To the extent that Confucianism and Taoism came out of the same spiritual roots, sharing in certain beliefs, rituals and values, one may speak here of *one* Chinese religion, but with multiple forms of expression. But this cannot include Buddhism, even when Buddhism has influenced so much the religiosity of the people. For this and other reasons, we have considered Buddhism as a religion of foreign origin.

The question of religion or religions is useful for recalling to mind the *shared* heritage called Chinese culture, which is inseparable from the religion(s), whether these be Confucianism, Taoism, or Buddhism. It also accounts for much that is common among the religions themselves, and for the phenomenon called popular religion. But we should not forget the existence of other traditions like Islam and Christianity in Chinese history and society, which have never been totally absorbed by the native culture. For the sake of clarity, we have opted for the plural, 'religions', in this book. Nevertheless, we are aware of a continuing process of syncretism among the traditions, both in the past and still taking place. We also realise that a Confucianism without rituals and a Taoism with a diminishing clergy are each becoming more muted in their current expression.

It is perhaps to be expected that the ruling dynasties of native origin would tend to favour Confucianism (and Taoism), whereas those of alien or mixed backgrounds offered more protection to Buddhism. Taoism and Buddhism offered a sense of escape and consolation during times of disunity, whereas Confucianism contributed more directly to social and political cohesion during times of national unity. The 'three religions' actually complemented one another, since they attended to different areas of human concern. During and after the Ming dynasty and until today, they converged in a syncretistic pattern; and Confucius, Lao-tzu and the Buddha have sometimes been linked in veneration and worship.

True, there was rivalry, even acrimony, among these three traditions, and yet it appeared that they were usually able to coexist and complement one another. We see here a spirit of harmony and reconciliation which, when compared to religious developments in the West (or the Middle East), is perhaps most characteristic of traditional Chinese culture – a harmony of parts within a whole, in which each religion serves a socially useful function. In Confucianism, such harmony has been directed to human social relationships; in Taoist *philosophy*, it has been turned to man's relationship with the rest of nature. Taoist *religion* presents a difficulty, since the desire for physical immortality prompted proto-scientific experiments in exploitation of nature, consciously undertaken *against* the spirit of harmony, to wrest from nature its precious secrets of life and longevity. In the case of Buddhism, the tradition offered an entirely new outlook on life and the world, only to become itself conditioned by the pervading Chinese culture. It filled a certain spiritual vacuum, by addressing questions largely ignored by both Confucianism and Taoism.

Even outside any particular syncretistic cult, many Chinese have found it possible to follow all three teachings at the same time. For example, a man could be a Confucian in his active life, responding to multiple social responsibilities, a *philosophical* Taoist in his leisure hours, reading poetry and enjoying nature and wine, while also practicing some health regimen associated with *religious* Taoism, and both he and his wife – or at least, she – would frequent the Buddhist temple to offer prayers for special intentions. The coexistence of all three religious traditions, and the possibility for the same people to be involved in all of them, testifies to a certain pluralism within the Chinese – and the East Asian – civilisation, a pluralism that was hardly known by Europe and the Middle East.

3   The Limitations of Harmony

Nevertheless, while contemplating the whole terrain of Chinese religions, I find myself drawn deeper and deeper beneath a rhetoric of harmony to a divergence of ideas and beliefs about human existence and its meaning. I detect certain fundamental shifts in the constellation of such ideas and beliefs. The first came between the Shang and the Chou times, contrasting an older religion of divination and shamanism with a newer humanism that distances itself from religion. The Han times represent synthesis and consolidation, while looking forward to a new shift – that involving the entry of Buddhism into the country. Another process of synthesis and consolidation followed, until our own times, with the introduction of Western thought and influence and the unparalleled consequences these have introduced.

Perhaps I might present a very different paradigm for understanding China's religious past and tumultous present – one borrowed from Goethe's *Faust*, a work that is said to show Chinese influence. In it, Dr. Faust, the hero, admits that two souls dwell within his breast, the one fain to separate itself from the other, thus echoing St. Paul's words: 'For I do not do the good I want, but the evil I do not want is what I do' (Rom. 7:19).

While prescinding from the moral choice that the above references imply, we may first assert that the Chinese soul is not that different from that of the Westerner, allegedly represented by both St. Paul and Dr. Faust – and in the latter case, being torn not only between good and evil, but also between the known limitations of the human condition and the call of the unknown, of dangerous adventure. The Chinese soul also desires both the ideals of goodness offered by Confucianism and the promises of immortality offered by religious Taoism. Within Taoism itself, the Chinese soul appears at times torn between harmony with nature (Taoist philosophy) and wrestling with nature (Taoist alchemy). And the Chinese soul finds fascinating the foreign world of beliefs that Buddhism offered, while wanting to keep the native ideas which are often diametrically opposed to those of alien origins.

True, the happy harmony of traditional Chinese society existed more as an ideal than as fact. Among other factors, the three major teachings were never the *only* religious traditions in China. As we have seen, the country has also known Islam and Christianity, although the adherents of these *Western* religions have always been a minority in the population, and Muslims have usually come from specific ethnic groups, refraining from making converts from the majority. In more recent times, China faced the onslaught of Western intrusions, both political and cultural. This has been a most severe test for the Chinese soul, and the occasion for a long period of self-doubt and self-criticism which has not yet ended. As traditional society found itself in the process of disintegration, Western ideas and beliefs were introduced – of religion as well as of science and government. The Chinese dilemma has been how to modernise *without* losing a cultural identity and a rich heritage, and how to distinguish between Western rationality and credulity, their excesses and limitations.

In this regard, Westerners have frequently commented on the lack of rational argumentation in the Chinese tradition – including the absence of arguments on questions such as God's existence and human freedom, and so on. On their part, Chinese intellectuals have wondered at Western beliefs as the Trinity, the virgin birth, and Resurrection, as being contrary to reason.

In the ensuing struggle, as we know, a particular Western ideology, that of Marxism, would emerge victorious and would combat traditional religious values, considered as outmoded and feudal forces keeping the country backward, as well as combatting the more recently introduced Christian religion, considered an ally of Western political and cultural imperialism. It appears as if Faustian man has taken over the destiny of Chinese culture, throwing caution to the winds, and ignoring ancestral advice on reconciliation and harmony.

4 Marxism and Chinese Religions

What happened to religion after the Communist victory in 1949? The Constitution of 1954, and each constitution promulgated since, has guaranteed religious freedom. This was in line with classical Marxist teachings, which assert that religion would wither away in a classless society, even if its demise might take many years. During the interval, a certain measure of freedom – narrowly defined as freedom of religious belief – is therefore allowed for political reasons.

Marxism had earlier shown a certain Western doctrinal intransigence and even militant aggressiveness that had not been found to the same extent in China's traditional religions. But the Cultural Revolution proved to be too extremist for most people, including most Communists. The death of Mao (1976) was followed by the fall of the 'Gang of Four'.[1] Then followed the implementation of a radically new policy with growing openness to the West. The new leadership also showed more readiness to permit a critical inheritance of traditional heritage, and a tolerance of religious practice. The most recent Constitution of 1982 would offer an improvement, including a tolerance of religious propaganda.

It appears at present that religion is both surviving and prospering, while a measure of harassment and persecution is also persisting in specific quarters. Obviously, the experiences of the recent past have created a real spiritual vacuum, and the revival of religious life, however minor, is one way by which this is being filled. We have mentioned the more positive reappraisal of Confucianism, and the signs of official support. Besides, many Taoist and Buddhist temples, Islamic mosques and Christian churches have been repaired and reopened, and the various groups are once more permitted and encouraged to educate recruits. Numerous conversions to Christianity are being reported. On the other hand, religious ignorance is widespread, folk 'superstitions' are returning, and a government frightened by the alleged role played by religion in the dissolution of Communist Eastern Europe and the Soviet Union is strictly monitoring religious activities.

With the greater efforts of modernisation, even Westernisation, will China find Western religion, especially Christianity, more attractive, or will it prefer the religions of its own traditional past? This question was raised early in the twentieth century but was then superseded by the dominance of Marxism. Today, with the realisation that Marxism does not offer all the answers, it is once more being asked.

5 Christianity and Chinese Religions

Before answering this question directly, we shall first attempt to come to a conclusion regarding the basic similarities and differences between Chinese religions and Western religions, especially Christianity. We have alluded to these throughout the book. We have spoken about structural similarities. These include doctrinal beliefs, moral and ritual systems, spiritualities, as well as ecclesiastical organisations. We have also placed some emphasis on a certain running theme throughout the book: that of universal salvation (or sagehood). In that case, we have discussed the parallels between Confucian, Taoist and Buddhist concern for universal salvation and that of Christianity. We have pointed out the closer proximity between the more optimistic evaluation of human nature in Confucianism, Taoism and Ch'an Buddhism and that of the Greek Christian Fathers (hence more *jiriki*), and that between the presumably pessimistic evaluation in Pure Land Buddhism and in official Western Christianity, especially its Protestant version (hence more *tariki*).

Looking back, the religions of antiquity showed most similarities to pre-Christian religions of the Near East (Judaism, etc.) while Confucianism presents certain similarities to Christianity as an ethical religion, but lacks the other elements that constitute a church as this is known in the West. In its external 'gestalt', Taoist religion most resembles Catholic Christianity, with its beliefs in divine revelation (scripture), in sin and salvation, in deities (angels) and immortals (saints) as well as with its elaborate rituals (sacraments), its clergy (priests) and its Heavenly Masters (popes). But there are also differences: alchemy, divination and shamanism are hardly part and parcel of the Christian religion, Protestant or Catholic; besides, Taoists have a polytheistic inclination, and their popes belong to an hereditary lineage. Moreover, to the extent that today's popular religion possesses many of the features of institutional Taoism, it too may be described as a parallel to popular Christianity. But problems remain with polytheism, divination and shamanism. Even when echoes of these are found in the popular attachment to the cult of saints (resembling polytheism) and in the contemporary fascination with astrology, Christianity appears much more removed from practices that are central to Chinese popular religion. Lastly, with regard to questions relating to gender, we might remark here that comparatively speaking, women are accorded a higher place historically in Taoism and in the popular religion which it shaped, than in Confucianism or Buddhism. In the Christian case, the place of women is historically closer to that in Confucianism or Buddhism, although Protestant denominations have led the way in recent years by the ordination of women ministers.

Pure Land Buddhism has a resemblance to Protestant Christianity as a religion of grace (justification by faith) that also comes close to professing monotheism while also maintaining a kind of clergy. And if monastic celibacy is still the ideal for Chinese Buddhism, a married clergy is the rule in Japan and may even become so in the China of the future, where many monks are known to have abandoned the rule of celibacy during the Cultural Revolution. The differences here are: doctrinal fluidity (merging of Pure Land and Ch'an), devotion to a female figure Kuan-yin (more like Marian devotion), the use of beads (rosary), and tolerance for popular practices, including divination.

In many other ways, Chinese religious traditions show greater affinity to those Western traditions that preceded Christianity. This is the case with Confucianism and Stoic teachings, as missionaries recognised. This is also the case with popular religion and ancient Roman religion, with its pantheon and domestic rituals. There are also resemblances to those teachings that orthodox Christianity has considered heretical: certain Gnostic ideas and practices, including alchemy, are reflected in Taoism, but not Gnostic abhorrence of the material world; millenarian movements are found in popular Taoism as well as in Buddhism. The list can go on. But what sets Chinese religions most apart from Christianity is generally their reliance on experience rather than faith in divine revelation. This is true also of those traditions that make some claim of revelation, like Taoism and Buddhism. But even Pure Land Buddhism has incorporated experience into its system, especially by merging meditation and invocation. Moreover, in one crucial way, Chinese religious traditions have developed in a different political context than has

Western Christianity. I refer to the dominance of the state over religious matters, and the absence of a balance of power between church and state. More than most other previous governments, the Communist régime has controlled religious affairs, and, at least in the past, has placed in doubt the destiny of religion in China.

Once more: What future is there for religion in China? What will be its face? Will this be one, or many? Will it be the traditional religions, or Christianity?

I suppose that a clue may be found in the situation of Hong Kong and Taiwan, regions of rapid economic development where the Chinese tradition has never been formally rejected. Interestingly, while a significant number of people there have accepted Western Christianity, many more remain distanced from it. Some proclaim themselves secularists; others are satisfied with Confucian values as these are *now* understood, or remain loyal to Buddhism (which has also been undergoing transformation) or Taoism (which is more conservative, but also changing), or to all three teachings. A large number of people, the so-called masses, appear content with occasional participation in the ritual practices of popular religion. The future face of China, we may safely predict, will be shaped by a continuing transformation marked by syncretism. It will be pluralist and multiform. But what future?

6   What Future?

Let us return to a 'global' consideration of 'Chinese religion', by recalling to mind traditional China's self-consciousness as the centre of the civilised universe, indeed, of 'all under heaven', and its concomitant disdain of anything peripheral to this civilisation. Chinese values were considered to be *universally* valid, and Chinese culture had spread to the regions adjacent to the country, especially in the case of Japan, mainly as a result of the civilising efforts of these regions themselves. The late nineteenth century witnessed a rude awakening, when the Chinese discovered that theirs was only one country among others, and indeed, that their survival was being threatened by others. Consequently, the twentieth century has been a struggle for survival, the manifestation of Chinese nationalism – very much like nationalism elsewhere in Asia – *vis-à-vis* the imperialistic nationalism of the Western powers and of Japan. The entire cultural legacy was scrutinised in this struggle for national survival.

In this historical context, the religious situation of China takes on a new perspective. I speak of the tension between the universal and the particular, so important in all universal religions, including Christianity. Confucianism, for example, is a humanism, a cultural tradition with universalist claims. But it was rejected in early-twentieth-century China as irrelevant to national survival. Instead, Marxism was favoured – a system with universal claims but of foreign origin. And Marxism was given a particular task, that of saving China. In the process of carrying out this task, Marxism would increasingly assume a Chinese face, or rather several Chinese faces, identifying itself with the particular goals of this country, and of the stated policies of its successive leaderships. Today, Chinese Christianity, for example, is experiencing this same tension, being torn by its desire to serve the faithful through collaboration with the régime, and its consciousness of itself as part of a larger whole, a universal religion.

And as we look at China through the dimensions of time and space, we may conclude that religion was strongest in the earliest centuries. Measured by the percentage of the society actively participating, it is currently strong only in the peripheral regions such as Tibet and Central Asia. Does that mean that religion is no longer *central* to Chinese culture, and that it has not been so for a long time? And could this not be the result, at least in part, of the tendency toward harmony and syncretism, which makes 'secular humanism' out of formerly religious traditions?

Comparing the situation in China to the more overtly religious climate of both ritual worship and communal identification in present-day India, we have to answer Yes, that religion is less central to Chinese society and culture than it is to the Hindu, or the Muslim. But compared to the more secular or pluralist scene in Western Europe or North America, we find in China a tendency that is also at work in our West. We find a tendency toward secularisation that does not exclude religion, that accepts a multiplicity of religious faiths and practices, and that harmonises these with a humanism called liberal as well as secular.

But we are also saying that Chinese humanism itself, with its doctrine of self-transcendence in different forms (Confucianism, Taoism, Buddhism) points to *another* expression of human religiosity, which cannot simply be dismissed with the word 'secular'. It remains a great living tradition, a spiritual tradition undergoing critical transformation. In the last analysis, our contention is that the Chinese 'religions of harmony' also challenge all of us to redefine the word 'religion' itself. Observing them, we see religion not only as something not necessarily linked to a belief in God (as Buddhism has shown to be possible), but also and especially as a striving for human perfection or self-transcendence. This striving has remained open to the Great Ultimate (Taoism and Neo-Confucianism), to the True Self (Ch'an Buddhism), to the Pure Land (devotional Buddhism), and to Heaven and the Lord-on-high (ancient religion, popular religion and consciousness, Protestant Christianity). It may be open to as yet undisclosed spiritual horizons in the future.

Appendix:
The Chinese Liturgical Year

The Chinese almanac is itself a reflection of the syncretic character of popular religion and an indication of the close identification of the sacred and the profane which make up the 'liturgical year', somewhat like the way it was in Western Christendom before the secularisation process had set in. It follows a lunar calendar, with the first of the moon or month coinciding with the new moon and the fifteenth, coinciding with the full moon. It also parallels the agricultural cycle. Even with the official adoption of the solar calendar, the traditional Chinese almanac remains an important book.[1]

The cycle actually begins with preparations for the lunar New Year, usually taking place in late January or early February. For the Chinese, this festival has the combined meaning of Christmas as a religious and family celebration and New Year (January 1) as the turning of a new leaf in the book of time. About a week before the New Year, i.e., the first day of the first moon, the stove god, whose portrait decorates the kitchen, has to be sent off to heaven with his report on the family members. After he is bribed by having his lips smeared with honey or sticky rice or candy, his picture is removed and burnt. He returns on New Year's Eve when a new picture is pasted over the stove. In Chinese communities, dragon dances are performed to encourage rain and fertility and fire-crackers sound off to chase away demons. The New Year celebrations usually extend to the fifteenth of the month, and are called the Feast of the Lanterns. During that time, many pay visits to Taoist and other temples for divination and other rituals, and gifts are exchanged.

'Double Two' – the second day of the second moon – is reserved for the birthday of the local earth god, to whom incense, candles and paper offerings are made. He is considered as the local registrar for births, marriages and deaths. On the nineteenth day of the same moon is celebrated the birthday of Kuan-yin. She is sometimes represented as having a thousand eyes and a thousand hands – all the better to hear and respond to supplications.

The next big occasion on the calendar is in the spring: *Ch'ing-ming*, the clear and bright festival, falls 105 days after the winter solstice or two weeks after the spring equinox. This is the time for visiting the tombs, repairing them and sometimes offering sacrifices of cooked food there. In the seventh moon, the spirits of all the deceased are remembered, as with All Souls' Day in the Christian calendar. This happens in the Buddhist *p'u-tu/pudu* ritual which literally refers to 'ferrying across to the other shore' all souls of the departed. In the tenth moon, the ancestors are once more remembered during ritual visits to the tombs. Together with mock paper money, paper clothing is burnt, representing what is needed for the cold season.

In high spring, on the eighth day of the fourth moon, the Buddha Sakyamuni's birthday is celebrated. The principal rite is the 'bathing of the Buddha', in which a small Buddha image is cleansed with scented water in a ritual with Indian origins. In late spring, a well-known popular custom honours the ancient poet and minister Ch'ü Yüan who drowned himself in a river. I refer to the dragon boat festival on 'Double Five', the fifth day of the fifth moon, alleged to be a re-enactment of the search for the dead poet's body. Cooked rice, wrapped in palm leaves, is eaten on this day, commemorating the custom of offering food to the spirit of the tragic hero.[2]

'Double Seven' is a feast special to women, as it commemorates the story of the cowherd and the weaving maid. Allegedly the youngest daughter of the stove god, she fell in love with a mortal. Given only one reunion a year with her husband, she meets him on a bridge of magpies over the Milky Way. In the eighth moon, the harvest is celebrated as with the American Thanksgiving. In the Chinese context, this coincides with the full autumn moon, and so circular-shaped moon cakes are eaten. Formerly, women used to make offerings to the moon then, but now, it has become mainly a secular, family feast. The winter solstice, during the eleventh moon, has its importance. In the past, thanksgiving offerings were made at the family altar to Heaven and Earth, the household gods as well as the ancestors. And then, of course, the family would finish a sumptuous dinner, in the style of a North American Thanksgiving.

After that, the preparations for the lunar New Year soon begin the whole cycle once again. Not everyone today may adhere to everything in this liturgical calendar, but every family usually observes some of the festivals, especially the New Year. The parallel can be made with the post-Christian West, and its own yearly cycle that gives meaning and fulfilment to life itself. Even where Christmas is secularised, its observance indicates a need for meaning and fulfilment coming from a religious tradition that still inspires peace and sharing. After all, it is still part of human striving to achieve communication, harmony and even union with the supra-human, the heavenly, or the divine.

Notes

Introduction

1. Friedrich Heiler, *Prayer: A Study in the History and Psychology of Religion*, translated and edited by Samuel McComb (London: Oxford University Press, 1932).

2. Consult Fung Yu-lan, *A Short History of Chinese Philosophy*, edited by Derk Bodde (New York: Macmillan, 1962), ch. 8 on the School of Names and ch. 11 on the Later Mohists. For more information and for a selection of translated texts, consult also Wing-tsit Chan, *A Source Book in Chinese Philosophy* (Princeton: Princeton University Press, 1960), especially ch. 10.

3. Abe Masao, 'In Memory of Paul Tillich', *The Eastern Buddhist* n.s., I/2 (1966), 128–31. Nevertheless, Tillich returned to Europe enthusiastic about the encounter, and published the small but influential work, *Christianity and the Encounter of World Religions*, based on lectures he gave in 1961 in the United States. But time did not permit his fulfilling the intention of rewriting his own theology in the light of such an encounter.

4. For practical reasons, we have not alluded to the 'Common Era' in our chronology, but point out that this is not out of any lack of respect for Judaism or Islam, or even Chinese tradition itself.

5. In the case of popular religion, one might argue sometimes for historical influence from Christianity.

Chapter 1

1. Incidentally, 'dragon bones' are still used as medicine in today's China. We suppose that they no longer include early fossils or oracular records, but the powder from bones and shells continues to supply calcium and other substances that allegedly contribute to the healing of certain sicknesses.

2. Jao Tsung-i, 'Foreword: Speaking of "Sages": The Bronze Figures of San-hsing-tui', in Julia Ching and R. W. L. Guisso, *Sages and Filial Sons* (Hong Kong: Chinese University Press, 1991), pp. xiv–xx.

3. Consult Herbert Spencer, *Principles of Sociology* (first published, 1877–78. Westport, Ct.: Greenwood Press, 1974–75), vol. 1. See his chapter on ancestral worship.

4. Consult Maurice Freedman's Editorial Preface in Marcel Granet, *The Religion of the Chinese People*. Translated by Maurice Freedman (New York: Harper & Row, 1977), p. 19. In ancient China, the ancestral cult was practised only by the nobility. With time, it spread also among

the common people.

5. Hans Küng and Julia Ching, *Christianity and Chinese Religions* (New York: Doubleday, 1989), p. 37.
6. Arthur Waley, trans., *The Book of Songs* (New York: Grove Press, 1960), pp. 209–10. The *Book of Poetry* is sometimes called the *Book of Songs*, and sometimes the *Odes*.
7. Adamson E. Hoebel, *Anthropology: The Study of Man* (New York: McGraw-Hill, 1972), p. 376.
8. James Hsü, 'Unwanted Children and Parents', in Julia Ching and R. W. L. Guisso, eds, *Sages and Filial Sons*, op. cit., pp. 27–36.
9. Consult Hsü Chün-yüan, *et al.*, *Chung-kuo jen te hsing-shih* (Chinese clan names and surnames) (Hong Kong: South China Press, 1988), chs 1–2.
10. See quotations from original texts in Derk Bodde, 'Myths of Ancient China', in Charles LeBlanc and Dorothy Borei, eds, *Essays on Chinese Civilization* (Princeton: Princeton University Press, 1981), pp. 62–65.
11. Consult Derk Bodde, ibid., pp. 58–62.
12. For this entire subject, consult Kwang-Chih Chang, *Shang Civilization* (New Haven and London: Yale University Press, 1980), pp. 31–35.
13. Kwang-chih Chang, *Art, Myth and Ritual: The Path to Political Authority in Ancient China* (Cambridge, Mass.: Harvard University Press, 1983, p. 54.
14. David E. Aune, *Prophecy in Early Christianity and the Ancient Mediterranean World* (Grand Rapids, Mich.: William B. Eerdmans, 1983), p. 86.
15. Consult Derek Walters, *Chinese Astrology: Interpreting the Messages of the Celestial Messengers* (Wellingsborough, Northants: The Aquarian Press, 1987).
16. Roberto K. Ong, *The Interpretation of Dreams in Ancient China* (Bochum: Brockmeyer, 1985), pp. 18, 144–49.
17. Waley, *The Book of Songs*, p. 283.
18. David Hawkes, *Ch'u Tz'u: the Songs of the South* (Oxford: Oxford University Press, 1959), p. 89.
19. Hawkes, ibid., p. 90.
20. Consult Alfred Guillaume, *Prophecy and Divination among the Hebrews and Other Semites* (London: Hodder & Stoughton, 1938), pp. 107–10.

Chapter 2

1. Hans Küng and Julia Ching, op. cit., p. 100.
2. Henri Maspéro, *China in Antiquity*. Translated by Frank A. Kierman, Jr. (Amherst: University of Massachusetts Press, 1978), pp. 93–110.
3. Eng. trans. from Arthur Waley, *The Book of Songs*, p. 311. Duke Mu of Ch'in died in 621 B.C.
4. The stories are from the section T'an-kung. Consult James Legge, trans., *Li Ki*, in F. Max Müller, ed., *Sacred Books of the East* series, vol. 27 (Oxford: Oxford University Press, 1885), pp. 182; 183–84.
5. See Willard G. Oxtoby's overview article on priesthood (pp. 528–34)

and Baruch A. Levine's article on Jewish priesthood (pp. 534–36) in Mircea Eliade *et al.*, ed., *The Encyclopedia of Religion* (New York: Macmillan, 1987) vol. 11.

6. Consult I. M. Lewis, *Ecstatic Religion: An Anthropological Study of Spirit Possession and Shamanism* (Harmondsworth: Pelican, 1978).

7. Aune, op. cit., pp. 83–84. Reference especially to 1 Sam. 10:5; 19:20; 1 Kings 18:17–29; 22:5–10.

8. Morton Smith, *Jesus the Magician* (New York: Harper & Row, 1978), pp. 104–8.

9. *The Nine Songs* (Harmondsworth: Pelican, 1955), Introduction, p. 9.

10. See Arthur Waley, trans., *The Nine Songs: A Study of Shamanism in Ancient China* (London: Allen & Unwin, 1955), p. 27.)

11. See the *Book of Rites*, chapter on the Evolution of Rites.

12. David Hawkes, *Songs of the South*, pp. 104–7.

13. See *Wangdao ou la Voie Royale* (Paris, École Française d'Extrême-Orient, 1980), vol. 2, pp. 13–18.

14. The translations from the *Analects* are usually given after consulting translations by James Legge, D. C. Lau or Arthur Waley.

15. Georg Fohrer, *History of Israelite Religion*, translated from German by David E. Green (Nashville: Abingdon Press, 1972), p. 147.

16. Waley, *The Book of Songs*, pp. 283–84.

17. See 'Biography of the Japanese', in the *Chronicle of Wei*, a part of *Chronicle of the Three Kingdoms*, ch. 30. *Wo* was the Chinese name for the Japanese. The English translation is adapted from Ichiro Hori's chapter on Japanese shamanism, in *Folk Religion in Japan: Continuity and Change*, ed. by Joseph M. Kitagawa and Alan L. Miller (Chicago: University of Chicago Press, 1968), p. 188.

18. Waley, *The Book of Songs*, pp. 316–17.

Chapter 3

1. Karl Jaspers, *The Great Philosophers: The Foundations*, edited by Hannah Arendt, translated by Ralph Mannheim (New York: Harcourt, Brace & World, 1962), vol. 1, pp. 51–57.

2. The etymology of *ju* comes from the Han dynasty lexicon *Shuo-wen chieh-tzu* and has been made popular by Hu Shih (1930) in *Shuo ju* (On 'Ju') (Taipei: Yuan-liu, 1986), pp. 10–11.

3. On this and on other points, consult Julia Ching, *Confucianism and Christianity: A Comparative Study* (Tokyo: Kodansha International, 1977).

4. See the biography of Confucius by Julia Ching, in Mircea Eliade, ed., *The Encyclopedia of Religion*, vol. 4, pp. 38–42.

5. A useful source for more information is Burton Watson, *Early Chinese Literature* (New York: Columbia University Press, 1962), where the texts are explained under sections given as history, philosophy, and poetry.

6. See Carl Jung's Foreword to Richard Wilhelm *et al.*, trans., *The I Ching or Book of Changes* (Princeton: Princeton University Press,

1967), pp. xxi–xxxix. The Wilhelm / Baynes translation of the *I-ching* is considered superior.

7. C. K. Yang, *Religion in Chinese Society* (Berkeley: University of California Press, 1961), pp. 29–53.

8. William E. Soothill, *The Three Religions of China* (London: Oxford University Press, 1923), p. 232. See also the chapter on the Meaning of Sacrifice, in the *Book of Rites*, English translation in Legge, *Li Ki*, *Sacred Books of the East* series, vol. 28, pp. 210–20.

9. James Legge, *The Religions of China* (London: Hodder & Stoughton, 1880), pp. 43 ff.

10. John Shryock, *Origin and Development of the State Cult of Confucianism* (New York: The Century Co., 1932), p. 233.

11. Consult Yü Ying-shih, "'O Soul Come Back!'" A Study in the Changing Conceptions of the Soul and Afterlife in Pre-Buddhist China', *Harvard Journal of Asiatic Studies*, vol. 47 (1987), pp. 363–95.

12. James Legge, trans., *Li Ki, Sacred Books of the East* series, vol. 28, p. 430.

13. Herbert Fingarette, *Confucius: The Secular as Sacred* (New York: Harper & Row, 1972) p. 16.

14. This does not exclude the fact that military might usually decided the fate of historical dynasties. Nevertheless, the Chinese family's repugnance for military service for their sons endured, until the Communist government made efforts to change the attitude.

15. H. H. Rowley, *Prophecy and Religion in Ancient China and Israel* (London: Athlone Press, 1956).

16. Rowley, ibid., pp. 125–26.

17. Hans Küng and Julia Ching, op. cit., p. 111.

18. Max Weber, *The Religion of China: Confucianism and Taoism* (New York: Free Press, 1964), pp. 229–30.

Chapter 4

1. Burton Watson, trans., *Mo Tzu: Basic Writings* (New York: Columbia University Press, 1963), p. 125.

2. Watson, ibid., p. 82.

3. Wolfgang Bauer, *China and the Search for Happiness*, translated by Michael Shaw (New York: Seabury Press, 1976), p. 30.

4. *Chuang Tzu*, ch. 33. See Burton Watson, trans., *The Complete Works of Chuang Tzu* (New York: Columbia University Press, 1968), pp. 365–66.

5. The translations from Mencius are usually given after consulting those by D. C. Lau and James Legge.

6. Burton Watson, trans., *Hsün Tzu: Basic Writings* (New York: Columbia University Press, 1963), p. 85.

7. Watson, ibid., p. 82.

8. Ibid.

9. Taken from Gregory's *On the Inscriptions of the Psalms*, quoted in Paulos Mar Gregorios, *Cosmic Man: The Divine Presence: The Theology*

of St. Gregory of Nyssa (c. 330–395 A.D.) (New York: Paragon, 1988), 13.

10.   Paul Tillich, *Systematic Theology* (Chicago: University of Chicago Press, 1961–63), vol. 2, p. 42.

11.   Martin Buber, 'China and Us' (1928), in *A Believing Humanism: My Testament* (New York: Simon & Schuster, 1967), p. 189.

12.   Ibid., p. 157.

13.   Paulos Mar Gregorios, *Cosmic Man: The Divine Presence: The Theology of St. Gregory of Nyssa (c. 330–395 A.D.)* (New York: Paragon, 1988), chs 6–8. See also Julia Ching, 'The Mirror Symbol Revisited: Confucian and Taoist Mysticism', in Steven T. Katz, ed., *Mysticism and Religious Traditions* (New York: Oxford University Press, 1983), 154, 233–34.

14.   Consult Johann Auer's contribution to the article on grace in *Sacramentum Mundi*, ed. by Karl Rahner *et al.* (New York: Herder & Herder, 1968), 412–14; see also Henri de Lubac, *Surnaturel, Etudes historiques* (1946).

15.   Robert N. Bellah and Philip E. Hammond, *Varieties of Civil Religion* (San Francisco: Harper & Row, 1980).

16.   These altars, dedicated to the gods of the earth and of grain, represented the land itself.

17.   I am referring to the anonymous *Vindicae contra Tyrannos* (1579) and to Mariana's *De rege et regis institutione* (1598–99).

18.   Burton Watson, trans., *Han Fei Tzu: Basic Writings* (New York: Columbia University Press, 1964), pp. 17–18.

19.   Julia Ching, *Probing China's Soul: Religion, Politics, and Protest in the People's Republic* (San Francisco: Harper & Row, 1990), pp. 92–94.

20.   Léon Vandermeersch, *Le Nouveau monde sinisé* (Paris, Presses Universitaires de France, 1986), especially pp. 204–16.

21.   See Vandermeersch, ibid., pp. 161–203.

22.   Ibid., p. 167.

Chapter 5

1.   For a recent scholarly book, see Livia Kohn, ed., *Taoist Meditation and Longevity Techniques*, Michigan Monographs in Chinese Studies, vol. 61 (Ann Arbor: University of Michigan, Center for Chinese Studies, 1989). On the practical front, Mantak Chia, a disciple of Taoist masters, has published a series of books that offer a systematic unpacking of Taoist *ch'i-kung/qigong* practices, combining meditation and visualisation with physical exercises. The publisher of the series, Healing Tao Books, is in Huntington, New York.

2.   Gilles Quispel, 'Gnosticism', in *The Encyclopedia of Religion*, op. cit., vol. 5, pp. 566–74.

3.   Karl Jaspers, *The Great Philosophers*, ed. by Hannah Arendt, trans. by Ralph Mannheim (New York: Harcourt, Brace & World, 1966), vol. 2.

4.   Max Kaltenmark, *Lao Tzu and Taoism*, English translation by Roger

Greaves (Stanford: Stanford University Press, 1969), p. 8.

5. J. J. L. Duyvendak, *Tao Te Ching* (London: John Murray, 1954), p. 24; consult also Ellen Marie Chen, *Tao Te Ching: A New Translation with Commentary* (New York: Paragon, 1989), pp. 22–24. I presume that by magic power is meant a kind of charisma or 'grace'.

6. Unless otherwise noted, the translations from *Lao-tzu* are given after consulting either D. C. Lau or Arthur Waley.

7. *De Potentia*, q. 7, art. 5. English translation, *On the Power of God* (London: Burns, Oates & Washbourne, 1932–34), vol. 3, p. 33.

8. Martin Heiddeger, *On the Way to Language* (New York, Harper & Row, 1971), p. 92. Consult Hans Küng and Julia Ching, *Christianity and Chinese Religions* (New York: Doubleday, 1989), pp. 176–79.

9. English translation from Burton Watson, *The Complete Works of Chuang Tzu* (New York: Columbia University Press, 1968), pp. 57–58.

10. Ch. 6. Eng. trans. in Watson, ibid., pp. 90–91.

11. English trans. in Burton Watson, *The Complete Works of Chuang Tzu*, op. cit., p. 33.

12. See next chapter for further development.

13. English translation in D. C. Lau, op. cit., p. 85.

14. D. C. Lau, ibid., p. 113.

15. Consult Ellen M. Chen, op. cit., pp. 209–10.

16. Alan K. L. Chan, *Two Visions of the Way: A Study of Wang Pi and the Ho-shang Kung Commentaries on Lao Tzu* (New York: State University of New York Press, 1991).

17. Consult Fung Yu-lan, *A Short History of Chinese Philosophy*, edited by Derk Bodde (New York: Macmillan, 1962), chs 19–20.

18. Paul J. Lin, *A Translation of Lao-tzu's Tao Te Ching and Wang Pi's Commentary*, Michigan Papers in Chinese Studies, 30 (Ann Arbor: University of Michigan, 1977), p. 3.

19. English translation in A. C. Graham, *The Book of Lieh-tzu* (London: John Murray, 1960), pp. 140–41.

20. Ibid., p. 142.

21. Liu I-ch'ing, *Shih-shuo Hsin-yu*, trans. by Richard B. Mather as *A New Account of Tales of the World* (Minneapolis: University of Minnesota Press, 1976), pp. 372–73.

22. Quoted in Wolfgang Bauer, *China and the Search for Happiness*, p. 150.

23. See English translation in Donald Holzman, *Poetry and Politics: The Life and Works of Juan Chi, A.D. 210–236* (Cambridge: Cambridge University Press, 1976), p. 195.

24. *Pao-p'u-tzu* 48:190. Quoted in Bauer, op. cit., pp. 139–40. In the next chapter we shall pursue further the connection between Taoism and political protest.

25. Julia Ching, *Probing China's Soul: Religion, Politics, and Protest in the People's Republic* (San Francisco: Harper & Row, 1990), p. 90.

Chapter 6

1. Consult Fukui Kōjun, ed., *Dōkyō to wa nanika* (What is Taoism?), vol. 1 of *Dōkyō* (Tokyo: Hirakawa, 1984).
2. Henri Maspéro, *Taoism and Chinese Religion*. Translated by Frank A. Kierman, Jr. (Amherst: University of Massachusetts Press, 1981), especially pp. 309–430.
3. See Kristofer Schipper, *Le Corps taoïste: Corps mystique, corps social* (Paris: Fayard, 1982), pp. 22–25; John Lagerwey, *Taoist Ritual in Chinese Society and History* (New York: Macmillan, 1987).
4. Ilza Veith, trans., *The Yellow Emperor's Classic of Internal Medicine* (First published, 1949. Berkeley: University of California Press, 1972), pp. 97–98.
5. English translation adapted from Joseph Needham, *Science and Civilisation in China*, 6 vols (Cambridge: Cambridge University Press, 1954–86), vol. 5, part 2, p. 113.
6. I refer to the historical drama, Wu Han's *Hai-jui pa-kuan*, in which a Ming official sought to deter the emperor from favouring alchemists and elixirs, and lost his official position for doing so.
7. See Michael Loewe, *Ways to Paradise: the Chinese Quest for Immortality* (London: Allen & Unwin, 1979), chs 1–2.
8. Ssu-ma's name in *pinyin* is Sima Chengzhen. Consult Livia Kohn, 'Taoist Insight Meditation: The T'ang Practice of *neiguan*', in Livia Kohn, ed., *Taoist Meditation and Longevity Techniques* (Ann Arbor: Center for Chinese Studies, University of Michigan, 1989) Michigan Monographs in Chinese Studies, vol. 61, p. 199.
9. Livia Kohn, *Seven Steps to the Tao: Sima Chengzhen's Zuowanlun*, *Monumenta Serica* Monograph Series, 20 (Nettetal: Steyler Verlag, 1987).
10. See *Pao-p'u-tzu*, ch. 18. Consult the English translation by James Ware, *Alchemy, Medicine, Religion in the China of A.D. 320: The nei-p'ien of Ko Hung* (Cambridge, Mass.: M.I.T. Press, 1966), pp. 303–4.
11. Quoted by C. G. Jung in his commentary on Richard Wilhelm's translated text, *The Secret of the Golden Flower*. Translated by Cary F. Baynes (London: Kegan Paul, Trench, Trübner, 1931), p. 104. Richard Wilhelm himself suggests a possible Zoroastrian origin through Nestorian connections with the origins of such Taoist meditation on light. See p. 10.
12. We see evidence here of another feminine feature of religious Taoism, with the adept relating to new life as a mother to an infant. Consult Isabelle Robinet, 'Visualization and Ecstatic Flight in Shanqing Taoism', in Livia Kohn, ed., *Taoist Meditation and Longevity Techniques* op. cit., 160–62.
13. See the *Lao-tzu pien-hua ching*, (The Classic of the Transformations of Lao-tzu), a manuscript discovered at Tun-huang (Dunhuang); see also Anna Seidel, *La Divinisation de Lao-tseu dans le Taoïsme de Han* (Paris, École Française d'Extrême-Orient, 1969), pp. 59–128.
14. See Joseph Needham, *Science and Civilisation in China*, vol. 2, p. 160.
15. Anna K. Seidel, 'The Image of a Perfect Ruler in Early Taoist Messianism: Lao-Tzu and Li Hung', *History of Religions*, vol. 9

(1969–70), pp. 216–47.

16. Ernst Bloch, *Thomas Münzer als Theologe der Revolution* (München: K. Wolff, 1921; reissued Berlin: Aufbau-Verlag, 1960). Müntzer has been honoured as a precursor of Marxist revolutionaries.

17. See Julia Ching, 'The Idea of God in Nakae Tōju', *Japanese Journal of Religious Studies*, vol. 11 (December 1984), 299–301.

Chapter 7

1. Edward Conze, *Buddhism: Its Essence and Development*, 3rd edition (Oxford: Bruno Cassirer, 1957); Richard H. Robinson, *The Buddhist Religion* (Belmont, Calif.: Dickenson, 1970), chs 1–2; E. Zürcher, *Buddhism: Its Origin and Spread in Words, Maps and Pictures* (New York: St. Martin's Press, 1962), chs 1–3.

2. Ashoka's imperial order did not last as long as Constantine's. Within five decades of his death, his Mauryan dynasty was replaced by one more supportive of the Brahmanic tradition.

3. Donald Swearer, *Buddhism* (Niles, Ill.: Argus Communications, 1977), Parts I–II.

4. The 'Third order' is distinct from the monks (or friars) forming a 'first order' and the nuns forming a 'second order'. Some Catholic religious orders (like Carmelites) have their 'third orders' of lay supporters. Nevertheless, conflicts between the monastic order and its more numerous lay supporters marked the history of both Christianity and Buddhism.

5. Alfred North Whitehead, *Religion in the Making* (New York: New American Library, 1960), p. 50.

6. *Christianity and the Encounter of World Religions* (New York: Columbia University Press, 1963), p. 4.

7. See Donald S. Lopez Jr. and Steven C. Rockefeller, eds, *The Christ and the Bodhisattva* (Albany: State University of New York Press, 1987).

8. Arthur F. Wright, *Buddhism in Chinese History* (Stanford: Stanford University Press, 1959).

9. E. Zürcher, *The Buddhist Conquest of China: The Spread and Adaptation of Buddhism in Early Medieval China* (Leiden, E. J. Brill, 1959).

10. Wm. Theodore de Bary, *Sources of Chinese Tradition*, op. cit., pp. 312–30.

11. For more information, consult Kōgen Mizuno, *Buddhist Sutras: Origins, Development, Transmission* (Tokyo: Kosei, 1982).

12. As this is an edition by scholars and for scholars, the collection includes numerous commentaries, and even non-Buddhist texts mistaken to be Buddhist, such as texts of Manichaean or Nestorian origin. Consult Kenneth Ch'en, *Buddhism in China: A Historical Survey* (Princeton: Princeton University Press, 1964), ch. 13.

13. Zenryū Tsukamoto, *A History of Early Chinese Buddhism: From Its Introduction to the Death of Hui-yüan*, trans. from Japanese by Leon Hurvitz (Tokyo: Kodansha International, 1979), vol. 1, pp. 78–112.

14. James Legge, *A Record of Buddhistic Kingdoms: Being an Account by the*

Chinese Monk Fa-hien of His Travels in India and Ceylon (A.D. 319–414) in Search of the Buddhist Books of Discipline (Oxford, Clarendon, 1886 edn, New York, Paragon reprint, 1965). This includes his biography in Chinese. Consult also Latika Lahiri, *Chinese Monks in India* (Delhi: Motilal Banarsidass, 1986).

15. Hans Klimkeit, 'Christian–Buddhist Encounter in Medieval Central Asia', in G. W. Houston, ed., *The Cross and the Lotus: Christianity and Buddhism in Dialogue* (Delhi: Motilal Banarsidass, 1985), pp. 9–24.
16. Consult Mizuno, op. cit., ch. 4.
17. Mizuno, op. cit., ch. 5.
18. See Anthony Yu's translation, *The Journey to the West* (Chicago: University of Chicago Press, 1977–83), 4 vols.
19. I have in mind the Buddhist notion of *upāya* (skill-in-means), which subordinates doctrine to the more pragmatic needs of salvation.
20. See Kenneth Ch'en, op. cit., p. 84.
21. Consult W. Liebenthal, trans., *Chao Lun: The Treatises of Seng Chao* (Hong Kong: Hong Kong University Press, 2nd rev. edn, 1968); Richard H. Robinson, *Early Madhyamika in India and China* (Delhi: Motilal Banarsidass, 1976).
22. Kenneth Ch'en, op. cit., p. 323.
23. For more information on Buddhism in recent times, see Holmes Welch, *The Practice of Chinese Buddhism, 1900–1950* (Cambridge, Mass.: Harvard University Press, 1985).
24. Kenneth Ch'en, op. cit., pp. 309–11; David W. Chappell, ed., *T'ien-t'ai Buddhism: An Outline of the Fourfold Teachings* (Tokyo: Daiichi Shobo, 1983).
25. See Garma C. C. Chang, *The Buddhist Teaching of Totality: The Philosophy of Hwa Yen Buddhism* (University Park: Pennsylvania State University Press, 1971), p. 24.

Chapter 8

1. English translation adapted from Philip B. Yampolsky, *The Platform Sutra of the Sixth Patriarch: The Text of the Tun-huang Manuscript* (New York: Columbia University Press, 1967), pp. 130–32.
2. Fung Yu-lan, *A Short History of Chinese Philosophy*, op. cit., ch. 22.
3. Daisetz Teitaro Suzuki, *Mysticism: Christian and Buddhist* (London: Allen & Unwin, 1957), and 'An Interpretation of Zen Experience' (1939), in *Studies in Zen* (London: Rider, 1955), pp. 74–75; Heinrich Dumoulin, *A History of Zen Buddhism*. Translated from the German by Paul Peachey (New York: McGraw-Hill, 1965), pp. 18–22.
4. These include, for example, Dom Aelred Graham, William Johnston, and Hugo Enomiya-Lassalle.
5. Consult the product of collaboration between Daisetz Teitaro Suzuki, Erich Fromm and Richard De Martino, entitled *Zen Buddhism and Psychoanalysis* (New York: Grove Press, 1963).
6. See Heinrich Dumoulin, *History of Zen Buddhism*, trans. by James W. Heisig and Paul Knitter (London: Macmillan, 1988–90), vol. 1, Part

2, ch. 8.

7.   A third important scripture regards the meditation of Amitābha, also known as Amitayus.

8.   Karl Barth, *Church Dogmatics*. Translated from the German by G. T. Thompson, Harold Knight, vol. 1, part 2 (Edinburgh: T. & T. Clark, 1956), pp. 340–44. For Barth of course, Christianity is the only true religion and the name of Jesus alone is salvific.

9.   Alfred Bloom, *Shinran's Doctrine of Pure Grace* (Tucson: University of Arizona Press, 1965), p. 88.

10. Its best known exponent is St. Gregory Palamas (d. 1356), who was even excommunicated for a few years for his defence of Hesychasm.

11. Kenneth Ch'en, op. cit., pp. 357–64; Chang Chung-yuan, trans., *Original Teachings of Ch'an Buddhism* (New York: Grove Press, 1969), Foreword, p. vi.

12. Consult David Snellgrove, *Indo-Tibetan Buddhism: Indian Buddhists and their Tibetan Successors* (Boston: Shambhala, 1987), especially vol. 2, ch. 5.

13. Kurt Rudolph, 'Mystery Religions', in *Encyclopedia of Religion*, op. cit., 231.

14. They are: Akshobhya in the east, Amitābha in the west, Amoghasiddhi in the north and Ratnasambhava in the south.

15. They include the old Nyingma lineage going back allegedly to the late eighth-century figure Padmasambhava the wonder-worker, and the Kagyu lineage identified with the great saint-poet Milarepa (1040–1123), sometimes compared to Francis of Assisi for his love of nature and animals.

16. Consult David Snellgrove, *Indo-Tibetan Buddhism*, op. cit., vol. 2.

17. *Culla-Vagga*, English translation adapted from Henry Clarke Warren, *Buddhism in Translation* (Cambridge, Mass.: Harvard University Press, 1896; New York: Atheneum reprint, 1963), p. 444. I have substituted 'monk' for 'priest' and 'nun' for 'priestess'. These terms have become standard in the twentieth century. Warren's translation is older.

18. Nancy Shuster Barnes, 'Buddhism', in Arvind Sharma, ed. *Women in World Religions* (Albany: State University of New York Press, 1987), 107.

19. Leon Hurvitz, trans., *Scripture of the Lotus Blossom of the Fine Dharma* (New York: Columbia University Press, 1976), p. 201. Consult Diana Y. Paul, *Women in Buddhism: Images of the Feminine in Mahayana Tradition* (Berkeley: Asian Humanities Press, 1979), p. 113.

20. It has been said that women in traditional China benefited from the social custom of visiting temples and paying homage to Buddha statues. But this was at best a side effect; and even here, the usual custom was for women of good families to visit these places in isolation from the crowds.

21. Jerrold Schecter, *The New Face of Buddha: Buddhism and Political Power in Southeast Asia* (New York: Coward-McCann Inc., 1967), ch. 9; William R. LaFleur, *Buddhism* (Englewood Cliffs, N.J.: Prentice-Hall, 1988), pp. 137–43.

22. *Milindapañha*, in Warren, op. cit., p. 437. Where Warren gives 'Priests', I have substituted 'Monks'.
23. Hurvitz, op. cit., pp. 294–95.
24. Consult the English translation to the 'Memorial on the Bone of Buddha', in Wm. Theodore de Bary, ed., *Sources of Chinese Tradition*, op. cit., p. 428.
25. E. Dale Saunders, *Buddhism in Japan: With an Outline of Its Origins in India* (Philadelphia: University of Pennsylvania Press, 1971).
26. Frederick Francke, *The Buddha-Eye: An Anthology of the Kyoto School* (New York: Crossroad, 1982).

Chapter 9

1. Consult Max Weber, *The Religion of China: Confucianism and Taoism.* Translated by Hans H. Gerth (Glencoe, Ill.: Free Press, 1964).
2. For early political theology, see Jürgen Moltmann, 'The Cross and Civil Religion', in Moltmann *et al.*, *Religion and Political Society* (New York: Harper & Row, 1974), pp. 24–25.
3. *Ch'un-ch'iu fan-lu*, trans. in W. T. de Bary, *Sources of Chinese Tradition* (New York: Columbia University Press, 1960), p. 179.
4. Ibid., p. 181.
5. Hu Shih, *Shuo Ju*, op. cit., pp. 48–63.
6. The kingship-motif is also prominent in the cult that developed around the historical Buddha and around Maitreya, the future Buddha. Consult A. L. Basham, 'Ideas of Kingship in Hinduism and Buddhism', *Kingship in Asia and Early America*, ed. by A. L. Basham (Mexico City: El Colegio de México, 1981), pp. 115–32.
7. Joseph Needham, *Science and Civilisation in China* (Cambridge: Cambridge University Press, 1956), vol. 2, pp. 243–46.
8. Consult Julia Ching, *To Acquire Wisdom: The Way of Wang Yang-ming* (New York: Columbia University Press, 1976), Introduction.
9. *Chu-tzu ch'üan-shu* (Complete Works of Chu Hsi) (1714 edn), ch. 42. The quotation within is from the *Book of History*. See James Legge, trans., *The Chinese Classics* (London: Oxford University Press, 1861–72), vol. 3, p. 185. See also Julia Ching, 'God and the World: Chu Hsi and Whitehead', *Journal of Chinese Philosophy* 6 (1979), 275–95.
10. A. N. Whitehead, *Process and Reality: An Essay in Cosmology* (Cambridge: Cambridge University Press, 1929; reprinted New York: Free Press, 1969), pp. 410–11.
11. Pierre Teilhard de Chardin, *The Divine Milieu: An Essay on the Interior Life*, trans. by Bernard Wall (New York, Harper & Row, 1960), p. 114.
12. Consult Julia Ching, 'The Problem of Evil and a Possible Dialogue Between Neo-Confucianism and Christianity', *Contemporary Religions in Japan* 9 (1968), 161–93.
13. Jacques Leclerq, *The Inner Life*, trans. by F. Murphy (New York: P.J. Kennedy, 1961), p. 118.

14. Consult Julia Ching, 'What Is Confucian Spirituality?' in Irene Eber, ed., *Confucianism: The Dynamics of Tradition* (New York: Macmillan, 1986), pp. 73–74.
15. Consult Julia Ching, '"Authentic Selfhood": Wang Yang-ming and Heidegger', *The Monist* 61 (1978), 3–27.
16. *Hsiang-shan ch'üan-shu* (Complete Works of Lu Chiu-yüan), ch. 22. English translation adapted from Wing-tsit Chan, *A Source Book in Chinese Philosophy* (Princeton: Princeton University Press, 1963) p. 580.
17. *Ch'uan-hsi lu*, part 1. English translation adapted from Wing-tsit Chan, *Instructions for Practical Living* (New York: Columbia University Press, 1967), pp. 80–81.
18. Consult Julia Ching, *Confucianism and Christianity*, 135–36; Julia Ching, *To Acquire Wisdom: The Way of Wang Yang-ming* (New York: Columbia University Press, 1976), chs 5–6.
19. *Meister Eckhart*, ed. by F. Pfeiffer, trans. by C. de Evans, 2 vols. (London: J. M. Watkins, 1924–31), Tractate 8, p. 338.
20. Ibid., p. 366.
21. English translation in *How to Be a Good Communist* (Beijing: Foreign Languages Press, 1951), p. 24.
22. See Carsun Chang, *The Development of Neo-Confucian Thought* (New York: College & University Press, 1963), vol. 2, Appendix.
23. This is given in the Ceremonials (*I-li*), in the section on mourning apparel.
24. Maruyama Masao, *Studies in the Intellectual History of Tokugawa Japan* (Princeton: Princeton University Press, 1974).
25. Robert N. Bellah, *Tokugawa Religion: The Values of Pre-Industrial Japan* (Boston: Beacon Press, 1957), pp. 8, 185–97; Wm. Theodore de Bary and Irene Bloom, eds, *Principle and Practicality: Essays in Neo-Confucianism and Practical Learning* (New York: Columbia University Press, 1979), Introduction, pp. 1–35; Minamoto Ryoen, 'Jitsugaku and Empirical Rationalism in the First Half of the Tokugawa Period', pp. 375–470.
26. In his article, Shmuel Noah Eisenstadt argues that the Confucianism found in today's Japan and the Asian Pacific Rim has itself undergone successful transformation. See 'Some Observations on Relations between Confucianism, Development and Modernization', in Silke Krieger and Rolf Trauzettel, eds, *Confucianism and the Modernization of China* (Mainz: v. Hase & Koehler, 1991), pp. 360–66.

Chapter 10

1. Donald D. Leslie, *Islam in Traditional China: A Short History to 1800* (Canberra: Canberra College of Advanced Education, 1986), p. 33.
2. Consult Donald Daniel Leslie, *The Survival of the Chinese Jews: The Jewish Community of Kaifeng* (Leiden: E. J. Brill, 1972), pp. 11, 15.
3. Samuel N. C. Lieu, *The Religion of Light: An Introduction to the History of Manichaeism in China* (Hong Kong: University of Hong Kong,

1979), ch. 1; consult also Lieu's larger work, *Manichaeism in the Later Roman Empire and Medieval China* (Manchester: Manchester University Press, 1985), chs 7–9.

4. Lieu, op. cit., p. 25.

5. Archaeological discoveries in today's Turfan, Chinese Central Asia in an area today's Muslim Uighurs still inhabit, as well as findings of Manichaean texts at Tun-huang, testify to the religion's earlier prosperity.

6. Consult Wu Han, *'Ming-chiao yü Ta-Ming ti-kuo'* (The Religion of Light and the Great Ming Empire) *Ch'ing-hua hsüeh-pao* 13 (1941), pp. 49–85.

7. The author of this book had the good fortune to visit there in 1984. The shrine, now Buddhist, could barely contain our group of about twenty people at a time.

8. Assuristan in West Asia.

9. Quoted in Lieu, op. cit., p. 24.

10. *Kephalaia*, CLIV, trans. by J. Stevenson, quoted in Lieu, *The Religion of Light*, 11.

11. Quoted in Donald Daniel Leslie, *The Survival of the Chinese Jews*, pp. 8–9. The name 'Magians' refers to the Zoroastrians.

12. Consult William Charles White, *Chinese Jews*, second edition (Toronto: University of Toronto Press, 1966). The first edition was in 1942. A recent Chinese book on the subject is by Jiang Wenhan, *Chung-kuo ku-tai Chi-tu-chiao chi Kaifeng Yu-t'ai jen* (Christianity in ancient China and the Jews of Kaifeng) (Shanghai: Chih-shih Press, 1982.)

13. Today, the street name has been changed to 'Reading the Scriptures' which sounds close to 'Extracting the Sinews'. I visited them in 1981 in the company of my husband and Catherine Maudsley.

14. The historic Waqqas, uncle of the Prophet, was a great soldier and governor of Iraq (638–c. 645). Possibly, he was part of the delegation of 651, although there is no proof whatsoever. Consult Leslie, *Islam in Traditional China*, p. 75. See also George Fadlo Hourani, *Arab Seafaring in the Indian Ocean in Ancient and Early Medieval Times* (Princeton: Princeton University Press, 1951), pp. 61–79.

15. *Ancient Accounts of India and China by Two Mohammedan Travellers Who Went to Those Parts in the Ninth Century*, translated by Eusebius Renaudot, quoted in E. R. Hughes and K. Hughes, *Religion in China* (London: Hutchinson, 1950), pp. 100–103. As Muslims usually refrain from portraying the prophet, it is interesting that portraits of him existed in the ninth century.

16. See Leslie, *Islam in Traditional China*, op. cit., pp. 43–45. In 1984, I visited Quanzhou, and saw the mosque, some tombstones, as well as the graves of the Muslim sages, dated to about the twelfth century.

17. This occurred in the thirteenth century.

18. Leslie, *Islam in Traditional China*, pp. 94–96.

19. Consult Jean-François Billeter, *Li Zhi: Philosophe maudit (1527–1602)* (Geneva: Droz, 1979); and Hok-lam Chan, *Li Chih, 1527–1602, in Contemporary Chinese Historiography* (New York: M. E. Sharpe, 1980). Consult also Chen Yuan, *Western and Central Asians in*

China under the Mongols: Their Transformation into Chinese, translated by Ch'ien Hsing-hai and L. Carrington Goodrich (first published by Monumenta Serica, Los Angeles, 1966; Nettetal: Steyler Verlag, 1989 reprint).

20. There are numerous ethnic groups in China. One mainland publication gives a description of about fifty-five of them. See *Chung-kuo shao-shu min-chu* (The Ethnic Minorities of China) (Beijing: Renmin, 1981). This book is edited by the National Minorities Committee of the State Council.

21. In the 1980s, many mosques were repaired, as I myself witnessed during my travels in China and in Sinkiang in 1981.

22. If the figure is around forty million, China's Muslims would rank with Egypt, Iran and Nigeria; if ninety million, with Pakistan, Bangladesh or India. Among national states today only Indonesia exceeds these in Muslim population. For a general account of Islam in China, consult Morris Rossabi's article in *The Encyclopaedia of Religion*, edited by Mircea Eliade, *et al.* (New York: Macmillan, 1987), vol. 7, pp. 377–90. Marshall Broomhall's *Islam in China* (London: Morgan & Scott, for the China Inland Mission, 1910), is sketchy and out of date, but there is no one-volume historical study to replace it. Raphael Israeli's *Muslims in China: A Study in Cultural Confrontation* (London: Curzon Press, 1980) has a politically inflammatory rhetoric with its predictions of a coming vast Muslim rebellion.

23. For works on Islam in China and Chinese Muslims, consult also Donald Daniel Leslie, 'Islam in China to 1800: A Bibliographical Guide', *Abr-Nahrain* 16 (1976), 16–48, and his *Islamic Literature in Chinese: Late Ming and Early Ch'ing Books, Authors and Associates* (Canberra: Canberra College of Advanced Education, 1981).

24. Joseph Fletcher, 'Central Asian Sufism and Ma Ming-hsin's New Teaching', in *Proceedings of the Fourth East Asian Altaistic Conference*, ed. by Ch'en Chieh-hsien (Taipei: 1975), 75–96.

25. See an article by Paul Pelliot, 'Les Sources de Matteo Ricci', in William Charles White, *Chinese Jews*, 2nd edition, Part III, p. 16. In this context I am also referring to my own family, as my maternal grandmother remembers her family's Muslim background. We have been told that an early nineteenth-century ancestor who did well in the examinations was honoured with pork from the imperial court which he was unable to decline.

26 Consult Barbara L. K. Pillsbury, 'Being Female in a Muslim Minority in China', in *Women in the Muslim World*, edited by Lois Beck and Nikki R. Keddie (Cambridge, Mass.: Harvard University Press, 1978).

Chapter 11

1. I. de Rachewiltz, *Papal Envoys to the Great Khans* (London: Faber & Faber, 1971).

2. F. Hirth, *China and the Roman Orient* (Shanghai and Hong Kong, 1885; reprinted New York: Paragon, 1966); G. F. Hudson, *Europe & China: A Survey of Their Relations from the Earliest Times to 1800* (London: E. Arnold, 1931), ch. 1.

3. David Mungello, *Curious Land: Jesuit Accommodation and the Origins of Sinology* (Stuttgart: F. Steiner, 1985).

4. A. C. Moule, *Christians in China before the Year 1550* (London: Society for Promoting Christian Knowledge, 1930); John Joseph, *The Nestorians and Their Muslim Neighbors: A Study of Western Influences on Their Relations* (Princeton: Princeton University Press, 1961); Paul Carus, ed., *The Nestorian Monument: An Ancient Record of Christianity in China, with Special Reference to the Expedition of Fritz V. Holm* (Chicago: Open Court, 1909); consult also Saeki Yoshiro, *Nestorian Monument in China* (London: Society for the Promotion of Christian Knowledge, 1916). I visited the museum which houses the Monument in Xi'an in 1981.

5. For the various scripts, consult David Diringer, *The Alphabet: A Key to the History of Mankind* (London: Hutchinson, 1948), pp. 316–19.

6. G. Rosenkranz, *Die älteste Christenheit in China in den Quellen-Zeugnissen der Nestorianertexte der Tang-Dynastie* (Berlin: Verlag des Ostasien-Mission, 1939), p. 6.

7. Donald W. Treadgold, *The West in Russia and China: Religious and Secular Thought in Modern Times* (Cambridge: Cambridge University Press, 1973), chs 1–2.

8. Georg Schurhammer, S. J., *Das kirchliche Sprachproblem in der japanischen Jesuiten-mission des 16. und 17. Jahrhunderts: Ein Stück Ritenfrage* (Tokyo: Deutsche Gesellschaft für Natur- und Völkerkunde Ostasiens, 1928).

9. Julia Ching, *Confucianism and Christianity*, op. cit., pp. 23–25; see also A. S. Rosso, *Apostolic Legations to China of the Eighteenth Century* (South Pasadena: P. D. & I. Perkins, 1948), pp. 138–43.

10. Ludwig von Pastor, *History of the Popes* (London: Kegan Paul, Trench, Trübner, 1941), vol. 33, p. 428.

11. Julia Ching and Willard G. Oxtoby, eds, *Moral Enlightenment: Leibniz and Wolff on China*, Monumenta Serica Monograph Series, 26 (Nettetal: Steyler Verlag, 1992).

12. Still, it may be observed that until the early part of the twentieth century, many people fleeing wars carried their heavy ancestral tablets with them as their most valuable possessions.

13. Consult Marshall Broomhall, *The Bible in China* (London: China Inland Mission, 1934; reprinted, San Francisco: Chinese Materials Center, 1977).

14. Today, the two most numerous groups of Chinese Christians are Catholics and evangelical Protestants.

15. Consult Paul A. Cohen, *China and Christianity: the Missionary Movement and the Growth of Chinese Antiforeignism, 1860–1870* (Cambridge,

Mass.: Harvard University Press, 1963).

16. Consult Robert G. Orr, *Religion in China* (New York: Friendship Press, 1980); Angelo S. Lazzarotto, *The Catholic Church in Post-Mao China* (Hong Kong: Holy Spirit Study Centre, 1982).

17. See *China Heute* 10 (1991), 151–52. Unofficial figures in 1992 put the number of Christians at about thirty million, which would make the growth under Communist rule quite phenomenal.

18. For the pre-modern history of Christianity in Japan, consult Neil S. Fujita, *Japan's Encounter with Christianity: The Catholic Mission in Pre-modern Japan* (New York: Paulist Press, 1991).

19. Jacques Gernet calls the missionary effort an 'enterprise of seduction', See *China and the Christian Impact: A Conflict of Cultures*, translated by Janet Lloyd (Cambridge: Cambridge University Press, 1985).

Chapter 12

1. See article on Chinese Popular Religion by Alvin P. Cohen, in *The Encyclopedia of Religion*, op. cit., vol. 3, pp. 289–96.

2. David K. Jordan and Daniel L. Overmyer, *The Flying Phoenix: Aspects of Chinese Sectarianism in Taiwan* (Princeton: Princeton University Press, 1986), p. 16.

3. See Alan J. A. Elliott, *Chinese Spirit-Medium Cults in Singapore* (London: Royal Anthropological Institute, 1955), p. 170.

4. See Elliott, ibid., p. 63. The climbing of a sword-ladder is a widespread practice, also found in Japan, and may symbolise the shaman's 'magical flight'.

5. David K. Jordan, *Gods, Ghosts and Ancestors: The Folk Religion of a Taiwanese Village* (Berkeley: University of California Press, 1972), p. 84.

6. Consult also Jack M. Potter, 'Cantonese Shamanism', in Arthur P. Wolf, ed., *Religion and Ritual in Chinese Society* (Stanford: Stanford University Press, 1974), pp. 207–31.

7. Jordan and Overmyer, op. cit., p. 36, pp. 63–81.

8. E. J. Eitel, *Feng-shui: Principles of the Natural Science of the Chinese* (Hong Kong and London: Trübner, 1873), p. 22, quoted in Laurence Thompson, *Chinese Religion*, p. 23. Consult also Joseph Needham, *Science and Civilisation in China*, op. cit., vol. 2, p. 42, vol. 4, p. 26(i).

9. Laurence G. Thompson, *Chinese Religion: An Introduction*, 4th edn (Belmont, Calif.: Wadsworth, 1989), pp. 68–72.

10. Arthur P. Wolf, 'Gods, Ghosts and Ancestors', in *Religion and Ritual in Chinese Society*, p. 131. His research was focused along the south-western edge of the Taipei Basin.

11. Wolf, ibid., pp. 136–39.

12. Anne S. Goodrich, *Peking Paper Gods: A Look at Home Worship* (Nettetal: Steyler Verlag, 1991), pp. 43–49.

13. Anne Goodrich, ibid., pp. 60–64.

14. *South China Morning Post*, 7 February 1992.

15. Ibid., p. 140. This god is among the clan ancestors of the author of

this book. Consult Frank Ching, *Ancestors: Nine Hundred Years in the Life of a Chinese Family* (New York: Morrow, 1988), ch. 4, where the name is transliterated according to *pinyin* as Qin Yubo.

16. Wolf, op. cit., pp. 143–45. Consult also Thompson, op. cit., ch. 4, p. 70.
17. For more information, consult Francis L. K. Hsü, *Under the Ancestor's Shadow* (New York: Columbia University Press, 1948), 182–91.
18. Jordan, op. cit., pp. 31–38.
19. Cheng Chih-min, *Tai-wan min-chien tsung-chiao lun-chi* (On Popular Religion in Taiwan) (Taipei: Student Bookstore, 1984), 67–71.
20. Consult Jordan, op. cit., p. 28.
21. Daniel L. Overmyer, *Folk Buddhist Religion: Dissenting Sects in Late Traditional China* (Cambridge, Mass.: Harvard University Press, 1976), 99–102.
22. V. R. Burkhardt, *Chinese Creeds and Customs* (Hong Kong: South China Morning Post, 1953–58), vol. 3, 158–60, E. T. C. Werner, *Myths and Legends of China* (London: Harrap, 1924) ch. 11.
23. In Taiwan, Taoist priests entitled to carry out higher rituals in the official liturgy are called 'Blackheads' on account of their official caps, while lower level exorcists and sorcerers are called 'Redheads' on account of their red scarves. Michael Saso, *The Teachings of Taoist Master Chuang* (New Haven: Yale University Press, 1978), p. 195.
24. Consult Anne S. Goodrich, *Chinese Hells: The Peking Temple of Eighteen Hells and Chinese Conceptions of Hell* (St. Augustin, Monumenta Serica Series, 1981), especially ch. 2.
25. Teitaro Suzuki and Dr Paul Carus, trans. *T'ai-shang Kan-ying P'ien* (Chicago: Open Court, 1906).
26. Judith Berling, *The Syncretic Religion of Lin Chao-en* (New York: Columbia University Press, 1980), 111–15.
27. See Cheng Chih-ming, *Chung-kuo shan-shu yu tsung-chiao* (Chinese Morality Books and Religion) (Taipei: Student Book Store, 1988), ch. 13.
28. Ibid., ch. 14.
29. Jordan and Overmyer, op. cit., 210–60.
30. Overmyer, *Popular Buddhist Religion*, pp. 105–8; Cheng Chih-min, op. cit., 64–79.
31. English translation given in Jordan and Overmyer, op. cit., 262–63.
32. Cheng Chih-min, op. cit., p. 79.
33. A stronger parallel may be found in the religion that Christianity supplanted: the religion of ancient Rome, with its many domestic deities, its temples and religious festivities. See Alain Hus, *Greek and Roman Religion* (New York: Hawthorn Books, 1962), 99–102, 116–17.
34. For popular religion in Japan, consult also Carmen Blacker, *The Catalpa Bow: A Study of Shamanistic Practices in Japan* (London: Allen & Unwin, 1975).

Chapter 13

1. Reference is to Mao's widow Jiang Qing and her three associates, accused of having usurped power during the Cultural Revolution.

Appendix: The Chinese Liturgical Year

1. For a sense of continuity between the present and the historical past, consult Derk Bodde, *Festivals in Classical China: New Year and Other Annual Observances During the Han Dynasty* (Princeton: Princeton University Press, 1975). Our own account owes much to V. R. Burkhardt, *Chinese Creeds and Customs*, vol. 3, pp. 152–61; Laurence Thompson's *Chinese Religion*, ch. 10.
2. See chapter 2 on divination in ancient religion.

Bibliography

I PRIMARY TEXTS IN TRANSLATION

1. Translations of the Five Classics include the following:

(i) for the *I-ching*:

James Legge, trans. *The Yi King* (*Sacred Books of the East*, ed. F. Max Müller, Vol. 16). Oxford: Clarendon, 1885.

Richard Wilhelm and Cary F. Baynes, trans. *The I Ching or Book of Changes*. Princeton: Princeton University Press, 1967.

(ii) for the *Shu-ching*:

James Legge, trans. *The Shu King* or the Book of Historical Documents. In Legge, *The Chinese Classics*, Oxford: Clarendon, 1893–95. 2nd edn, 7 vols. Reprinted, Hong Kong: University of Hong Kong, 1960. Vol. 3.

Bernhard Karlgren, trans. 'The Book of Documents'. In *Bulletin of the Museum of Far Eastern Antiquities*, No. 22 (1950), 1–81. A partial translation.

(iii) for the *Shih-ching*:

James Legge, trans. *The She King*. In Legge, *The Chinese Classics*, 1893–95. 2nd edn, 7 vols. Reprinted, Hong Kong: University of Hong Kong, 1960. Vol. 4.

Arthur Waley, trans. *The Book of Songs: The Ancient Chinese Classic of Poetry*. First published, 1937; 2nd edition, London: Allen & Unwin, 1952.

Bernhard Karlgren, trans. *The Book of Odes*. Stockholm: Östasiatiska Museet (Museum of Far Eastern Antiquities), 1950.

(iv) for the ritual texts:

James Legge's translation of *Li-chi* (the *Book of Rites*) is the *Li Ki* (*Sacred Books of the East*, ed. F. Max Müller, vols 27–28). Oxford: Clarendon, 1886.

John Steele's translation of the Ceremonial is *The I-li or Book of Etiquette and Ceremonial*. London: Probsthain, 1917. Reprinted, Taipei: Ch'eng-wen, 1966, 2 vols.

(v) for the *Ch'un-ch'iu* (and the *Tso-chuan*):

James Legge translated the *Ch'un Ts'ëw* (*Spring-Autumn Annals*) and the *Tso Chuen* (Tso commentary) in Legge, *The Chinese Classics*, 1893–95. 2nd edn, 7 vols. Reprinted in Hong Kong, 1960. Vol. 5.

2. English translations of the Four Books:

(i) For the *Analects*:
D. C. Lau, trans. *Confucius: The Analects*. Harmondsworth: Penguin Books, 1979.
James Legge, trans. *The Chinese Classics*, 1893–95. 2nd edn, 7 vols. Reprinted in Hong Kong, 1960. Vol. 1.
Arthur Waley, trans. *The Analects of Confucius*. London: Allen & Unwin, 1938.

(ii) for the *Book of Mencius*:
James Legge, in *The Chinese Classics*, 1893–95. 2nd edn, 7 vols. Reprinted in Hong Kong, 1960. Vol. 2.
D. C. Lau, trans. *Mencius*. Harmondsworth: Penguin Books, 1970.

(iii) for the *Great Learning* and the *Doctrine of the Mean*:
James Legge, in *The Chinese Classics*, 1893–95. 2nd edn, 7 vols. Reprinted in Hong Kong, 1960.
Wing-tsit Chan, in Chan, *A Source Book in Chinese Philosophy*. Princeton: Princeton University Press, 1963, pp. 84–94, 95–114.

3. English translations from Taoist texts include the following:

(i) for the *Lao-tzu*:
Ellen Marie Chen, trans. *Tao Te Ching: A New Translation with Commentary*. New York: Paragon, 1989.
J. J. L. Duyvendak, trans. *Tao Te Ching*. London: John Murray, 1954.
D. C. Lau, trans. *Lao Tzu: Tao Te Ching*. Harmondsworth: Penguin, 1963.
James Legge, trans. *The Texts of Taoism* in *Sacred Books of the East series*, Vol. 39.
Arthur Waley, trans. *The Way and Its Power: A Study of the Tao Te Ching and Its Place in Chinese Thought*. London: Allen & Unwin, 1949. Reprinted, New York: Grove Press, 1958.

(ii) for the *Chuang-tzu*:
Burton Watson, trans. *The Complete Works of Chuang Tzu*. New York: Columbia University Press, 1968.
James Legge, trans. *The Texts of Taoism* in *Sacred Books of the East series*, Vol. 40.

(iii) for the *Lieh-tzu*:
A. C. Graham, trans. *The Book of Lieh-tzu*. London: John Murray, 1960.

(iv) for other texts:
Jay Sailey. *The Master Who Embraces Simplicity*, A.D. *283–343*. San Francisco: Chinese Materials Center, 1978.
James Ware. *Alchemy, Medicine, Religion in the China of* A.D. *320: The nei-p'ien of Ko Hung*. Cambridge, Mass.: M.I.T. Press, 1966.

Richard Wilhelm and Cary F. Baynes, trans. *The Secret of the Golden Flower: A Chinese Book of Life.* London: Kegan Paul, Trench, Trübner, 1931.

James Legge, trans. *T'ai-shang Kan-ying P'ien.* in *The Texts of Taoism,* Vol. 40. Another translation is by Teitaro Suzuki and Paul Carus. *T'ai-shang Kan-ying P'ien.* Chicago: Open Court, 1906.

Ilza Veith. *Huang ti nei ching su wen: The Yellow Emperor's Classic of Internal Medicine.* Baltimore: Williams & Wilkins, 1949; reissued, Berkeley: University of California Press, 1960.

4. English translations of Buddhist texts include:

David W. Chappell, ed. *T'ien-t'ai Buddhism: An Outline of the Fourfold Teachings.* Tokyo: Daiichi-Shoho, 1983.

Chang Chung-yuan, trans. Tao-Yuan, *Original Teachings of Ch'an Buddhism, Selected from the Transmission of the Lamp.* New York: Pantheon, 1959.

Leon Hurvitz. *Scripture of the Lotus Blossom of the Fine Dharma.* New York: Columbia University Press, 1976.

James Legge. *A Record of Buddhistic Kingdoms: Being an Account by the Chinese Monk Fa-hien of his Travels in India and Ceylon (A.D. 319–414) in Search of the Buddhist Books of Discipline.* Oxford: Clarendon Press, 1886. Reprinted, New York: Paragon, 1965.

W. Liebenthal. *Chao Lun: The Treatises of Seng Chao.* Hong Kong: Hong Kong University Press, 2nd rev. edn, 1968.

Philip B. Yampolsky. *The Platform Sutra of the Sixth Patriarch: The Text of the Tun-huang Manuscript.* New York: Columbia University Press, 1967.

Henry Clarke Warren. *Buddhism in Translations.* Cambridge, Mass.: Harvard University Press, 1896. Reprinted, New York: Atheneum, 1963.

5. English translations of other texts include:

Burton Watson. *Hsün Tzu: Basic Writings.* New York: Columbia University Press, 1967.

Burton Watson. *Mo Tzu: Basic Writings.* New York: Columbia University Press, 1967.

Burton Watson. *Han Fei Tzu: Basic Writings.* New York: Columbia University Press, 1967.

Richard B. Mather. (trans. from Liu I-ch'ing). *Shih-shuo Hsin-yu: A New Account of Tales of the World.* Minneapolis: University of Minnesota Press, 1976.

David Hawkes. *Ch'u Tz'u: The Songs of the South.* Oxford: Clarendon Press, 1959.

Donald Holzman. *Poetry and Politics: The Life and Works of Juan Chi, A.D. 210–236.* Cambridge: Cambridge University Press, 1976.

Arthur Waley. *The Nine Songs.* London: Allen & Unwin, 1955.

6. Translations in Anthologies

William Theodore de Bary, *et al.,* eds. *Sources of Chinese Tradition.* New York: Columbia Univerity Press, 1960.

Wing-tsit Chan. *A Source Book in Chinese Philosophy*. Princeton: Princeton University Press, 1963.

II   GENERAL READINGS

Bauer, Wolfgang. *China and the Search for Happiness*. Translated by Michael Shaw. New York: Seabury Press, 1976.

de Bary, William Theodore. *East Asian Civilizations: A Dialogue in Five Stages*. Cambridge, Mass.: Harvard University Press, 1988.

Chan, Wing-tsit. *Religious Trends in Modern China*. New York: Columbia University Press, 1954.

Eliade, Mircea. *Shamanism: Archaic Techniques of Ecstasy*. New York: Bollingen Foundation, 1964.

Eliade, Mircea. *A History of Religious Ideas*, 3 vols. Chicago: University of Chicago Press, 1978–85.

Fung Yu-lan. *A History of Chinese Philosophy*, 2nd edn. Trans. by Derk Bodde. Princeton: Princeton University Press, 2 vols, 1952–53.

Fung Yu-lan. *A Short History of Chinese Philosophy*. Edited and translated by Derk Bodde. New York: Macmillan, 1958.

Graham, A. C. *Disputers of the Tao: Philosophical Argument in Ancient China*. La Salle, Ill.: Open Court, 1989.

Granet, Marcel. *The Religion of the Chinese People*. Edited and translated by Maurice Freedman. Oxford: Basil Blackwell, 1975.

Heiler, Friedrich. *Prayer: A Study in the History and Psychology of Religion*. Translated and edited by Samuel McComb. London: Oxford University Press, 1932.

Jaspers, Karl. *The Great Philosophers*, Vol. 1: *The Foundations*. Translated by Ralph Manheim. New York: Harcourt, Brace & World, 1962.

Kitagawa, Joseph M. *Religions of the East*. Philadelphia: Westminster Press, 1960.

Kitagawa, Joseph M. *Religion in Japanese History*. New York: Columbia University Press, 1966.

Küng, Hans and Julia Ching. *Christianity and Chinese Religions*. New York: Doubleday, 1988.

Legge, James. *The Religions of China*. London: Hodder & Stoughton, 1880.

Lewis, I. M. *Ecstatic Religion: An Anthropological Study of Spiritual Possession and Shamanism*. Harmondsworth: Penguin Books, 1971.

Needham, Joseph. *Science and Civilisation in China*, 6 vols. Cambridge: Cambridge University Press, 1954–86.

Robinson, Richard H. *The Buddhist Religion*. Belmont, Calif.: Dickenson, 1970.

Schecter, Jerrold. *The New Face of Buddha: Buddhism and Political Power in Southeast Asia*. New York: Coward-McCann, 1967.

Smith, D. Howard. *Chinese Religions*. London: Weidenfeld and Nicolson, 1968.

Soothill, William E. *The Three Religions of China*. London: Oxford University Press, 1923.

Thompson, Laurence. *Chinese Religions: An Introduction*. Encino, Calif.: Dickenson, 1975.

Wach, Joachim. *Sociology of Religion*. Chicago: University of Chicago Press, 1944.
Waley, Arthur. *Three Ways of Thought in Ancient China*. London: Allen & Unwin, 1946.
Weber, Max. *The Religion of China: Confucianism and Taoism*. Translated by Hans H. Gerth. Glencoe, Ill.: Free Press, 1964.
Yang, C. K. *Religion in Chinese Society*. Berkeley: University of California Press, 1961.

III SPECIAL READINGS

For the Introduction:
See 'General Readings' above.

For Chapters 1 and 2 (ancient religion):

Bodde, Derk. *Essays on Chinese Civilization*, edited by Charles LeBlanc and Dorothy Borei. Princeton: Princeton University Press, 1981.
Chang, K. C. *Art, Myth and Ritual: The Path to Political Authority*. Cambridge, Mass.: Harvard University Press, 1983.
Chang, K. C. *Shang Civilization*. New Haven: Yale University Press, 1980.
Ching, Julia and R. W. L. Guisso, eds. *Sages and Filial Sons: Archaeology and Mythology in Early China*. Hong Kong: Chinese University Press, 1991.
Keightley, David. *Sources of Shang History*. Berkeley: University of California Press, 1978.
Maspéro, Henri. *China in Antiquity*. Translated by Frank A. Kierman, Jr. Amherst: University of Massachusetts Press, 1978.
Roberto K. Ong. *The Interpretation of Dreams in Ancient China*. Bochum: Brockmeyer, 1985.
Vandermeersch, Léon. *Wangdao ou la voie royale*, 2 vols. Paris: École Française d'Extrême-Orient, 1980.
Walters, Derek. *Chinese Astrology: Interpreting the Messages of the Celestial Messengers*. Wellingborough, Northants: Aquarian, 1987.

Readings for Comparative Purposes:
Aune, David E. *Prophecy in Early Christianity and the Ancient Mediterranean World*. Grand Rapids: Eerdmans, 1983.
Fohrer, Georg. *History of Israelite Religion*. Translated by David E. Green. Nashville: Abingdon Press, 1972.
Guillaume, Alfred. *Prophecy and Divination among the Hebrews and Other Semites*. London: Hodder & Stoughton, 1938.
Smith, Morton. *Jesus the Magician*. New York: Harper & Row, 1978.

For Chapters 3 and 4 (Confucianism and its early rivals):

Bellah, Robert N. and Philip E. Hammond. *Varieties of Civil Religion*. San Francisco: Harper & Row, 1980.

Ching, Julia. *Confucianism and Christianity: A Comparative Study*. Tokyo: Kodansha International, 1977.

Creel, Herlee G. *Confucius: The Man and the Myth*. New York: John Day, 1949.

Eber, Irene, ed. *Confucianism: The Dynamics of Tradition*. New York: Macmillan, 1986.

Fingarette, Herbert. *Confucius: The Secular as Sacred*. New York: Harper & Row, 1972.

Hu Shih. *Shuo Ju*, in *Hu Shih tso-ping chi* (Collected works of Hu Shih), Vol. 15. Taipei: Yuan-liu, 1986.

Krieger, Silke and Rolf Trauzettel, eds. *Confucianism and the Modernization of China*. Mainz: v. Hase & Koehler, 1991.

Schwartz, Benjamin I. *The World of Thought in Ancient China*. Cambridge, Mass.: Harvard University Press, 1985.

Shryock, John. *Origin and Development of the State Cult of Confucius*. New York: The Century Co., 1932.

Vandermeersch, Léon. *Le Nouveau monde sinisé*. Paris: Presses Universitaires de France, 1986.

Yü Ying-shih, '"O Soul Come Back!" A Study in the Changing Conceptions of the Soul and Afterlife in Pre-Buddhist China', *Harvard Journal of Asiatic Studies* 47 (1987), 363–95.

Readings for Comparative Purposes:
Buber, Martin. *A Believing Humanism*. New York: Simon & Schuster, 1967.

Ching, Julia. *Confucianism and Christianity: A Comparative Study*. Tokyo: Kodansha International, 1977.

Jaspers, Karl. *The Great Philosophers*, volume 1: *The Foundations*, edited by Hannah Arendt, translated by Ralph Mannheim. New York: Harcourt, Brace & World, 1962.

Lee, Peter K. H., ed. *Confucian-Christian Encounters in Historical and Contemporary Perspective* (Religions in Dialogue, 5). Lewiston, N.Y.: Edwin Mellen Press, 1991.

Mar Gregorios, Paulos. *Cosmic Man: The Divine Presence: The Theology of St. Gregory of Nyssa (c. 330–395 A.D.)*. New York: Paragon, 1988.

Rowley, H. H. *Prophecy and Religion in Ancient China and Israel*. London: Athlone Press, 1956.

Tillich, Paul. *Systematic Theology*, 3 vols. Chicago: University of Chicago Press, 1957–65.

Weber, Max. *The Religion of China: Confucianism and Taoism*. New York: Free Press, 1964.

For Chapters 5 and 6 (Taoist philosophy and religion):

Chan, Alan K. L. *Two Visions of the Way: A Study of the Wang Pi and the Ho-shang Kung Commentaries on Lao Tzu*. Albany: State University of New York Press, 1991.

Creel, Herlee G. *What Is Taoism? and Other Studies in Chinese Cultural History*. Chicago: University of Chicago Press, 1970.

Fukui Kojun, ed., *Dōkyō to wa nanika* (What is Taoism?), Vol. 1 of *Dōkyō*. Tokyo: Hirakawa, 1984.

Huard, Pierre, *et al. Chinese Medicine.* Translated by Bernard Fielding. New York: McGraw-Hill, 1968.

Kaltenmark, Max. *Lao Tzu and Taoism.* Translated by Roger Greaves. Stanford: Stanford University Press, 1969.

Kohn, Livia. *Seven Steps to the Tao: Sima Chengzhen's Zuowanlun (Monumenta Serica* Monograph Series, 20). Nettetal: Steyler Verlag, 1987.

Kohn, Livia, ed. *Taoist Meditation and Longevity Techniques* (Michigan Monographs in Chinese Studies, 61). Ann Arbor: University of Michigan, Center for Chinese Studies, 1989.

Lagerwey, John. *Taoist Ritual in Chinese Society and History.* New York: Macmillan, 1987.

Loewe, Michael. *Ways to Paradise: The Chinese Quests for Immortality.* London: Allen & Unwin, 1979.

Maspéro, Henri. *Taoism and Chinese Religion.* Translated by Frank A. Kierman, Jr. Amherst: University of Massachusets Press, 1981.

Schipper, Kristofer. *Le Corps taoïste: Corps mystique, corps social.* Paris: Fayard, 1982.

Saso, Michael and David Chappell, eds. *Buddhist and Taoist Studies I* (Asian Studies at Hawaii, 18). Honolulu: University Press of Hawaii, 1977.

Sivin, Nathan. *Chinese Alchemy: Preliminary Studies.* Cambridge, Mass.: Harvard University Press, 1968.

Welch, Holmes and Anna Seidel, eds. *Facets of Taoism: Essays in Chinese Religion.* New Haven: Yale University Press, 1979.

Welch, Holmes, *et al.* 'Symposium on Taoism'. *History of Religions* 9 (1969–70), No. 2 / 3.

Readings for Comparative Purposes:

Heiddeger, Martin. *On the Way to Language.* New York: Harper & Row, 1971.

Jaspers, Karl. *The Great Philosophers*, Vol. 2, ed. by Hannah Arendt, trans. by Ralph Mannheim. New York: Harcourt, Brace & World, 1966.

Quispel, Gilles. 'Gnosticism'. In *The Encyclopedia of Religion*, ed. Mircea Eliade *et al.* New York: Macmillan, 1977. Vol. 5, pp. 566–74.

For Chapters 7 and 8 (Buddhism):

Bloom, Alfred. *Shinran's Doctrine of Pure Grace.* Tucson: University of Arizona Press, 1965.

Ch'en, Kenneth S. *Buddhism in China: A Historical Survey.* Princeton: Princeton University Press, 1964.

Conze, Edward. *Buddhism: Its Essence and Development*, 3rd edn. Oxford: Bruno Cassirer, 1957.

Dumoulin, Heinrich. *A History of Zen Buddhism.* Translated by Paul Peachey. New York: McGraw-Hill, 1965.

Dumoulin, Heinrich. *History of Zen Buddhism*, 2 vols. Trans. by James W. Heisig and Paul Knitter. London: Macmillan, 1988–90.

Houston, W., ed. *The Cross and the Lotus.* Delhi: Motilal Banarsidass, 1985.

LaFleur, William R. *Buddhism.* Englewood Cliffs: Prentice-Hall, 1988.

Paul, Diana Y. *Women in Buddhism: Images of the Feminine in Mahayana Tradition.* Berkeley: Asian Humanities Press, 1979.

Robinson, Richard H. *Early Madhyamika in India and China*. Delhi: Motilal Banarsidass, 1976.

Saunders, E. Dale. *Buddhism in Japan: With an Outline of its Origins in India*. Philadelphia: University of Pennsylvania Press, 1971.

Swearer, Donald. *Buddhism*. Niles, Ill.: Argus Communications, 1977.

Takasaki Jikido. *An Introduction to Buddhism*. Trans. by Rof W. Giebel. Tokyo: The Toho Gakkai, 1987.

Tsukamoto Zenryū. *A History of Early Chinese Buddhism*, 2 vols. Translated from Japanese by Leon Hurvitz. Tokyo: Kodansha International, 1979.

Welch, Holmes. *The Practice of Chinese Buddhism, 1900–1950*. Cambridge, Mass.: Harvard University Press, 1985.

Zürcher, Erik. *Buddhism: Its Origin and Spread in Words, Maps and Pictures*. London: Routledge & Kegan Paul, 1962.

Zürcher, Erik. *The Buddhist Conquest of China: The Spread and Adaptation of Buddhism in Early Medieval China*. Leiden: E. J. Brill, 1959.

Readings for Comparative Purposes:

Barth, Karl. *Church Dogmatics*, 5 vols. in 14. Edinburgh: T. & T. Clark, 1956–77). See especially 'The Revelation of God as the Abolition of Religion', Vol. 1, part 2, section 17.

Graham, Aelred. *Zen Catholicism: A Suggestion*. New York: Harcourt, Brace & World, 1963.

Lopez, Donald S., Jr. and Steven C. Rockefeller, eds. *The Christ and the Bodhisattva*. Albany: State University of New York Press, 1987.

Sharma, Arvind, ed. *Women in World Religions* Albany: State University of New York Press, 1987.

Suzuki, Daisetz Teitaro. *Mysticism: Christian and Buddhist*. London: Allen & Unwin, 1957.

Tillich, Paul. *Christianity and the Encounter of the World Religions*. New York: Columbia University Press, 1963.

Whitehead, Alfred North. *Religion in the Making*. New York: Macmillan, 1926. Reprinted, New York: New American Library, 1960.

For Chapter 9 (Neo-Confucianism):

Bellah, Robert N. *Tokugawa Religion: The Values of Pre-Industrial Japan*. Boston: Beacon Press, 1957.

Chan, Wing-tsit, ed. *Chu Hsi and Neo-Confucianism*. Honolulu: University Press of Hawaii, 1986.

Chang, Carsun. *The Development of Neo-Confucian Thought*, 2 vols. New York: College & University Press, 1962.

Ching, Julia. *To Acquire Wisdom: The Way of Wang Yang-ming (1472–1529)*. New York: Columbia University Press, 1976.

de Bary, Wm. Theodore and Irene Bloom, eds. *Principle and Practicality: Essays in Neo-Confucianism and Practical Learning*. New York: Columbia University Press, 1979.

Graf, Olaf. *Tao und Jen: Sein und Sollen im sungchinesischen Monismus*. Wiesbaden: Otto Harrassowitz, 1970.

Liu Shaoqi. *How to Be a Good Communist*. Beijing: Foreign Languages Press, 1951.

Maruyama Masao. *Studies in the Intellectual History of Tokugawa Japan.* Princeton: Princeton University Press, 1974.

Readings for Comparative Purposes:
Basham, A. L., ed. *Kingship in Asia and Early America.* Mexico City: El Colegio de México, 1981.
Pfeiffer, Franz. *Meister Eckhart,* trans. by C. de Evans. London: J. M. Watkins, 1924–31.
Teilhard de Chardin, Pierre. *The Divine Milieu: An Essay on the Interior Life.* Trans. by Bernard Wall. New York: Harper & Row, 1960.
Whitehead, Alfred North. *Process and Reality: An Essay in Cosmology.* Cambridge: Cambridge University Press, 1929.

For Chapter 10 (Islam):

Billeter, Jean-François. *Li Zhi: Philosophe maudit, 1527–1602.* (Geneva: Droz, 1979.
Chan, Hok-lam. *Li Chih, 1527–1602, in Contemporary Chinese Historiography.* New York: M.E. Sharpe, 1980.
Chen Yüan. *Western and Central Asians in China under the Mongols: Their Transformation into Chinese.* Translated by Ch'ien Hsing-hai and L. Carrington Goodrich. Los Angeles: Monumenta Serica, 1966. Reprinted, Nettetal: Steyler Verlag, 1989.
Israeli, Raphael. *Muslims in China: A Study in Cultural Confrontation.* London: Curzon Press, 1980.
Leslie, Donald Daniel. *The Survival of the Chinese Jews: The Jewish Community of Kaifeng.* Leiden: E. J. Brill, 1972.
Leslie, Donald Daniel. *Islamic Literature in Chinese: Late Ming and Early Ch'ing Books, Authors and Associates.* Canberra: Canberra College of Advanced Education, 1981.
Leslie, Donald Daniel. *Islam in Traditional China: A Short History to 1800.* Canberra: Canberra College of Advanced Education, 1986.
Lieu, Samuel N. C. *The Religion of Light: An Introduction to the History of Manichaeism in China.* Hong Kong, University of Hong Kong, 1979.
White, William Charles. *Chinese Jews,* second edition. Toronto: University of Toronto Press, 1966. The first edition was in 1942.

Readings for Comparative Purposes:
Lieu, Samuel N. C. *Manichaeism in the Later Roman Empire and Medieval China.* Manchester: Manchester University Press, 1985.

For Chapter 11 (Christianity):

Broomhall, Marshall. *The Bible in China.* London: China Inland Mission, 1934; reprinted, San Francisco: Chinese Materials Center, 1977.
Cary-Elwes, C. *China and the Cross: A Survey of Missionary History.* New York: P. J. Kenedy, 1957.
Ching, Julia and Willard G. Oxtoby, eds. *Moral Enlightenment: Leibniz*

and Wolff on China (*Monumenta Serica* Monograph Series, 26). Nettetal: Steyler Verlag, 1992.

Diringer, David. *The Alphabet: A Key to the History of Mankind.* London: Hutchinson, 1948.

Fujita, Neil S. *Japan's Encounter with Christianity: The Catholic Mission in Pre-modern Japan.* New York: Paulist Press, 1991.

Gernet, Jacques. *China and the Christian Impact: A Conflict of Cultures.* Translated by Janet Lloyd. Cambridge: Cambridge University Press, 1985.

Hirth, F. *China and the Roman Orient.* Shanghai and Hong Kong, 1885; reprinted, New York: Paragon, 1966.

Hudson, G. F. *Europe & China: A Survey of Their Relations from the Earliest Times to 1800.* London: E. Arnold, 1931.

Lazzarotto, Angelo S. *The Catholic Church in Post-Mao China.* Hong Kong: Holy Spirit Study Centre, 1982.

MacInnis, Donald E. *Religion in China Today: Policy and Practice.* Maryknoll, New York: Orbis, 1989.

Mungello, David. *Curious Land: Jesuit Accommodation and the Origins of Sinology.* Stuttgart: F. Steiner, 1985.

Orr, Robert G. *Religion in China.* New York: Friendship Press, 1980.

de Rachewiltz, I. *Papal Envoys to the Great Khans.* London: Faber & Faber, 1971.

Rosso, A. S. *Apostolic Legations to China of the Eighteenth Century.* South Pasadena: P. D. & I. Perkins, 1948.

Treadgold, Donald W. *The West in Russia and China: Religious and Secular Thought in Modern Times.* Cambridge: Cambridge University Press, 1973.

Wickeri, Philip L. *Seeking the Common Ground: Protestant Christianity, Three-Self Movement, and China's United Front.* Maryknoll, New York: Orbis, 1988.

Readings for Comparative Purposes:

Joseph, John. *The Nestorians and Their Muslim Neighbors: A Study of Western Influences on Their Relations.* Princeton: Princeton University Press, 1961.

von Pastor, Ludwig. *History of the Popes*, Vol. 33. London: Kegan Paul, Trench, Trubner, 1941.

For Chapter 12 (popular religion):

Berling, Judith. *The Syncretic Religion of Lin Chao-en.* New York: Columbia University Press, 1980.

Blacker, Carmen. *The Catalpa Bow: A Study of Shamanistic Practices in Japan.* London: Allen & Unwin, 1975.

Bodde, Derk. *Festivals in Classical China: New Year and Other Annual Observances During the Han Dynasty.* Princeton: Princeton University Press, 1975.

Burkhardt, V. R. *Chinese Creeds and Customs*, 2 vols. Hong Kong: South China Morning Post, 1953–58.

Ching, Frank. *Ancestors: Nine Hundred Years in the Life of a Chinese Family.* New York: Morrow, 1988.

Eitel, E. J. *Feng-shui: Principles of the Natural Science of the Chinese.* Hong Kong and London: Trübner, 1873.

Elliott, Alan J. A. *Chinese Spirit-Medium Cult in Singapore.* London: Royal Anthropological Institute, 1955.

Hsü, Francis L. K. *Under the Ancestor's Shadow.* New York: Columbia University Press, 1948.

Jordan, David K. *Gods, Ghosts and Ancestors: The Folk Religion of a Taiwanese Village.* Berkeley: University of California Press, 1972.

Jordan, David K. and Daniel L. Overmyer. *The Flying Phoenix: Aspects of Chinese Sectarianism in Taiwan.* Princeton: Princeton University Press, 1986.

Kitagawa, Joseph M., and Alan L. Miller, eds. *Folk Religion in Japan: Continuity and Change.* Chicago: University of Chicago Press, 1968.

Overmyer, Daniel L. *Folk Buddhist Religion: Dissenting Sects in Late Traditional China.* Cambridge, Mass.: Harvard University Press, 1976.

Saso, Michael. *The Teachings of Taoist Master Chuang.* New Haven: Yale University Press, 1978.

Thompson, Laurence G. *Chinese Religion: An Introduction*, 4th edn. Belmont, Calif.: Wadsworth, 1989.

Werner, E. T. C. *Myths and Legends of China.* London: Harrap, 1924.

Wolf, Arthur P., ed. *Religion and Ritual in Chinese Society.* Stanford: Stanford University Press, 1974.

Readings for Comparative Purposes:

Hus, Alain. *Greek and Roman Religion.* New York: Hawthorn Books, 1962.

IV   OTHER INFORMATION

A recent reference work often consulted in this book is *The Encyclopaedia of Religion*, edited by Mircea Eliade *et al.*, 16 vols. New York: Macmillan, 1987.

For quotations from the Old and New Testaments, the Revised Standard Version (R.S.V.) has been consulted.

Index–Glossary:
Selected Chinese Terms

General Index